D0077175

PARTY DECLINE IN AMERICA

PRINCETON STUDIES IN AMERICAN POLITICS:
HISTORICAL, INTERNATIONAL, AND COMPARATIVE PERSPECTIVES

SERIES EDITORS

IRA KATZNELSON, MARTIN SHEFTER, AND THEDA SKOCPOL

*Labor Visions and State Power: The Origins of Business Unionism
in the United States* by Victoria C. Hattam

The Lincoln Persuasion: Remaking American Liberalism
by J. David Greenstone

*Politics and Industrialization: Early Railroads in the United States
and Prussia* by Colleen A. Dunlavy

Political Parties and the State: The American Historical Experience
by Martin Shefter

*Prisoners of Myth: The Leadership of the Tennessee Valley Authority,
1933–1990* by Erwin C. Hargrove

*Bound by Our Constitution: Women, Workers, and the Minimum
Wage* by Vivien Hart

*Experts and Politicians: Reform Challenges to Machine Politics
in New York, Cleveland, and Chicago* by Kenneth Finegold

*Social Policy in the United States: Future Possibilities in Historical
Perspective* by Theda Skocpol

Political Organizations by James Q. Wilson

*Facing Up to the American Dream: Race, Class, and the Soul
of the Nation* by Jennifer L. Hochschild

Classifying by Race edited by Paul E. Peterson

From the Outside In: World War II and the American State
by Bartholomew H. Sparrow

*Kindred Strangers: The Uneasy Relationship between Politics
and Business in America* by David Vogel

*Why Movements Succeed or Fail: Opportunity, Culture,
and the Struggle for Women Suffrage* by Lee Ann Banaszak

The Myth of the Legislative Veto by Jessica Korn

Party Decline in America: Policy, Politics, and the Fiscal State
by John J. Coleman

PARTY DECLINE IN AMERICA

POLICY, POLITICS, AND THE FISCAL STATE

John J. Coleman

PRINCETON UNIVERSITY PRESS   PRINCETON, NEW JERSEY

Library of Congress Cataloging-in-Publication Data

Coleman, John J., 1959–
Party decline in America : policy, politics, and the fiscal state /
John J. Coleman
p.   cm.—(Princeton studies in American politics)
Includes bibliographical references and index.
ISBN 0-691-02731-5 (cl : alk. paper)
1. Political parties—United States—History—20th century.   2. United States—
Politics and government—1933–1945.   3. United States—Politics and government—
1945–1989.   4. United States—Politics and government—1989– .   5. United
States—Economic policy.   6. Finance, Public—United States—1933– .   I. Title.
II. Series.
JK2261.C69 1996   96-6801
324.273′09′04—dc20   CIP

This book has been composed in Sabon

Printed in the United States of America by
Princeton Academic Press

10 9 8 7 6 5 4 3 2 1

For my parents —————————————————————

Contents

Figures and Tables _____

Figures

Tables

Preface and Acknowledgments _____

FOR MUCH of the postwar period, scholars argued that American political parties were in decline. More recently, however, scholars have pointed to signs of party revival in Congress and party organizations, and there is a new and important literature of "resurgence" in both these areas. Among the citizenry, however, the status of parties remains grim whether one focuses on such behavior as voting turnout and split tickets or on opinions toward the performance of the two-party system and the contributions of parties to contemporary democracy. This paradox of parties—revival with decline—challenges our theories of parties and our understanding of American political development.

The status of party in American politics is tied intimately to its state setting, including particularly the major policy at the center of a given era and the institutional structure that articulates and resolves that policy. Thus, the significance and salience of parties depends on state-building episodes that are themselves subject to the influence of parties. This book is most directly concerned with the status of party after World War II, and particularly the decline of party in that period. The structure and policy concerns of the state before the 1930s encouraged stronger and more meaningful parties than did the structure and policy after the 1930s. In the "fiscal state" after the 1930s, parties were left on the periphery of economic management, which was the fundamental concern of the era. Losing control of policy weakens the political party. With economic management centered in the executive branch, implemented through automatic stabilizers and other structural devices, and tending toward Keynesian convergence, the legislative parties—the linchpin of the party system—were decreasingly significant in this area and were seen as such by voters. This structure opened up opportunities for candidate-centered campaigning by members of Congress, but it also weakened the status of party in American politics. Only when the structure and policy of the fiscal state began to erode would the parties be able to revive. This process, I argue, began in the late 1970s with stagflation. Under what many saw as crisis conditions, the logic of fiscal state economic management unraveled and the party organizations found substantially increased numbers of donors willing to contribute to party coffers. In Congress, the erosion of the fiscal state allowed for increased party polarization. But enough of the fiscal state remained in place to limit the impact of this elite-level change on the public. It was this dynamic that produced the paradox of revival with decline. Party resurgence depends on the erosion of fiscal state structural and policy limits on parties. Through the early to mid-1990s that erosion was partial, as was the resurgence of party. The interregnum between the weakening of the fiscal state and the establishment of a new political settlement could not last indefinitely, however, and by 1992 and 1994 signs pointed toward a new state and a new system of party competition. As this point suggests, one advantage of the state-based approach is that it does not treat party development as a linear process in which parties are either irreversibly declining or continually adapting and prospering in new circumstances. Instead, because state building is an inherently political act, the condition of parties can change with the breakdown of previously held assumptions and the demands for new policy-making arrangements in response to crisis.

In suggesting that the role of the state and policy is of central importance to understanding changes in the status of American political parties, I follow a path opened by such scholars as Stephen Skowronek, Joel Silbey, Theda Skocpol, Martin Shefter, and Richard McCormick. My intellectual debts to the work of these students of politics are legion. Charles Stewart, Suzanne Berger, and Walter Dean Burnham brought their diverse methodologies, probing questions, and substantive interests to bear in this book's early incarnation as a dissertation at MIT. They saved me from numerous miscues. Dean Burnham stoked my interest in historical analyses of political parties and took an early interest in me and my work. I am deeply thankful for his personal and professional support and friendship. I also acknowledge George Billias, Douglas Little, Ronald Formisano, Sharon Krefetz, and Scott Taylor for nurturing my interest in political science and history as a professional endeavor. Professor Billias in particular instructed me in the research process, imparted in me his love of historical inquiry, and is a special friend. The following individuals offered helpful commentary on various versions and parts of the manuscript: Kristi Andersen, John Chubb, Melissa Collie, Leon Epstein, Charles Franklin, Charles Jones, Robert Katzmann, Ira Katznelson, Anne Khademian, Kathleen Knight, Herbert Kritzer, Robert Luskin, Karen Orren, Frances Fox Piven, Gretchen Ritter, Annalee Saxenian, Jean Schroedel, Steven Rathgeb Smith, Bartholomew Sparrow, Joseph White, and John Witte. I also received considerable assistance from anonymous reviewers of article and chapter drafts. I trust they will see many of their suggestions incorporated in the book. David Yoffie deserves special thanks for giving me a rich education in trade politics. Finally, Malcolm Litchfield, editor at Princeton University Press, took an early interest in this project. His commitment and willingness to assist me made this a better book.

For research assistance, I appreciate the help of the staffs at the Brookings Institution, John F. Kennedy Presidential Library, Lyndon Baines

Johnson Presidential Library, Gerald R. Ford Presidential Library, Jimmy Carter Presidential Library, the National Archives, and the library staff at MIT, the University of Texas at Austin, and the University of Wisconsin-Madison. I also thank Jack Pitney for allowing me to roam through the library at the Republican Party National Headquarters. Financial assistance was provided by MIT, the Brookings Institution, the University of Texas, the University of Wisconsin, and the Lyndon Baines Johnson Presidential Library. Substantial portions of chapter 2 originally appeared as "State Formation and the Decline of Political Parties: American Parties in the Fiscal State," in *Studies in American Political Development* 8 (1994): 195–230 (© 1994 Cambridge University Press); it is reprinted with the permission of Cambridge University Press.

Finally, I owe the greatest debt to my family for encouragement and the occasional reality check. June Coleman has been supportive in a multitude of ways. Her love and understanding made my work easier. Andrew, Danny, and Laura pulled me away from the book on many occasions. I do not regret it.

PARTY DECLINE IN AMERICA

1

The Past and Present of American Political Parties

POLITICAL PARTIES make policy; political parties take policy. To understand changes in the status of American political parties, one needs to begin from this point. When parties control policy, they are better able to act as vital linkage institutions. When they lose control, they weaken. The content of policy and the making of policy have concrete effects on the ability of parties to appear centrally important in the legislative process. By affecting whether parties appear to control a policy domain, policy substance and state structure in turn affect whether the public focuses on parties or on individuals when voting, and they tell citizens which political players deserve their attention. But the status of parties is not fixed. The changing significance of parties and their contribution to American political development have been of central interest to political participants, observers, and scholars across American history.

Because state structure and dominant policy concerns can change, the role, perceptions, and centrality of political parties can also change. From the 1870s to the 1930s, for example, party competition was based substantially but by no means exclusively on trade policy. This policy, both in content and in the way it was made, tied voters to the parties and tied the parties to meaningful policy differences. Parties controlled the making of trade policy, they differed significantly, and voters cared about the differences. In contrast, the fiscal policy–based party system of the postwar period was far less supportive of parties that play central legislative roles and that appear important to the public. A "fiscal state" emerged from several key institutional debates from the mid-1930s to the mid-1940s. By institutionalizing fiscal policy, introducing new components of policy making, and encouraging plebiscitary voting, this state set in place the long-term conditions for party decline and, I argue, the keys to party renewal.

To explore how the fiscal state affects parties, I take up one particular aspect of party performance: How do the parties respond to economic downturns? Given the relation of economic downturns to the creation of the new party system of the 1930s, it is a key question. Downturns are also important because the structure and policy of the state are potentially most malleable and public attention to politics is heightened. But the parties, not in control of macroeconomic policy, serve more as policy takers than policy makers. During downturns, major areas of potential party contestation are effectively off-limits and, in those areas where parties do act, widespread Keynesian understandings of the way the economic world works push the parties to adopt similar solutions. The Keynesian revolution in economic thought argued that government had an active, ongoing role to play in the economy. Rather than hewing persistently to a balanced budget orthodoxy and allowing the economy to repair itself, government should use budget deficits to stimulate economic growth during recessions. Similarly, government should reduce deficits or run budget surpluses to combat inflation. This change in economic thinking had an impact on party actions. An analysis of budget-related roll-call votes shows that with economic decline, parties become less distinctive. Precisely when voters can use more policy choice, they hear more echo. A qualitative look at how parties respond to recessions reinforces this conclusion by showing that the parties choose from a narrow range of policy options and converge fairly quickly on which of these tools to employ.

Saying that policy matters and the state matters is important because it suggests that forecasts of inexorable decline (or improvement) for party are likely to be unreliable. When either the policy content or policy-making structure underlying party competition become less viable, a reconstituted party politics is possible. Predictions of dealignment or party decline as the irreversible result of postindustrialism, affluence, education, media, geographical mobility, or some other megatrend have not been sensitive enough to what has made American parties important in the past. The partial improvement in the parties position in the 1980s and early 1990s can, for example, be tied to the increasingly less tenable prescriptions of Keynesian analysis, not to any reversal of these broad historical trends. Policy content changed. But the *limited* nature of this improvement through the early 1990s—for example, voters remained distinctly unimpressed with the parties—reflected the relatively modest changes in state structure. Revitalized parties require a new policy basis for party competition and a new structure of policy making that places parties as central actors. Without both, the rebirth of American political parties will be stillborn. Factors such as changing communications media have no doubt influenced the status of parties. An adequate explanation of party decline and resurgence, however, must consider changes in the state.[1]

My analysis of party decline and resurgence employs Chambers's definition of party: "a relatively durable social formation which seeks offices or power in government, exhibits a structure or organization which links

---

[1] Chapter 2 defines in more detail the conceptualization of the state in general and the fiscal state in particular. Lake (1988a) offers an excellent discussion and elaboration of the concept.

leaders at the centers of government to a significant popular following in
the political arena and its local enclaves, and generates in-group perspectives or at least symbols of identification or loyalty" (1975: 5). With this
kind of party, politicians should get a more predictable marketplace of
voters, and voters should get more predictable results from politicians. At
bottom, the story told in this book is most specifically about congressional
parties and changes in their role and behavior, but congressional parties
are the means to an analytical end: I focus on congressional parties because they are linchpins that connect the operation of parties in the government, parties in the electorate, and parties in relationship to policy
arenas. Changes in congressional parties have ripple effects on the rest of
the party system. Focusing on the congressional party and the key institutional debates redefining its role casts light on the postwar position and
salience of party in Congress, in the polity, and among voters.

Party Decline in the Postwar Period

A large group of political scientists warned about the decline of American
political parties in the late 1970s and early 1980s. Many implied the decline was irreversible. The concern about the status of political parties was
wide ranging; virtually everything about the parties seemed to be going
wrong. Writers pointed to difficulties in the electorate, Congress, party organizations, and the political system that decreased the salience, significance, and meaning of party.[2] Party decline need not mean decline from
some "ideal" condition of parties, but rather a decline from what parties
had been doing in the past.[3]

More recently, scholars have pointed to at least partial party revital-

[2] For indicators of decline in the electorate, see Nie, Verba, and Petrocik 1979; Burnham
1982; Lipset and Schneider 1983, 1987; Crotty 1984; Flanigan and Zingale 1985; and Fiorina 1980, 1987, 1990. For Congress, see Burnham 1975; Clubb and Traugott 1977; Cooper
and Hurley 1977; Brady, Cooper, and Hurley 1979; Collie and Brady 1985; Brady 1990.
For party organizations, see Kirkpatrick 1979; Ranney 1975; and Polsby 1983. For decline
in the system, see Schlesinger 1984; Finer 1984; and Ginsberg and Shefter 1990. These examples are representative of the literature but are by no means exhaustive.

[3] Assumptions about whether parties should be emphasizing clear ideological programs
and punishing transgressors—the responsible party (Schattschneider 1942; APSA 1950)—
or whether parties should be primarily concerned with integrating society and serving its
other functions such as recruiting candidates—the functional party (Herring 1940; Eldersveld 1982)—influenced what analysts found dissatisfying about American parties and
where they saw "decline" (Orren 1982). Nonetheless, both groups saw serious deficiencies
in the workings of American political parties. V. O. Key showed that these two perspectives
could be brought together. His famous work on one-party factionalism (1949), for example, shows an interest in the functional concerns of party while his work on realignment and
the electorate evinces connections with responsible party concerns (1955, 1959, 1966).

ization. Congressional parties have become more distinctive and cohesive in their roll-call voting. Party organizations have increased the array of services they offer candidates.[4] To be sure, the improvements in Congress were from a historically low base and the party organizations, for all their improved service vending, could encourage but not select their party's candidates, did not normally exert much pressure on legislative party members, and had modest impacts on voting turnout and the public's attitudes toward parties.[5] Even with these significant shortcomings, there was genuine improvement in the status of party in Congress and in organizations in the 1980s and early 1990s.

Decline has persisted more securely, however, in the electorate and in the overall centrality of party to the political system. On the positive side, some of these trends temporarily bottomed out in the 1980s and some voters, notably in the South, realigned their party identification with their policy views (Lipset and Schneider 1987; Petrocik 1981, 1987; Wattenberg 1990: ch. 9; Sundquist 1983–1984; Cavanagh and Sundquist 1985; Dennis 1986). But by the 1990s, party loyalty was still low, perceptions of the parties were highly cynical, neutral or indifferent perceptions of parties were common, and a fifth of the electorate in 1992 cast its vote for an unconventional independent presidential candidate offering a distinctly antiparty message (Dennis and Owen 1994).[6] Parties were seen as part of politics-as-usual, and that kind of politics was in severe disfavor.[7]

---

[4] Among the most significant treatments of resurgence in Congress are Rohde 1991, Kiewiet and McCubbins 1991, and Cox and McCubbins 1993. Others are cited in chapter 3. For party organizations, see Cotter and Bibby 1980; Bibby, Gibson, Cotter, and Huckshorn 1983; Gibson, Cotter, Bibby, and Huckshorn 1983; Cotter, Gibson, Bibby, and Huckshorn 1984; Advisory Commission on Intergovernmental Relations 1986; Gibson, Cotter, Bibby, and Huckshorn 1985; Reichley 1985; Huckshorn, Gibson, Cotter, and Bibby 1986; Kayden and Mahe 1985; Sabato 1988; Baer and Bositis 1988, 1993; Patterson 1989; Gibson, Frendreis, and Vertz 1989; Bibby 1990; Frendreis, Gibson, and Vertz 1990; Kazee and Thornberry 1990; Frantzich 1989; Crotty 1991; Longley 1992; Freindreis, Gitelson, Flemming, and Layzell 1993; Herrnson 1986, 1988, 1990; Jacobson 1985–1986; Wilcox 1989; Sorauf and Wilson 1990; Dwyre 1992; Gibson and Scarrow 1993; Shea and Green 1994.

[5] Sorauf and Wilson conclude that the rise of legislative campaign committees provides "greater autonomy for legislative parties . . . without interference from the party organization" (1990: 203). Wright (1994) makes the strongest case for party organizational elites providing the basis for voting cues for members of Congress.

[6] Wattenberg (1990; cf. Advisory Commission 1986: 52) shows that the public was not so much alienated from parties or dissatisfied with parties as they were ignoring them; they were neutral, not negative. He charts a growing indifference to party among people to whom the concepts of partisanship and independence have no real meaning. These people are not necessarily apolitical; they are simply detached from the parties. Careful analysis of opinion surveys seems to bear this out: The trend toward more neutral views of party began as early as 1952 and was not dependent on the political turmoil of the 1960s. Stanga and Sheffield (1987) argue that Wattenberg overstates the evidence.

[7] Survey research provides numerous indicators of public discontent with the parties. Louis Harris and Associates found in 1992 that 69 percent of the public felt that the United

Despite an increase in 1992, turnout remained low, especially at subpresidential levels. Any celebration of voters shifting their party allegiance more in line with their views must be tempered by the simultaneous withdrawal of voters from the electoral universe. The centrality of party to the political discourse following the 1994 election is a promising sign that is discussed further in chapter 6.

Studies of decline and studies of resurgence provide many insights about the condition of parties, but they also share common problems.[8] Both have relied too heavily on the tripartite approach to parties (party in the electorate, party in government, party as organization) and fail to illuminate how changes in one part of the party system might encourage

States should either eliminate party labels from election ballots or have additional significant parties. In a 1991 *USA Today* survey, 41 percent of all respondents volunteered that "neither" party came closer to sharing their values. A 1990 *USA Today* survey found that 51 percent of the public agreed that "neither political party represents my views anymore" (Source: University of North Carolina, Institute for Social Research Public Opinion Index, online).

[8] Despite numerous variations on a theme, four approaches predominate in the party decline literature: the breakdown of confidence, realignment and dealignment, institutional displacement, and Keynesianism and the politics of growth. The level of analysis differs: Breakdown of confidence theories and realignment theories begin with the role and behavior of individuals; institutional displacement theories begin with the role, capacity, and behavior of institutions; and politics of growth theories take policy and coalitions as their benchmark. Confidence theories argue that voters were increasingly detached from parties that failed to confront several concrete political and economic events in ways beneficial to their supporters. In short, a "crisis of confidence" in parties, party leaders, and politicians and government more generally led to less consistent party voting. The various stripes of realignment analysis agree that party decline on both the voter and system level should accelerate a generation or so following a realignment as issues, emotions, and environmental stimuli fade. Institutional displacement theory argues that parties declined as other institutions, such as the media or interest groups, adapted better to the changes of the twentieth century or, alternatively, as changes such as greater educational levels decreased the need for cue-givers. Changes made by Congress to allow construction of member enterprises and candidate-centered campaigning, such as staff increases, travel allowances, franking privileges, district offices, and so on, fall in this latter category (Loomis 1988). Politics of growth studies assert that systems oriented around Keynesian management techniques and operating under some notion of a labor-management accord progressively squeeze allowable debate into narrow parameters. Society is seen as a firm trying to optimize the ratio of output to input, and the state's task is to manage the firm. The questions of importance are focused on expertise in macroeconomic and administrative management; parties can offer little of distinctive significance in such a system. Studies that employ aspects of these approaches include Broder 1972; Alt 1984; Crewe, Sarlvik, and Alt 1977; Ladd 1977, 1978; Burnham 1981b, 1982: chs. 1–2; Lawrence and Fleisher 1987; Schneider 1984; Nie, Verba, and Petrocik 1979; and Dionne 1991 on the decline of confidence; Key 1955; Burnham 1970; Trilling and Campbell 1980; Nexon 1980; Williams 1984; Sundquist 1983; Kleppner 1981; Clubb, Flanigan, and Zingale 1989; Brady 1978, 1980, 1988; Brady and Stewart 1982; Ginsberg 1976; Seligman and King 1980; Meier and Kramer 1980; Hansen 1980; Adamany 1980; Macdonald and Rabinowitz 1987; A. Schlesinger 1984; Silbey 1990; Carmines and Stimson 1981, 1984, 1986, 1989; Carmines, McIver, and Stimson 1987; P. Beck 1974, 1984;

or retard change in another part.[9] Failing to focus on meaningful historical periods is another common weakness. Some studies of decline begin at the turn of the twentieth century and imply that all subsequent changes in party status derive from that historical turning point. Others, perhaps acknowledging that the forces behind changes in party status differ across historical periods, employ alternative starting years but do not indicate why these years are significant. Party resurgence studies, particularly those focusing on party organizations, suffer from a similar weakness. A related problem with much of the decline literature from the 1960s and 1970s that is now emerging in the resurgence literature is selection bias on the dependent variable: Taken from a slice of history, all party measures are apt to show a downward trend. Similarly, in models constructed to explain a decline in a particular measure of party strength, less attention is given to variables that might lead to party resurgence. This creates a dilemma: Models suggesting that parties decline as the media proliferates or geographical mobility accelerates, for example, look plausible on the surface, but they are hard-pressed to account for party resurgence (a change in the dependent variable) as these large trends (the independent variables) continue unabated. Explanations suggesting an ever improving trajectory for the fortunes of parties based on recent improvements are equally problematic.

An adequate explanation of postwar party status should incorporate some reversal of decline, explain why some signs of decline emerge early in the postwar period, and plausibly link together decline (and its reversal) at different levels and roles of party. The major lines of research into resurgence and decline fail on at least one of these points. To their credit, several studies do provide analyses that point to events antedating the 1960s. Most of the theories, however, are unidirectional and stress the slippery slope of decline or resurgence. And some are more adept than others in integrating different kinds of party decline or resurgence. Although there have been some recent attempts to integrate party theory from the perspective of party organization (see Cotter, Gibson, Bibby, and Huckshorn 1984; Baer and Bositis 1988, 1993; Schlesinger 1991), these

---

Abramson 1976; Ferguson 1982, 1984; and Ferguson and Rogers 1981, 1986 on the many varieties of realignment (see also Huntington 1981); Nie, Verba, and Petrocik 1979; Inglehart 1977; Ladd and Hadley 1975; Phillips 1975; Sabato 1981; Blumenthal 1982; Piven and Cloward 1977; Offe 1987; Baer and Bositis 1988; Berger 1981; Pizzorno 1981; Lowi 1979; Huntington 1973; Dodd and Schott 1979; Milkis 1981, 1984, 1993; Shefter 1994: ch. 3; Aldrich 1995; and Skowronek 1982, 1993 on institutional displacement; Skidelsky 1979; Poggi 1978; Offe 1983, 1984; Mollenkopf, O'Connor, and Wolfe 1976; and Wolfe 1977 on the politics of growth. See Coleman (1992: ch. 2) for an extended discussion of these alternative schools, including weaknesses specific to each approach.

[9] Ware (1985) terms this model the "unholy trinity." See also Baer and Bositis (1988).

attempts have largely left out the public. To the extent that the public is considered, cynical beliefs about the parties and withdrawal from the electorate are dismissed as relatively unimportant.[10]

With evidence of both decline and renewal, the data are now available to overcome these problems. Approaching parties from the perspective of the state makes sense of key points in other theoretical approaches, avoids unilinear analyses, and helps connect developments in different portions of the party system. By following the thread of the fiscal state across postwar American party politics, I hope to show that considering the relationship of the state and parties is vital to understanding the status of party in a particular era.

Why is the state's role so crucial? First, state structure places boundaries around the responsibilities of different institutions and the types of policies adopted. Structure does not drop from the sky: The structure that emerges reflects the policy range and actors' roles favored by the dominant political coalition at a particular time, tempered by existing institutions and policy legacies that provide a cumulative sense of what is feasible.[11] Second, state structure builds public perceptions about where policy responsibility lies. When the state had relatively little institutionalized policy from one administration to the next and a relatively circum-

---

[10] Cotter, Gibson, Bibby, and Huckshorn (1984), for example, devote only one paragraph to the public, and the tone is dismissive of public criticisms of the parties. Baer and Bositis (1988, 1993) argue that the parties have incorporated the public by incorporating social movements. Although developing an important argument about party elites, the authors are unable to show finally that this incorporation of social movement elites has had any effect on, or support in, the public. They also dismiss the significance of declining turnout. Finally, Schlesinger (1991) argues that party loyalty in the electorate and the need for strong party organization are inversely related; the improvement in party organization, he argues, results from the uncertainties caused by increased voter volatility. It is plausible (though hardly inevitable) to link an uncertain environment with moves toward stronger party cohesion and party organization. Schlesinger, however, does not explain why voter behavior changed in the first place. And again, exit from the electorate is considered unimportant, except as it might affect the uncertainty of the political environment.

[11] This statement links together two schools of thought that have been in a sharp debate over explaining why the United States (or any country) ends up with policy x and not policy y. On one side are the coalition theorists such as Kurth (1979), Gourevitch (1986), and Ferguson (1984), who see political coalitions as explaining policy choice. On the other side are the more state-centric analysts such as Skocpol and Weir, who argue that one needs to explain policy by looking at the state institutions, the interests of state managers, and the limits posed on innovation by previous policy legacies (cf. Moe 1989). But it seems to me that Skowronek has effectively bridged the debate in his analysis of the 1880–1920 period. In a sense rather different from Marx, Skowronek is echoing one of his dictums: Coalitions can make their structure, but not exactly the structure they please. It is on this point that Skowronek's 1982 work on bureaucracy and his recent (1993) work on the presidency most profoundly intersect. See also Orren and Skowronek's (1994) development of a multilayered perspective to American political development, and Chubb and Peterson (1985).

scribed role for the central government, people saw parties as the locus of responsibility. When policies, programs, and procedures become institutionalized into the state and the president takes the lead role in policy initiation, however, the perception of party importance declines and partisan identification is more fleeting. Parties find it more difficult to challenge the new regime, as Joseph Harris, a research staff director on the President's Commission on Administrative Management, noted in 1936: "We may assume the nature of the problems of American life are such as not to permit any political party for any length of time to abandon most of the collectivist functions which are now being exercised. This is true even though the details of policy programs may differ and even though the old slogans of opposition to governmental activity will survive long after their meaning has been sucked out" (cited in Milkis 1984: 13). Third, the outcome of state policies changes the political environment within which political parties and other organizations operate. For example, the success or perceived success of the state's management can shape the political environment.

In short, the state shapes the relationship between the people, policies, politicians, and the parties. This "shaping" raises important questions: Does the state interfere with party links to voters? What happens to policy control? What conditions make parties "strong"? Are these conditions made less likely by the state? By asking questions such as these, an analysis viewed through the lens of the state can be sensitive to both the limits and opportunities facing parties. Today, American political parties witness both improvement and decline. These diverging paths of resurgence and decline taken by different "parts" of the parties in the present period present an excellent opportunity to understand how these components of the parties fit together.[12]

What Are American Political Parties?

The short answer to this question is that American parties, while not programmatic, have been strongly policy oriented and that this policy orientation matters to both the mass voters and elites (James 1992; Bridges 1994; cf. Bailey 1959: 4). It is also indisputable that American

[12] See Baer and Bositits (1988: chs. 1–2) for an excellent overview of the weaknesses of tripartite theorizing. What was gained from the tripartite model was a rich, extensive, empirical literature on several aspects of American political parties that allowed for finely-tuned, low-to-mid-level theory building. What was lost was the sense that the whole of party was more than the sum of these three parts. Baer and Bositis's analysis suggests that an integrated theory ideally has some notion of "party," how party affects relations between mass and elite, the broad impact of party on politics, and the likelihood of change in party.

parties have assumed over time the "constituent" roles depicted by Theodore Lowi (1975). By this term, Lowi means roles that are constitutive of the political system, functions without which the political system would not operate. Such tasks include overcoming the constitutional separation of powers and branches, keeping conflict within boundaries, monitoring the rules of the game to keep them "fair," integrating new citizens into politics, recruiting and training candidates, running campaigns, and informing voters. In both policy considerations and political roles, then, political parties have been a central element of political life in the United States for both officeholders and the public. The decrease in this centrality is the core of the notion of party decline.

Does Policy Matter?

Party scholars generally agree that American political parties have been predominantly constituent rather than programmatic. Skowronek (1982), for example, argues that through the late nineteenth century the American state was a "state of courts and parties." Party, in his view, was exceptionally strong in this era: Parties linked the national government to each locale, linked the discrete units of government horizontally in a territory, and organized government institutions internally. Parties were less notable for their programs than for the "procedural unity" they lent the state. It was a party structure and party system designed to integrate national government services into local centers of governing activity. Consequently, "building a winning electoral coalition on a national scale substantially reduced the prospects for implementing a positive national program" (Skowronek 1982: 26).[13]

Despite the obvious importance of these constituent functions, it is not obvious that short of programmatic parties the policy consistency of parties must be written off altogether. Although American parties may not have been programmatic and ideological, they have been strongly issue oriented over time; one might label them "policyist." Broad thematic differences have separated the parties over time (Jensen 1981b; Silbey 1984; Hibbs 1987; Budge and Hofferbert 1990; Hofferbert 1993; Stewart and Weingast 1992).[14] Clusters of issue concerns have defined various eras in American political history (Sundquist 1973; Ferguson 1982; Ladd and Hadley 1975; Hahn 1983; Bensel 1990; Aldrich 1995). And nineteenth

---

[13] Jaenicke (1986), largely through the vision of Martin van Buren, presents a concise overview of the early struggle to institutionalize parties in national politics, including the balance between ideology, policy, and commitment to party organizational practices.

[14] Silbey (1984) argues that parties verged on the responsible party model at certain times in the nineteenth century, perhaps most prominently in the 1830s and 1840s.

century congressional voting displayed high levels of party cohesion and interparty conflict, particularly in the latter part of the century.

Not only have parties had some issue content but links between the parties and the populace have been issue related as well.[15] The pre–Civil War party system was critical for the development of the working class (Bridges 1986). Workers, as a minority, found it necessary to work with partisan coalitions at the state and federal level. With unionism not a possible strategy for craftsmen, and militant unionism an unacceptable strategy for others (because of their fear of immigration), workers could be mobilized into cross-class coalitions. Both "ostentatious paternalism" and the tariff that promised to protect American labor from British labor facilitated this process. Indeed, the tariff was "the policy cement of the view that labor and capital shared the same interest" (Bridges 1986: 187) After the Civil War, parties promoted visions of society to create reliable majorities. Partisan solidarities made workers American. Partisanship embraced ethnicity, class identity, and visions of social relations. Partisan identity was "larger" than class or ethnicity, not simply reflective of them. And the choice was firmly embedded in concrete issues: "Workers became Republicans and Democrats not as the result of symbolic or ritualistic activities but in the service of quite objective working-class goals" (Bridges 1986: 192).

The parties organized around issues that "were deeply meaningful to most workers" (Shefter 1994: 145), especially the tariff. Democrats argued that the Republican impulse to tax every article workers consumed (and to elevate blacks to a position of equality with whites) was tantamount to telling people "what they could or could not do on [their] Sundays." Republicans replied that Democrats were indifferent to the plight of workers by being unwilling to assist industry. These appeals held real meaning to citizens. Even if not programmatic, the way that parties and policies were intertwined was what made them significant to the public. The salience of party depended on both their constituent functions and their evident policy relevance. Issues like trade were important not only to the business or agricultural elite or to agricultural laborers but to the growing industrial workforce as well.

One way scholars have explored the link between policy and parties is by making a distinction between distributive and regulatory issues and how these affect parties. This dichotomy can be overdrawn (McCormick 1986: 197–227; Lowi 1975). Distributive issues are said to be "easy" for parties while regulatory issues are difficult and cut across coalitions. But looking more closely at distributive issues makes them appear less easy. If

---

[15] In the late nineteenth century, Jensen writes, "The typical voter relished an articulate long speech unravelling the complexity of national monetary, trade, or constitutional policy" (1981b: 67).

"there were never enough of the choicest resources and privileges to go around" (McCormick 1986: 207), then parties had to make difficult decisions. If the hard times of the late nineteenth century led to great dissatisfaction among elites and demands for widespread retrenchment in the government and in the economy, then it is not so simple to give alternative forms of distributive largesse to groups excluded from a particular distributive benefit.

Even if party conflict were more muted in regulatory than distributive policies, there *were* party differences and they were differences over an increasingly important area of policy. Because elites demanded action, because these were key areas of public concern, and because party members wanted the party to be relevant to the public's and elite's political calculations, parties did not simply avoid regulatory issues after the turn of the century. And despite the mutual appearance of declining party conflict and the onset of regulation at the turn of the century, postwar party conflict had declined for years before the surge of social regulation issues arrived in the 1970s. In short, the importance of a policy to elites and the public, the existence of party divisions, and the ability of the parties to control policy making are key considerations when examining policy.[16] Labeling an issue as regulatory or distributive is not sufficient.

There will be some ebb and flow in how issues play into party competition, and this fluctuation is an important contributor to party status across time. Key notes that party distinctiveness changes over time as parties move from controversy to convergence in the ongoing process he labels "dualism in a moving consensus" (1964: 222–27). Similarly, a key problem in the contemporary West is that the ideal of economic growth "gained an overwhelming grip on the public imagination. It was unanimously endorsed (at any rate in their rhetoric) by political leaders of all persuasions, who treated it on the one hand as utterly self-justifying, and on the other as validating whatever burdens the state might impose on so-

---

[16] Unfortunately, discussions of parties and policy often get tangled up in discussions of the responsible party model. But these are separate considerations. When he argues that American parties "have almost never been 'responsible,' policy-making parties," Lowi (1975: 241) merges two concepts. Responsible parties campaign more or less as a cohesive team on policies, enact those policies when in office, and take responsibility for the results in the next election. So a responsible party is not only a policy-making party and a policy-making party is not necessarily responsible. Policy-making can occur through parties even if the parties are not necessarily responsible. I do not assert that this is desirable, only that it is possible. Otherwise, it is difficult to understand why wealthy individuals and interests pour so much money into political parties. Assuming these people are not irrational and that they do not thrive on the visceral thrills of empty victories, it is reasonable to assume that they see some concrete policy functions of the parties. Whether the parties responsibly campaigned on these policy differences or will mention them in the following campaign is another question.

ciety" (Poggi 1978: 133). The growth of the growth idea, with growth seen as a technical issue, "diminishes the relevance of the parties ideological heritage" and encourages parties to ask voters for ever-vaguer mandates (Poggi 1978: 141). As I suggest, the ebb and flow of these economic management issues help make sense of the decline and partial resurgence of postwar parties.

When Are American Parties "Strong"?

Most discussions of American parties depend on some notion, whether implicit or explicit, of the characteristics of "strong" and "weak" parties. Typically, this designation applies not to individual parties but to all parties in a political system (cf. Alt 1984). That is, it is intended to suggest something about the role, importance, and functioning of parties on a systemic level. American observers often consider parties in the United States to be weak, while those in Europe are said to be strong. But a general perusal of the literature on European parties often reveals the same lamentations about weak, irrelevant, and declining parties that have been common in the United States.[17] This comparison suggests three things: Unless it is defined, the use of strong party/weak party may mask more than it reveals; the sources of party decline may be broader than particularistic events in one country;[18] and the parties may change. On this last point in particular, it does not explain party decline after the New Deal to say that American parties have traditionally been weak. Nor are the events and forces that caused party decline around the turn of the century necessarily the same events and forces that led to later decline. Recognizing change in parties is important: Except for strong contending ideologies, most of what is considered "strong" about European parties can be found at some point in American history.[19]

Putting first things first, how should a strong party be defined? I sug-

---

[17] See, for example, the articles (and bibliography) in Dalton, Flanagan, and Beck (1984); Crewe, Sarlvik, and Alt (1977); Wilson (1979); the essays in Dalton and Kuechler (1990); Esping-Andersen (1990); Mair (1990); Richardson (1991); and Reiter (1991), among many others.

[18] Theoretical treatments of "party government" that focus especially on Europe are essays by Wildenmann, Katz, Pasquino, Freddi, and Smith (all 1986) in an edited volume by Castles and Wildenmann. The second volume of the series (Katz 1987) presents country case studies. For a look at party decline, see Poguntke (1993).

[19] By "strong contending ideologies" I refer simply to the familiar notion that the United States has never had a major party based on nonliberal (for example, socialist) ideas. Even within a liberal consensus, party differences can be dramatic. Defining terms such as "property" and "liberty" and the means to achieve these goals invites contention; occasionally such efforts lead to revivals of republicanism (Morone 1990).

gest a modest understanding of party strength that is synonymous with "healthy" party. The periods of party strength in the United States are notable for three factors. First, the parties had control over a policy domain; second, that policy served to divide the parties consistently over time; and third, it was an area about which voters and elites cared. In other words, strong or healthy parties are parties that provide meaningful cues for the achievement of both individual and collective goals for voters, politicians, and other elites.[20] This conception describes the systemic strength of party rather than the unique characteristics of any individual party. No doubt individual parties will enjoy varying levels of success. But the idea of party decline and the discussion of party in American political development is concerned with the systemic party.[21] Policy areas differ in the likelihood they will support systemically strong parties.

This policy-oriented definition of party strength thus emphasizes concerns that contrast with those expressed in other conceptions of party. Unlike some of the party analyses in the Congress literature, it does not necessarily matter in the policy-oriented definition if parties are strong because of assertive leadership; parties can provide meaningful cues—and be meaningful representative devices—even if leaders are relatively passive. Leaders of a cohesive party may not need to do much leading. This definition also leaves out features that party organization scholars might include in a definition of party strength, such as control over nominations or the amount of ongoing party activity during and between campaigns. Features such as control over nominations may make policy control and party cohesion more possible; in that way these organizational features may assist strength as defined here, but they neither substitute for nor guarantee it.

Since this conception of strength assumes that there is some virtue to party differences, it is appropriate to ask whether voters want the parties to be cohesive and different. While the performance of some "extreme" contemporary presidential candidates—Barry Goldwater, George

[20] Despite the insistence of many strong-party advocates, there is no particular need for the party divisions to be class-based. That is one possible division. But one is reminded that even Antonio Gramsci, surely an advocate of "strong" parties, recognized the effectiveness of cross-class coalitions. Sartori (1990) points out the difficulties inherent in the discussions of class-party links.

[21] Strong individual parties are those that are particularly successful in these strong party periods—they win elections, appear to have the backing of public opinion, and organize effectively to build political debate around policies voters care about and in a fashion that voters find relevant to their lives. It may well be, as Ferguson (1982) suggests, that the messages voters receive are instigated by powerful investors in the parties and not anything that arises from the voters themselves. But voters are not likely to be mobilized for long on a set of issues in which they have no interest. Therefore, the issues still have to have some connection to voter interests.

McGovern—suggests voters veer away from extremes, there is some evidence that voters prefer a choice. Reclassifying data gathered by Martin Wattenberg on public evaluations of the parties, Konda and Sigelman (1987) build positivity indexes for the two American parties together and the Democratic and Republican parties individually. I compared these indexes (which examine voters' "likes" and "dislikes" about the parties in election years from 1952 to 1984) with indexes of intraparty cohesion and interparty dissimilarity in House roll-call votes. The result is a moderate, substantial relationship: The positivity ratings of the two parties correlates with party dissimilarity at .63. The individual positivity indexes correlate with cohesion at .67 and .41 for Democrats and Republicans, respectively. In other words, the more cohesive and distinctive the parties over this thirty-year period, the more positive the public view of the parties in general and the two parties specifically.[22] A more extensive comparison of party distinctiveness with likes/dislikes evaluations from 1952 through 1990 paints the same picture (see table 1.1). Parties are more salient (that is, generate more like/dislike observations from respondents) and attract firmer support when they are distinctive. "Directional" theories of voting reinforce this argument. Rather than favoring parties to move toward a moderate median, voters are primarily interested that public policy head in a direction that they approve (Rabinowitz, Macdonald, and Listhaug 1993). This "directional" behavior means that voters prefer parties to move toward the extremes, though not to be extreme. Supportive attitudes about parties increase when the public is offered two strong, competitive, active party organizations (Coleman 1994). Similarly, periods of high turnout—when voters believe political involvement has some payoff—and periods of high cohesion and conflict have historically tended to coincide. For example, from 1862 through 1970, the congressional turnout rate outside the South correlated with party conflict in the House of Representatives at .50. The relationship is stronger when the fluctuation caused by presidential elections is controlled. In presidential election years, conflict and turnout correlate at .58; in off-year elections, the correlation increases to .69.[23] These various findings make perfect Downsian (1957) sense: More distinctive parties are likely to increase an

[22] The correlations are not spurious. When I compared the positivity indexes with the cohesiveness or dissimilarity of parties at years t-1 and t-2, the correlations dropped anywhere from 50 to 75 percent in magnitude for all three cases (both parties, Democrats only, Republicans only).

[23] Party conflict is measured as the percentage of roll-call votes that pit a majority of Democrats against a majority of Republicans. Scores are calculated for each two-year Congress, not for each year separately. The conflict scores are then compared to the voting turnout outside the South in the subsequent congressional election. For example, conflict in the 1921–1922 Congress is matched with turnout for 1922. Party conflict data is from Clubb and Traugott (1977); turnout data is from Burnham (1987).

Table 1.1
Party Salience and Party Conflict, 1952–1990

	Party Votes	Authorizations Party Votes
Democratic Party Salience	.56*	.60**
Republican Party Salience	.45*	.62**
Overall Party Salience	.53*	.63**
Strength of Partisanship	.60**	.66**

Source: American National Election Studies Cumulative Data File 1952–1990, variables v317, v321, v323, v305. Party votes calculated by the author.

Notes: Entries represent the Pearson correlation between the mean of each salience or strength measure for an election year and the percentage of House budget-related roll-call votes with opposing party majorities in that year. Authorizations party votes indicate the percentage of authorizations votes pitting party majorities against each other. I separate these because they are, arguably, more likely to receive media scrutiny and public attention than are appropriations votes. Salience measures the total number of likes and dislikes a respondent offers for a particular party; strength of partisanship classifies the strength of a respondent's party identification.
*$p \leq .05$; **$p \leq .01$. N = 20.

individual's calculation of the benefit from voting, *if* it is believed that the parties control key policy areas.

All three elements of party health—control of a policy area, contrasting party positions, and the salience of the policy to voters and elites—are relevant in considering the rise of fiscal issues in the 1930s and 1940s. In all three respects, the fiscal state made the prospect of healthy parties in postwar America problematic.[24]

From the Old Deal to the New: Moving Partisan Trade Politics to the Periphery

Before moving to an analysis of the fiscal state, the notion of healthy parties will be made clearer by looking to the past. One need not downplay the other important issues facing parties from the period between Reconstruction and the Great Depression to suggest that trade policy was the most important issue consistently dividing the parties and defining their coalitions. When the parties wanted to express a vision of state-economy

[24] From 1976 through 1982, at least half of the electorate believed that there was no difference in the parties' ability to handle unemployment and inflation (Parker 1986: 394). Cotter (1985) concurs that the decline of partisan identification is most strongly related to a perception that the parties are no longer relevant.

relations and the proper interaction of industry and government, they relied most often on the measures and symbols of trade policy. To be sure, trade was not the only policy separating the parties, but most studies agree that it was the most enduring, crossing even the otherwise momentous party system changes of 1896 (Ferguson 1982, 1984; Bensel 1984; Terrill 1973; Jensen 1981b; McCormick 1986: 57, 210; Shefter 1994: ch. 4; Bridges 1986; O'Halloran 1994; Verdier 1992). Congressional parties developed and defined trade policy; they differed significantly on policy preferences; and voters, including newly mobilized portions of the electorate, understood and cared about the differences. Acknowledging that this era, like others, had serious democratic deficiencies, party scholars at the same time look with favor at the period's cohesive and distinctive parties, extremely high voter turnout, deep public interest in politics and issues, and emphasis on party labels and linkage in campaigning and governing. Trade policy tied together disparate levels of the parties.

Prior to fiscal policy and economic management, the American party system revolved around issues concerning foreign trade and economic development. Tariff politics provided an integration of sorts to the political order. Parties mobilized farmers, businesspersons, and workers and defined their interests in terms of trade issues (Bridges 1986). Tariffs pervaded other issues facing government. On budgetary policy, for example, tariff politics had both direct and indirect effects. A direct effect was a surge in government revenue. Republicans favored increasing spending so that this tariff-induced surge would not create huge budget surpluses. Increasing spending more rapidly than might have been the case under a less hidden tax is an example of the tariff's indirect budgetary effect (Stewart 1989: 63–66).

Ferguson (1982, 1984) has presented the most comprehensive accounts linking trade policy differences to party divisions; other studies also confirm the importance of the division to the party systems of the nineteenth and early twentieth centuries. Party divisions on trade were key for policy outcomes and for party competition for most of the country's history before World War II, according to Barrie (1987). O'Halloran's (1994) statistical analysis of tariff rates demonstrates that party control exerted an independent effect on tariff rate levels. McCormick notes that "Both parties enjoyed dispensing, and fighting about, policies benefiting particular constituencies, but both opposed any significant expansion of public authority. The perennial question of how much tariff protection to place on scores of separate products perfectly fit the major parties of the late nineteenth century" (1986: 173; see also Kleppner 1987; Silbey 1991). Verdier (1992) more narrowly depicts trade policy as salient, divisive, and controlled by congressional parties in the period from 1888 to the New Deal, with a brief executive-led interlude during World War I. Poulshock

(1965), unlike Verdier, suggests the 1880s featured pitched trade battles between the parties. Bensel (1990: 428–29) argues that there were two conflicts over wealth in late-nineteenth-century American politics: One was interregional in which northern workers and capitalists united to expropriate wealth from the South; another was intraregional in which northern capitalists and workers argued over distribution of wealth. In party politics, this latter conflict was subsumed by the former. Interregional issues like tariffs and trade defined the party system. These studies differ from Bauer, Pool, and Dexter's (1963) classic portrayal of the member of Congress as free from the external control of parties, the executive branch, or business, but it is important to remember that they were describing the trade policy system of the late 1950s and early 1960s.

Studies of trade policy suggest several benefits of trade politics for the parties that were not duplicated by postwar macroeconomic policy. First, trade policy was centered in Congress rather than the presidency. Congressional control created a stronger sense that policy positions were *party* positions, not individual or administration positions, and that parties were responsible for the policies adopted. Some recent studies suggest that the executive branch had more importance in trade policy than the literature generally recognizes (Lake 1988b; Frieden 1988), but Congress's position is still critical (Destler 1992).

Second, trade issues would seem to have a more concrete and more understandable impact on a typical voter's livelihood than do fiscal policy and economic management. Where grasping the different impact of a $20 billion and $50 billion budget deficit, or how fiscal policy is offset by monetary policy, or the effect of a myriad of tax change proposals would understandably be difficult and abstract, the difference between protection and no protection or a high tariff and a low tariff for one's industry is easier to grasp.

In turn, voters are more likely to view fiscal policy but not trade policy as a plebiscitary matter. Americans favor low unemployment and low inflation and are not particularly focused on just how these results are achieved. But if one's industry does poorly under protection, the response of the affected individuals—if we can infer from industry political actions (and public opinion data in contemporary periods)—is not to turn to free trade but to demand more protection. Unlike in fiscal policy, "trying something new" has relatively low appeal in trade politics, unless the "something new" is a more vigorous application of an existing policy. The policy tool chosen, not merely the result, is of major interest. Opinions on fiscal policy techniques are likely to be fleeting; on trade policy, stable. At the systemic level, these processes support persistent party conflict on trade with little likelihood of convergence.

A fourth difference is that trade politics, as practiced before the New

Deal, was more closely akin to distributive policies than was later fiscal policy. Although scholars imply incorrectly that distributive policies are easy policies, distributive policies do have some potential benefits for parties. Parties could produce distributive trade policies to retain the loyalty of key economic sectors. Fiscal policy and economic management per se did not enjoy this easy divisibility. Budget policy and tax breaks traveled more along the distributive track than did broader macroeconomic policy, and these are important in postwar politics. But it was the ability to forestall recession and to promote growth that defined the new state and played a dominant role in party campaigning beginning in the 1930s. Democratic reminders of the "Hoover Depression" made a point about the willingness to use government to stanch economic decline; the goal was only secondarily about which budget categories Hoover favored and which ones he ignored. Public knowledge of government spending patterns (the realm of budget policy) is in any case generally low, but the public is generally well aware of the macroeconomic problems of the day (the realm of macroeconomic policy).[25] Public attitudes and political behavior relate more to macroeconomic conditions than to budget shares or personal financial conditions (Kiewiet 1983; Lewis-Beck 1988).

Finally, trade policy fit well into the sectional and cultural molds of American politics. Because industry was sectionally differentiated and because ethnic groups tended to cluster into certain industries and occupational types, politicians tapped into sectional or ethnocultural loyalties to rouse support for particular trade policies. These tactics were more successful after the Civil War than before because of the increased sectionalism in party coalitions after the Civil War. Before the Civil War, parties encountered difficulty building cross-sectional trade policy positions (Ratner 1972). The Democrats, for example, were especially split along class and sectional lines during the administration of Andrew Jackson. Politics at the national level was often more ideologically consistent about tariff and currency issues than politics at the state and local level (McCormick 1986: 210; Reynolds 1988). After the Civil War, partisan policy differences coincided with sectional differences in party strength (Schattschneider 1935: 9). But it is important to recognize that sectional policy preferences were not uniform, and within sections the parties represented significantly different views (Ratner 1972: 18–21). It is also important that economic management was not as well suited for integration into these preexisting sectional and ethnocultural molds.

These trade and fiscal policy comparisons suggest that the linkage of policy to parties is multifaceted and does not lie only in party conflict over

[25] One 1992 study showed that the public considered the relatively small spending areas of welfare and foreign aid (domestic and international handouts in the eyes of many) to be the largest areas in the federal budget (Lewis and Morgan 1992).

policy preferences, although these conflicts are important, or in any one factor. Indeed, while there is substantial evidence of varying levels of partisan conflict across policy areas (see Fenno 1973: 84–85), partisan conflict does not always coincide with public concerns.[26] Partisan differences are particularly high on procedural issues, for example, but these issues hold little if any public interest (Lowi 1975: 273).

How did these trade issues filter down to the electorate? Trade was important for the parties because it allowed a party to "identify itself clearly with a national issue that might give them the internal cohesion necessary to counter the centrifugal forces of sectionalism, ethnic and religious differences, dynamic but uneven economic change, or perspectives limited by the boundaries of a neighborhood or small community" (Terrill 1973: 9; see also McCormick 1986: 57). The tariff linked the interests of labor and capital (Bridges 1986: 187). These "mutualist" sentiments were reflected in national support for the Republican party. Yet ethnocultural historians such as Ronald Formisano, Richard Jensen, and Paul Kleppner argue that economic issues such as trade were important largely for their symbolic content.[27] According to this school, "party rhetoric on particular economic issues could convey to voters a message about where the party stood on cultural issues close to their daily lives" (McCormick 1986: 37). Democrats in the 1890s could paint Republicans high-tariff views as another example of Republican meddling and paternalism (Shefter 1994: 145–46). This dispute over how nineteenth-century parties appealed to the public and, less explicitly, how economic policies were made, is a fascinating one but it should not obscure the central point: the widespread agreement that the tariff issue played a special role in delineating the two parties and that trade was, during that period, a widely perceived and encouraged demarcation. Indeed, trade issues seemed a constant. "Other issues come and go," a journalist wrote at the end of the nineteenth century, "but the tariff issue goes on forever" (cited in Terrill 1973: 36). Divisions over trade policy had been a key difference between the political parties for over a century, and the parties in Congress had control over trade policy (Jensen 1981b). William M. Springer (D-Illinois), chair of the

---

[26] Fenno points out how partisanship varies across committees and how partisanship was interwoven with institutional struggles in the appropriations process (Lowery, Bookheimer, and Malachowski 1985). Formal models of parties typically assume that policy matters for parties, even if only as a means to the greater end of holding power. Studies extending these points are cited in chapter 3.

[27] On the other side, historian Virginia Yans-McLaughlin (1977: 121) suggests that Italian voters in Buffalo's Little Italy at the turn of the twentieth century were not monolithic in their party identification and switched their party voting depending on concrete pragmatic interests. She describes the situation as one of "bitter factionalism" involving rival Italian community leaders. Other recent contributions to this debate include Reynolds (1988), Oestreicher (1988), Argersinger (1992: chs. 1, 8), and Formisano (1994).

House Ways and Means Committee in the fifty-second Congress, published a four hundred-page book of speeches and writings in 1892 focused specifically on tariff reform. Copies of the book were to be distributed by the Democratic National Committee (Springer 1892). The latent function of trade policy, one might say, was party building.

Given the advantages of trade policy for the parties, it is puzzling that in the 1930s the parties would increasingly grant control over trade policy to the executive branch and abandon trade policy as the central point of partisan contention. Beginning with the Reciprocal Trade Agreements Act of 1934 (RTAA), Congress transferred the role of trade policy initiator to the president.[28] Table 1.2 indicates how dramatically things changed after 1934. The table tallies changes in trade laws and regulations as designed to either increase or restrict presidential autonomy. These trade law provisions are weighted equally; the table presents a tally of changes, not a tally of the relative importance of each change. Prior to the New Deal, Congress had in small portions given presidents flexibility in trade negotiations and tariff setting. The column indicating what Congress "took back" is empty for these years because there were in effect so few permanent powers that the president could forfeit. After 1934 the pattern changes. The presumption now is that the president has autonomy in trade policy, and that every few years Congress gives the president more latitude on the one hand while trying to provide some restrictions on the other. Recent studies (Lohmann and O'Halloran 1991; O'Halloran 1994; Martin 1994) reinforce the findings of earlier accounts (Barrie 1987; Destler 1992) that Congress had not handcuffed itself regarding trade policy and that delegating power does not necessarily mean abdicating power. But setting parameters for acceptable policy via delegation is not the same as intensive microcontrol of policy details and is less visible to the public for use as cues. Congress did not abdicate trade policy entirely, but it retained substantially less control over this policy domain than it had before 1934, especially over the fate of individual industries.[29] It increasingly sought to mandate not outcomes but rather access. Revisions in the trade law constituted an incremental approach that allowed more and more interests structured and predictable access into trade policy. Par-

[28] To be sure, Congress, in an environment of emergency, transferred several powers to the president that one would not expect in more "normal" times. But these other areas did not have the emotional resonance of the trade issue and had not been an underlying factor in party divisions for over 130 years.

[29] One reason for Congress's willingness to increase the president's role in trade policy seems to be the particularly close relations important members of Congress shared with Secretary of State Cordell Hull, who was the most important and persistent administration proponent of liberalizing trade and passing the Reciprocal Trade Agreements Act (Karl 1983: 209). Hull's views are presented in Hull (1934a, 1934b, 1935).

Table 1.2

Congressional and Presidential Power in Major Trade Policy
Acts, 1790–1984

Year	Congress Increases President's Autonomy	Congress Restricts President's Autonomy
1790	1	0
1815	1	0
1823	1	0
1824	1	0
1890	1	0
1897	3	0
1909	2	0
1922	1	0
1934	3	5
1937	1	0
1940	1	0
1943	1	0
1945	1	0
1948	1	1
1949	2	0
1951	1	4
1953	1	4
1954	1	0
1955	2	3
1958	1	4
1962	11	7
1963	1	0
1974	8	21
1979	2	0
1984	1	1

Source: Yoffie (1989) and author's calculations.

ticular outcomes were more rarely ordered, although institutional rules
(for example, how one defines "injury") were sometimes altered to make
successful outcomes more likely. Congress's attempts to place some restrictions on the widespread power it had given the president is indicated
in the length of trade bills. The trade act in 1934 ran 2 pages; in 1958,
8 pages; 1962, 32 pages; 1974, 99 pages; 1979, 173 pages; 1984, 102
pages (Baldwin 1986: 38). But the president's power to negotiate re-

mained flexible.[30] Congress did not attempt to regain the kind of control over trade policy it held before 1934.

Why did Congress loosen control over this jealously guarded policy turf? Several reasons seem plausible. First is the fact of the economic crisis itself. The infamous Smoot-Hawley tariff, instituted in reaction to the economic downturn, was a failure from nearly any perspective. It did not stanch the decline. Although it did not initiate the period of economic difficulties, it made things worse. Under these conditions, possibilities widen for dramatic policy change as old coalitions are scattered and old definitions of interests no longer appear tenable. As long as the RTAA seemed to work satisfactorily, there would be little incentive to return to the old system.[31]

But economic crisis is not enough. Previous crises did not lead to major change in the parties control over trade policy. Perhaps this crisis was different because currency devaluation had provided an opening for a free trade policy: Import sensitive industries would be protected, and exporters would (in theory) see their international position improve (Yoffie 1989). These exporters, located in the now dominant Democratic

[30] Destler best describes this "System of '34." He identifies seven major components (1992: ch. 2). First, the "bargaining tariff" replaced the statutory and inflexible tariff of the past. The president would have the authority to initiate and negotiate tariff changes within broad parameters outlined by Congress. Second, the "bicycle theory" stressed the importance of export promotion rather than import protection. During periods of ongoing negotiations, American officials used the negotiations themselves as a tool to deter protectionist demands. If protectionism was pushed during negotiations, these officials would argue, the long-term benefit of open international markets would have been sacrificed for a transient short-term advantage. The idea was that, like a bicycle, "the trade system needed to move forward, liberalize further, or else it would fall down, into new import restrictions. It could not stand still" (Destler 1992: 17). The next component was an "executive broker" to balance domestic and foreign concerns. Cordell Hull first played this role; after 1962, the role was filled by the Special Trade Representative. "Rules" and "objective" procedures for relief, the fourth component, set up administrative channels through which petitioners could seek some kind of trade relief. Channels included, among others, countervailing duty and antidumping procedures, national security exceptions, and escape clause procedures for industries needing a respite from foreign competition. Remedies included tariffs, quotas, and adjustment assistance. In two of the channels, countervailing duty and antidumping, relief bypassed the political arena altogether as an industry that argued a successful case before the proper executive agency received protection automatically. Rules occasionally are politically burdensome, so the system allowed political deals for special cases such as steel, textiles, and so on. Aside from their raw political muscle because of their size, these industries, if they were so inclined, could tie up the administrative channel by filing a flood of complaints. The steel industry took just this path in 1982. The sixth component of the system was strong congressional committees such as Ways and Means and the Senate Finance Committee that could keep product-specific bills and amendments off the House and Senate floors. And finally, the system rested on an assumption of nonparty competition. To Destler (1992: 68), "open U.S. trade policies had been founded, in part, on closed politics."

[31] See Fisher (1972) and Haggard (1988) for the establishment of the RTAA.

party, finally had a reliable institutional vehicle with which to pursue their interests (Ferguson 1984; Ferguson and Rogers 1986; Gourevitch 1986: chs. 3–4). In short, the conjunction of crisis and devaluation with a powerful coalition made liberal trade a potent idea.

Surely a liberalized trade policy could have emerged from a Democratically controlled Congress (Pastor 1980). Why make the executive branch the policy initiator in trade? The most plausible reason why liberalization and presidential autonomy coincided was that the two branches reached an implicit bargain: By giving the president control over trade policy, Congress expected the president to protect members from the kind of special-interest onslaught that produced the Smoot-Hawley tariff (Pastor 1980; Yoffie 1989; Destler 1992). Stated differently, Congress needed to resolve a collective action problem in which district-minded behavior threatened to produce suboptimally high levels of protection (Lohmann and O'Halloran 1991; O'Halloran 1994).[32] To be successful, supporters of liberalization had to provide compensation for opponents of this policy change (Haggard 1988; Goldstein 1988: 187), namely, administrative avenues for firms to get trade relief without employing massive logrolling.[33] And the process has worked. In the postwar period, only a handful of American industries have successfully circumvented the administrative channels of the International Trade Commission and obtained protection directly through Congress or the president (Hufbauer and Rosen 1986).

[32] Schattschneider (1935) remains the single best portrait of the legislative proceedings that led to the tariff.

[33] In contrasting the political significance of tariffs in the nineteenth century and the contemporary era, McKeown makes the interesting point that in the nineteenth century, tariffs were more significant politically because of the lack of alternative policy instruments. Tariffs carried a heavy political burden because "actors deprived in this issue could not readily be compensated by payoffs in other areas" (1984: 231). McKeown also notes that the tariff issue can be evaded today by direct foreign investment. The effect of these two changes, is, first, to "reduce the degree to which the preferences of firms are likely to constrain a government's choices of tariff policies" (1984: 233), and second, to lead to a situation where the same level of economic difficulty would not produce the same level of protection in the twentieth century that it did in the nineteenth. The first conclusion is better supported by his points on compensation and has been a major and occasionally overwrought theme in the state autonomy literature. On the other hand, the availability of alternative forms of compensation cannot alone explain the change in protection from one "equivalent" period to another. One would also need to consider the structure of policy making (for example, the System of '34), the demands of coalitions (Gourevitch 1986), and the demands of industry (Milner 1988; Milner and Yoffie 1989). If the party systems of the nineteenth century were based largely on distributive issues, many writers would question whether alternative compensation was such a new feature of the 1930s. Distributive politics are often viewed as not a zero-sum game. Quoting historian Harry Scheiber, McCormick points out that in a system dominated by distributive politics, "repeated trips to the public trough are possible, both for those who come away empty-handed and for those already well fed" (1986: 208).

Are these sufficient reasons to transfer to the president a potent organizational issue that the parties controlled for over a century and that encouraged party discipline and party affiliation? Probably not. Even the bizarre special-interest carnival of the Smoot-Hawley tariff should not, by itself, have dislodged such a potent system. The relationship between the *nature* of the pleading that went on with Smoot-Hawley and the organizational power of the trade issue is the missing link.[34] One advantage accruing from the old system of trade politics was stability and dependability. Firms, industries, agriculture, and the workers and communities tied to them had fairly stable demands in trade policy. With stable demands, coalition building is somewhat simplified. Logrolling itself can become almost routinized. In the early 1930s, however, members of Congress faced a new *confusion* in trade demands. Accounts of the period (Schattschneider 1935; Ferguson 1984) suggest that industry and company positions on trade were highly undependable by the early 1930s and that the prospect of building stable coalitions likely appeared daunting to the typical member of Congress (Haggard 1988: 104–7). At the least, it was not clear that a division existed that was relevant in the existing partisan terms, as Verdier notes (1992, 1994). While he disagrees that changing industry demands resulted in changes in party politics, arguing instead that the converse is true, Verdier shows that farmers were a wild card that disrupted the existing party business coalitions. Democrats, he suggests, believed that the executive branch could more effectively balance the trade demands of industry and farmers; again, the president was helping Congress solve its collective action problems (O'Halloran 1994). Trade had lost its great organizational advantages for the parties. It was not the onslaught of demands alone that made abandoning trade policy appealing to Congress; it was the disorganized and unpredictable nature of the onslaught. Except for a few industries whose demands changed slowly if at all after World War II—steel and textiles, for example—members of Congress found that administrative channels for protection provided adequate protection for local industries and absolved the member of Congress of any blame should protection not be granted (Coleman and Yoffie 1990).

With the transfer of trade policy responsibilities to the executive branch, trade declined as a central issue of contention between the parties. After World War II, the two major parties became more alike in their views toward trade policy, at least as reflected in roll-call behavior.[35] From

---

[34] Organizational is used here in two senses—that trade was useful for organizing constituencies and that trade was useful for the party organizations.

[35] From 1934 to 1940 no more than five Republicans in either chamber voted for reciprocal trade, but they supported thirteen of sixteen such roll calls from 1943 to 1958 (Fisher 1972: 147). Some of the increased Republican support was due to support for the new peril

1947 to 1964, 60 percent of all trade-related votes in the House were party votes (votes where a majority of one party opposes a majority of the other). From 1965 through 1975 this figure dropped to 49 percent. Party votes declined even further from 1976 to 1982, totaling 44 percent of all votes. But party votes increased to 72 percent from 1983 to 1992. Although conflict substantially increased, it peaked in the first half of this period and tailed off thereafter. I consider in chapter 6 whether this recent polarization may be a harbinger of important and positive changes in the party system.[36]

Moving the party vote cutpoints to 75 percent—defining a party vote as 75 percent or more of one party voting yes while 75 percent or more of the other party votes no—provides another measure of partisan divisions over trade. Using this criterion, 34 percent of all trade-related roll-call votes from 1947 to 1964 were party votes. From 1965 to 1975, 8 percent qualify as party votes, decreasing further to 1 percent from 1976 to 1982, and then increasing to 29 percent from 1983 to 1992. Other measures confirm these impressions. The index of party dissimilarity, a measure of the voting distance between the parties, averages 49 on trade votes from 1947 to 1964, 29 from 1965 to 1975, 27 from 1976 to 1982, and 47 from 1983 to 1992, on a scale of 0 (equal party proportions vote in the same direction) to 100 (parties are unified and vote in opposite directions). Looking at annual averages, from 1947 to 1964 party dissimilarity exceeded 50 five times and exceeded 70 three times. From 1965 to

---

point and escape clauses, more so than an advocacy for free trade. The measures of party cohesion and conflict are discussed more fully in chapter 3.

[36] Data are grouped because of the relatively small number of roll calls in some years (n = 332 for the period from 1947 to 1992). The cutpoints closely coincide with what are generally considered the most momentous changes in postwar trade policy: the granting of authority in 1963 for massive tariff reduction, the reassertion of congressional power in the 1974 Trade Act, and the Trade Act of 1984. As with most analyses of party cohesion, consensus votes—votes where 90 percent of Democrats vote in the same direction as 90 percent or more of Republicans—were eliminated from these calculations. Of the 394 trade-related votes, 62 (15.7 percent) qualified as consensus votes. Years toward the end of the sample have a higher proportion of consensus votes than earlier years, but one cannot necessarily assume that this reflects weaker parties. The implementation of electronic roll-call voting in the House in 1973 plus the increased ability to demand recorded roll-call votes on amendments made roll calls, even on measures that were obviously headed for defeat or passage, easier and less time consuming. Therefore, the increase in consensus votes from 6 percent of the 1947–1964 roll calls to 13 percent of the 1965–1975 roll calls to about 20 percent of the 1976–1990 roll calls probably reflects, at least partly, the practice of electronic voting (cf. Collie 1988b). Including the consensus votes, the party votes percentages are 57, 43, 35, and 59, respectively, for the four time periods mentioned in the text. Eliminating the consensus votes avoids criticisms that roll-call votes make parties look more ineffectual than they really are.

1982, the index topped 50 once, never exceeding 70. From 1983 to 1992, it topped 50 twice but did not exceed 70.[37]

The dominant impression from these data is the declining salience of partisan divisions in voting on trade until the mid-1980s. General studies of trade politics concur with that assessment (Destler 1992, Nivola 1993).[38] Tariff and nontariff protection studies have had difficulty consistently linking the sectoral pattern of trade protection in the postwar United States to party differences. Ray's (1981) study of 225 industries, for example, indicates that tariff rates in the United States (as of 1970) were related positively to market concentration and labor intensity and negatively to the skill level of an industry's workforce. Nontariff barriers existed in capital-intensive industries producing homogenous products with low skill production, where tariff rates were high, and where foreigners also had nontariff barriers. They were not related to industry concentration or the level of imports. Other studies dispute parts of Ray's explanation of the pattern of protection. Despite this disagreement, there

[37] Chapter 3 provides more information on this measure. For now it is sufficient to note that the index runs from 0 to 100, with higher scores an indication of more party conflict. In the late nineteenth century, annual dissimilarity scores as high as 70, 80, or even 90 were not uncommon. After World War II, a score of 50 tends to be considered quite partisan. (As noted above, the annual figures must be interpreted cautiously because of the low number of roll-call votes in some years.) The figures presented in the text are rounded.

[38] Of course, even a cursory look at the party voting data indicates that party splits do not disappear. O'Halloran (1994) suggests that partisan differences on trade remained important in determining the amount of protectionism in United States trade policy from 1949 to 1990. Partisan differences on trade show up by contrasting policy during periods of unified and divided party control of government: Presidents during divided government face more restrictions on their trade authority than presidents in unified government periods, and restrictions lead to higher levels of protection. With only one two-year exception, all the unified government, lower-protection periods from 1949 to 1990 were Democratic and all the divided government scenarios featured a Republican president and Democratic Congress. In short, the partisan divisions between the institutions mattered. Lohmann and O'Halloran (1991) display a similar finding: Party control of Congress is not related to the level of protection unless unified and divided government are taken into account. Hansen and Powers (1994) suggest that their data show party conflict on trade issues to be higher in the 1980s than the 1880s, but some of this data is misread. For example, in their data, senators from unified states (both senators of the same party) were about 20 percentage points more likely to vote the same way on trade votes in the 1980s than the 1880s, thus giving a clear "party intensity" edge to the 1980s. But senators from split-control states were *also* about 20 points more likely to vote together in the latter period, suggesting partisanship was more intense in the earlier period—that is, split-control-state senators were less likely to vote together in the earlier period. These patterns suggest an overall increase in *consensus* on trade matters in the 1980s: Whether under split or unified control, senators were voting the same way more often. Hansen and Powers' data also show that if one looks only at votes in which 60 percent of each party's members voted the same, partisanship is clearly more notable in the earlier period: Compared to the 1980s, split-state senators in the 1880s were less likely to vote the same way and unified-state senators were more likely to vote together.

is only sketchy evidence in these critiques that party conflict, either in Congress or the White House, produced differing levels of protection across industries. O'Halloran (1994) makes the strongest effort to link party to the tariff rate structure, but her effort focuses on the period before 1934.[39]

The decreased centrality of trade divisions is evident and understandable in the post–New Deal period. Parties before the 1930s had domain over the trade policy area and fully appropriated any political benefits (or costs). With firm coalitions, stable industrial sector support, strong economic growth, and policy power clearly located in the parties, there was a strong incentive to support specific measures (a tariff, for instance) that explicitly distinguished between winners and losers. The other party would stand firmly and openly with an opposite view of the measure.

After the 1930s, the parties did not have each other as a trade policy foil. When trade policy leadership moved to the executive branch, interests organized within the parties were in flux and less predictable. With coalitions in flux, compromises within each party were increasingly necessary, and these internal compromises brought both parties toward the middle on trade issues and methods. These coalition-building strategies encouraged trade remedies that appeared dramatic but were not sharply disadvantageous to groups not involved in the protection.[40] With supporters in flux, there was less incentive for the parties to favor a trade remedy that sharply disadvantaged one group to benefit another (Coleman and Yoffie 1990: 141–42). These changes initiated in the 1930s do not mean that a party system oriented around trade policy has become impossible—indeed, in chapter 6, I suggest that divisions over trade policy could reemerge as a central and meaningful difference between the parties. What these changes do show is that trade did not play the same positive role for the parties after 1934 as it did prior to that period. When trade collapsed as the central dividing line between the parties, some other

[39] A representative sample of studies discerning the reasons that protection (or liberalization) looks the way it does includes Pincus (1977), Brock and Magee (1978), Ray (1981), Stone (1984), Conybeare (1983), Krasner (1979), Esty and Caves (1983), Hansen (1990), Gallarotti (1985), Finger, Hall, and Nelson (1982), Helleiner (1977), Gutfleish (1986), Baldwin (1986), Lavergne (1983), Hughes (1979), Goldstein (1986), and Lenway (1982). See Nelson (1988) for an excellent analysis of the theoretical literature. O'Halloran's (1994) study makes the case for the influence of party for overall tariff levels and for *changes* in the sectoral level of tariffs. From a group of sixteen sectors, in six sectors O'Halloran finds the two parties' effects on changes in tariff levels to be in opposite directions and significantly different from zero. In eleven sectors, the difference between the Democratic and Republican coefficients are significant. O'Halloran (1991) was less successful connecting party to the level, rather than the change in the level, of sectoral tariffs.

[40] Voluntary export restraints provided one of the more popular means to perform this balancing act (Coleman and Yoffie 1990).

issue could move to the surface. That issue was management of the economy, especially fiscal policy.

Conclusion

Because state building is a political act, taking the state seriously discourages ruminations on either the inevitable decline or inevitable resurgence of parties due to some "law" of development or economics or technology or adaptation. Rather, it is an approach that seeks to understand change in the status of parties by pointing to some of the macroconditions that improve or worsen that status. In the following chapters, I argue that looking at postwar parties through this lens suggests that a reversal of decline can be expected at particular levels of party when a specific fiscal-state constraint is reformulated, but a party renewal that sweeps through government, organizations, and the electorate depends on major changes in the state-economy relationship. Broad-scale challenges to the fiscal state proved to be electorally fruitless when that state was considered a success. Replacement or redefinition of that state became politically viable when the fiscal state was widely perceived to have failed by the late 1970s. But party renewal in the 1980s and early 1990s was partial because changes in the fiscal state were partial.

Focusing on politics and state building also stresses that at some historical points parties may be innovative and push political development rather than simply respond and adapt to a continuing flood of "forces." Sorauf's (1975) observation that parties "cannot step outside of the political system in order to get greater leverage on it" is probably true for most periods, but at times this leverage is greater than others and is reflected in the politics of state building. This need not mean a bigger, more encompassing state. The parties of the late nineteenth century made decisions about the relation between the state and economy. It is hard to believe that the populist movement would not have made significantly different choices (Goodwyn 1978) and effectively redirected American political development, but this is what much of the thinking about parties concludes (Schlesinger 1991).[41] Southern Democrats during the New

[41] Schlesinger (1991) makes a persuasive case about the importance of the goal of office seeking to the achievement of other party goals; he goes too far by suggesting that if policies are too dominant in a party's appeal, its electoral fortunes will suffer. Goodwyn's (1978) analysis suggests just the opposite—the decline of the People's party began when that party tailored its policy appeal to fit within the limits of the two dominant parties. The Populists proposed an alternative path to development, not a retrograde attempt to save the past. Their fortunes suffered as this agenda was watered down to meet the needs of the Democratic party.

Deal and immediately after surely had an important proactive effect on political development in areas such as social welfare and labor law. Simply put, while environmental factors including the state and policy will limit parties, there are times when parties can also influence and shape the environment.

This book focuses on the status of parties in postwar America, but parties have faced challenges in other periods. Some signs of party weakness—such as declining turnout and decreased party distinctiveness in Congress—emerged in the early decades of the twentieth century (Burnham 1981b). This decline can be viewed through the prism of a changing state. Changes in state structure do not necessarily produce party decline: Structural changes will have implications for parties that can be either positive or negative. Scholars have hinted at this connection. McCormick (1986) suggests that changes in the mix of policies being funneled through the state changed the status of parties, while Skowronek (1982) points to structural changes in the rise of the civil service system. Considering the major policy division discussed in this chapter, in the early decades of the twentieth century congressional parties still dominated trade politics, but the executive found ways to intervene in specific instances (Lake 1988a). There were signs of increased intraparty tensions on trade during portions of this period (Wolman 1992). In other major areas of congressional party concern, party control was also challenged and redefined. This challenge was most notable in currency with the formation of the Federal Reserve System in 1913, but also appears to a lesser extent with initial moves toward president-driven budgeting in the Budget and Accounting Act of 1921. Party organizations were also challenged as government began to integrate and absorb the party through reforms of ballots, elections, and party procedures. As noted above, reforms such as the direct primary weaken party organizations and perhaps produce less cohesive parties, but of greater importance to voters and the system is what parties do. To the extent that state redefinition led parties after the turn of the century to begin losing policy control, then it is not surprising to see signs of party weakness emerge in this period.

The remainder of this book makes the case for focusing on the state and policy in the study of postwar American parties. Chapter 2 explores the formation of the fiscal state between 1937 and 1946 and explores how this state constrains political parties and how it should affect party behavior. Reviewing several policy and institutional debates points out how the postwar position of the parties was importantly shaped by decisions made during this state-building period. The next two chapters explore how parties in the House of Representatives behave with the fiscal state in place from 1947 through 1990. Since I have suggested congressional parties are a linchpin in the party system, it is especially important to see what messages emerge from the parties when the economic system is under stress. In a system explicitly intended to manage the economy, what choices do the parties offer the public during economic downturns? Chapter 3 presents roll-call data and builds a model of aggregate party cohesion and conflict to test whether the parties behave in a pattern expected by fiscal state premises. Chapter 4 pushes this analysis further by considering two topics. First, sectionalism has been a central concern of students of American parties. At times it has been variously suggested that party splits simply overlapped sectional splits; at others, the sectional diversity within a single party has been seen as a more fundamental dynamic in politics than interparty competition. Because of the importance of sections in the study of American parties, I take the roll-call votes introduced in chapter 3 and examine the impact of North-South divisions in the Democratic party. Does sectionalism nullify the effectiveness of examining parties in the context of state structure and policy? Second, because the literature on the authorizations and appropriations aspect of government budgeting is often separated, I examine whether fiscal state expectations for party behavior hold across these different types of votes.

Chapter 5 returns to qualitative analysis to examine how parties in the fiscal state respond to three postwar recessions. I discuss substantive responses to economic problems and consider the relationship between the president and congressional parties. Finally, chapter 6 reviews the findings, suggests some implications of these findings for American politics, and considers the possibility of party revitalization in light of changes in political economy and the results of the 1992 and 1994 elections.

Why be so concerned with explaining the changing status of political parties? Certainly, most students of parties believe that parties perform sufficiently important roles in the political system that their declining relevance and impact presents a "hole" of sorts in the mediation between citizens and the state.[42] This "hole" in the representative system raises direct questions about the nature of American democracy. Ultimately, the point is the people and democracy. Poggi (1978: 144) asks of parliament, but one might well ask of party, "If it ceases to operate as an effective link, what or who can politically direct, control, and moderate the ever-growing mutual involvement between state and society?" If parties lose control of policy and the state, citizens lose as well.

[42] Or, more precisely, parties at least potentially play these roles under certain conditions. See King (1969), Rose (1980), and Schonfeld (1983) for skeptical views.

2

The Formation of the Fiscal State

DEFINED BY programs and institutions, the fiscal state emerged in an erratic sequence from 1937 to 1946. Similarly, the future place of party emerged not in any manifesto but in bits and pieces. Debates with significance for the role of party were sometimes explicitly framed as debates about parties and sometimes framed in terms of congressional power. This split is not surprising, because members of Congress had twin concerns. The first concern was maintaining Congress's independence: In a legislature becoming more "professional" (Polsby 1968) and more decentralized, threats to congressional autonomy would directly affect the electoral future of an individual representative. The second concern was to maintain the organizational strength and importance of congressional parties: Many members recognized that periods of congressional strength had also been periods of strong party cohesion. But the second concern was more complicated than the first. While all members recognized the value of congressional autonomy, most in this increasingly professionalized institution felt just as strongly about their autonomy from the parties. Members were often willing to voice their support for measures to keep Congress strong, but they were often not as vocal regarding measures to keep congressional parties strong. Ultimately, this split thinking weakened both institutions.

In this chapter, I examine several institutional debates from 1937 to 1946 that contributed to the development of the fiscal state. How did the role and fate of the parties enter discussions on the structure of postwar economic management? Did members of Congress link the changes in the political system to their effects on parties? What trade-offs were members willing to make? Rather than taking the battles solely on their own terms—did the recession of 1937 validate Keynesian dictums, for example—I ask what the debates meant for parties. Reviewing key institutional episodes over a ten-year period points out both the intentional and unintentional consequences for parties set in place by decisions made during the building of the fiscal state.[1] At times, questions concerning the importance of party were stated directly; at other times, questions about

[1] Katznelson and Pietrykowski (1991) independently have used similar language in their discussion of the "developmental" and "fiscalist" alternatives contending during the 1930s and 1940s. Our approaches are also compatible in that we both argue that one cannot meaningfully talk about state structure without also talking about policy (see also Coleman 1991).

Congress as an institution had implications for party. Most important, the willingness to tolerate presidential ascendancy over macroeconomic management in exchange for congressional party control over budgetary distribution proves to have especially important, negative consequences for the postwar parties.

I begin by explaining the concept of the fiscal state and indicating how this state constrains parties. These constraints were not in each case designed with the explicit intention of weakening parties; rather, as part of the process of institutional redefinition in this period, parties were sometimes affected inadvertently when other priorities predominated, sometimes directly when politicians made decisions about the role of parties with eyes open. In both instances, the consequences were significant for the future status of parties. Next, I turn to the case studies of key institutional debates concerning the recession of 1937, budgetary reform, executive reorganization, postwar planning, and legislative reorganization. Finally, because changes in the state can redefine and strengthen the position of political parties, I examine whether recent institutional changes have erased the limits of the fiscal state. Because the New Deal period is well-trod scholarly ground, I attempt here to focus tightly on the concerns listed above and avoid rewriting the extensive and well-known literature on the New Deal. Several of the longer sources cited provide useful, multifaceted review of the period.[2] I approach this chapter through debates to show the piecemeal construction of both structure and policy that built the fiscal state. None of these debates are unconnected with outcomes; some propose policy changes and introduce legislation while others pass legislation.

Political Parties and the State

Scholarly efforts to consider the interrelationship of the state and American parties have been conceptually informative, despite being small in number. Shefter's (1994: ch. 3) discussion of conflicts between political parties and government bureaucracies (also Shefter 1994: ch. 2; Ware 1988), Skowronek's (1982) depiction of the restructuring of state and destructuring of party in the Progressive period, and Milkis's (1981, 1984, 1993; cf. Eden 1993; Brand 1993) proposition that Franklin Roosevelt institutionalized programs in the executive branch in a deliberate effort to weaken the role of party all suggest key linkages between state structure—and to a lesser extent policy—and the status of parties (cf. Jensen

---

[2] For economy of space, my presentation of primary materials relies on archival records and the *Congressional Record*. Secondary sources cited make use of other primary resources.

1981b: 76–77).[3] None of these models is fully appropriate for understanding postwar party decline, and none assist in understanding party resurgence. Shefter asserts the onset of party decline but is unable to pinpoint its cause. Skowronek projects forward all party decline from one restructuring episode.[4] And because he does not trace out the implications of his important starting point, Milkis leaves open many questions. What kind of party decline is most instigated by these changes in structure? Is it possible for parts of the party system to be in decay while other parts seem to revive? Does specific policy content affect party status?

Politics of growth studies add the policy these state structure analyses ignore (see also Piven 1992: 242–45, 255–57). Growth studies argue that systems oriented around Keynesian policy techniques squeeze debate into narrow parameters (Skidelsky 1979; cf. Lipset 1968: ch. 7) and render legislative parties unimportant on the key issues of governance that rely on expertise in macroeconomic management (Poggi 1978). These two processes make parties less central to governing and citizens less likely to perceive them as relevant institutions (Offe 1984: ch. 7; Wolfe 1977). The impact of Keynesianism on parties is thus profound: "The issues and conflicts that remain to be resolved within the realm of formal politics (party competition and parliament) are of such a fragmented, nonpolarizing, and nonfundamental nature (at least in the areas of economic and social policy) that they can be settled by the inconspicuous mechanisms of marginal adjustments, compromise and coalition-building" (Offe 1983: 238–39).[5]

The Fiscal State

Although providing leverage for understanding party decline, these literatures are unilinear and undifferentiated: They explain neither the current revitalization of American parties nor the partial nature of this revitalization. Party decline is presented as irreversible and the various compo-

---

[3] An important early effort along these lines came from Huntington (1968: ch. 2), whose Tudor Polity argument illustrated (if not as its primary purpose) the limiting conditions imposed on American parties by the highly fractionalized structure of the American state. For example, in a manner that does not rely on the usual (albeit pertinent) observations about heterogenous diversity, the Tudor Polity thesis tells us much about the difficulties in building programmatic parties in the United States. Despite this promising start, most studies of parties emphasize how parties limit the state, not how the state might limit parties.

[4] With a different focus, Lewis-Beck and Squire 1991 also pinpoint this earlier period as more fundamental to public policy than the New Deal period.

[5] Along with signs of declining party saliency, Offe argues, one also sees a deradicalization of parties, more heterogeneity within parties, and increasing deactivation of the party's mass base.

nents of the party are assumed to decline together. Analysis based on the fiscal state attempts to overcome these weaknesses.

With the coming of the New Deal, particularly after the turn to a quasi-Keynesian policy in 1938 (Salant 1989; Winch 1989), state management of the economy concentrated on modifying the business cycles that were such a characteristic feature of the American economy.[6] The many institutional and policy innovations of the New Deal are well known (Hawley 1966; Stein 1969; Conkin 1975; Nash 1981),[7] but the whole of these innovations—which I label the "fiscal state"—are more important than the sum of the parts.

The "fiscal state" refers to the system of economic management established in the United States during the 1930s and 1940s. A workable concept of the state needs to include structure, dominant assumptions about state-economy relations, and policy concerns.[8] The fiscal state saw proactive economic management as *the* central domestic responsibility of government. It consists of the economic policy-making institutions in the government; the liberal values that motivate the actions of actors in these institutions, especially limited centralized intervention and the separability of the economic and political spheres; and macroeconomic regulation

[6] Government certainly had a role in the economy even before the New Deal. From feudal-like regulation of labor in the colonial era (Morris 1946) to financial assistance, land grants, and favorable legal interpretations during the nineteenth century (Horwitz 1977; Scheiber 1981), through the blossoming of economic regulation in the Progressive era (Kolko 1963) and the development of corporatist and associative arrangements in various industries in the 1920s (Hawley 1981; Keller 1987), governments at all levels, particularly the state and local level, assisted and promoted economic development. Katznelson argues that "Taking the state as a whole, the American formula . . . in the nineteenth century was not the development of a weak state (though, taken on its own, this is a reasonable appellation for the national state), but the development of a diffuse and complicated, but nevertheless supple and capable, state apparatus. This regime had three main elements: a balance between center and periphery in a continental state, the vesting of most state-market transaction rules at the state and city levels, and the creation of a strong set of localistic linkages to the state for white male voters" (1989: 47).

[7] See Scheiber (1981) for a discussion of these innovations; see a series of articles by Skocpol (Skocpol 1980; Skocpol and Finegold 1982; Skocpol and Ikenberry 1983; Weir and Skocpol 1985) for insightful examinations of the limits and possibilities of changes during the New Deal. Hacker (1947) suggests that the New Deal's tactics were: (1) restoration and maintenance of prices; (2) reduction of debt; (3) revival and expansion of credit; (4) raising of purchasing power of labor; (5) relief of needy, protection of dependents, and social security; (6) construction of homes; (7) protection of investor and saver; (8) rehabilitation of electric power industry; (9) revival of foreign trade; and (10) pump priming, lend and spend, deficit financing.

[8] Katznelson's notion of the state is similar: "The state is, simultaneously, a unit of decision-making authority, a set of social relations of power and social control, a normative order, and a legal and institutional order that represents, shapes, and manages conflict, and that organizes a framework for the market economy while acting to alter market outcomes" (1989: 47). See also Katznelson and Pietrykowski (1991).

of the business cycle based on an arm's-length transfer of cash from one economic sector to another. Structurally, the fiscal state featured presidentially led fiscal policy, congressional adjustment of presidentially suggested budget distribution, and less directly controllable (by Congress or the president) monetary policy. Within the executive, fiscal policy was built through varying collaborations of agencies (differing across presidencies), with a central theoretical and ideological role for the Council of Economic Advisers and a central implementation role for the Budget Bureau (later the Office of Management and Budget). Regarding policy preferences, the state began in 1933 to undergird the economy with a set of measures designed first to ensure stability and later to promote growth. Rather than merely react to crises this new state intended to *prevent* major economic upheavals like the ones in the 1890s and 1930s and to "smooth" the business cycle over time.[9] By following the policy prescriptions of Keynesian economics—running budget deficits to offset slow economic growth and running surpluses (or smaller deficits) to decrease growth—the state could produce consistent, stable levels of economic growth. Economic stability produced, it was believed, the attractive side benefits of social and political stability. The "fiscal" in "fiscal state" indicates not only the central position of fiscal policy and Keynesian ideas in

[9] Just how responsible the state was for the relative economic success of the postwar period has become a highly contentious issue. (Okun's study of Keynesianism's heroic years is one of the more optimistic accountings: "When recessions were a regular feature of the economic environment, they were often viewed as inevitable" (1970: 32). At the time Okun was writing, the economy had expanded for over one hundred months continuously. One might also note that in 1968 the Census Bureau changed the title of its monthly economic report from *Business Cycle Developments* to *Business Conditions Digest*.) There is no way to resolve that debate here. But three important points can be made. First, there does exist a rather impressive body of literature suggesting that the state and the nature of governing coalitions at least partly shape economic outcomes (Martin 1973; Hibbs 1977; Beck 1980; Cameron 1984a, 1984b; Eisner and Pieper 1984; Mahler and Katz 1984; Alesina and Rosenthal 1989; Nordhaus 1989; Budge and Hofferbert 1990). To be sure, this conclusion is not universally held. Rose (1980), Schmidt (1982), and Alt (1985) appropriately urge caution.

Second, even monetarist critics of fiscal policy admit that fiscal policy can have short-run beneficial effects, and the short-run may be what is important in practical politics.

Third, even if the state had nothing to do objectively with economic success, the widespread perception was that the state was indeed responsible for economic conditions. Shonfield (1965), Collins (1981), and the writers in Boltho (1982) make this case regarding business elites. They argue that business confidence in state management of the economy, whether justified or not, contributed to fairly steady economic growth and acquiescence to government policy (in the Western countries generally). Public opinion surveys in the United States throughout the postwar period make it clear that the general public considered the state and the government responsible for economic conditions. Even after years of economic problems and in the midst of deep stagflation, about 70 percent of the public in June 1980 believed that "a president of the United States can make a real difference" on preventing recession and cutting inflation (Louis Harris Survey, June 1980, study 802115).

managing the economy but also the nature of much of the stability and growth apparatus. In fiscal policy, a conservative, "commercial" Keynesianism (Collins 1981) that downplayed discretionary budget adjustments and spending increases in favor of "automatic" adjustments and tax cuts was at most times dominant. In other economic policy, the general idea in the fiscal state was not to intervene directly on a microlevel (although in certain instances this happened). Instead, government should restore order in an arm's-length fashion by providing cash, transfer payments, loan guarantees, and "bailouts," and defining rules and restrictions concerning cash flows, bank finances, stock transactions, and the like. If the fiscal state's macroeconomic measures produced growth by successfully manipulating the economic environment, the more drastic measures such as bailouts or direct microeconomic control of business activities should be infrequently needed. The fiscal state, then, is characterized by its policy preoccupations and the manner in which policy was made. Both policy and structure had implications for parties.

The Fiscal State and Its Constraints on Parties

As part of the environment affecting parties through the early 1990s, the fiscal state imposed constraints on parties and encouraged some actions more than others. What limits did the fiscal state place on parties? Five constraints are especially important. Some of these constraints built on features that were incipient, but weak, before the 1930s. The Federal Reserve, for example, began operations in 1913. And the Budget and Accounting Act of 1921 inaugurated a degree of presidentially led budgeting. But none of these constraints was cast in concrete or inevitable: The institutional debates discussed below indicate that other outcomes were possible. The fiscal state that emerged from these debates created a set a challenges for political parties.

First, fiscal policy in the fiscal state was centered in the executive branch. Obviously, Congress had some say on the distribution of funds. But the close congruence between presidential suggestions for total and departmental spending and subsequent congressional appropriations suggests that Congress rarely pushed a markedly different fiscal policy than the incumbent administration (Peterson 1985; Peterson and Rom 1989; Kiewiet and McCubbins 1991: 186–205). Particularly in the total level of spending and taxing, which is the crux of the Keynesian approach, Congress rarely differed significantly from the administration.[10] Kiewiet and

---

[10] Of course, within Keynesian theory, it does matter where the money goes: One wants the money to reside in the hands of those with relatively high marginal propensities to consume. In addition to the Peterson and Peterson and Rom studies, other works examining

McCubbins (1991) make a strong case that congressional delegation of spending power does not equate to abdication of that power; at the same time, their statistical analysis shows that Congress accommodated the president's requests and preferences on appropriations. The president's request, conversely, did not appear to take the congressional reaction into account.[11] Economic programs were commonly viewed as the programs of presidents ("Carternomics," "Reaganomics") rather than the program of the party itself. Presidents in the fiscal state reinforced this distinction between themselves and their congressional parties to an unusual degree. Hinckley (1990) shows that presidential speeches changed radically in the postwar period, as presidents sharply reduced their references to parties, elections, mandates, and the like. By contrast, earlier presidents emphasized in precise and frequent ways their connections to their congressional party, how they perceive their mandate, and what previous elections meant for the party and the president's position in it. Fiscal state presidents presented themselves as separate from and outside their parties; this presentation of self was perfectly suited to the economic management structure and policy of the fiscal state. Until changes in the 1970s (discussed below), Congress lacked some of the institutional tools to be the leading force in macroeconomic policy. Fiscal policy, unlike the trade policy that formed the major party divide in the nineteenth century, was less a domain of congressional parties and less under their control. To the public, the president appeared key.

Second, automatic fiscal policy weakened the link between parties and policy. "Uncontrollable" and entitlement spending—spending outside the normal appropriations process whose level is determined by formula rather than a specific budgetary allocation by the president and Congress—siphoned off large parts of potential party influence. "Automatic" countercyclical stabilizers kicked in without the specific instigation of the president or Congress when economic conditions warranted. For example, when unemployment increased and wages stagnated, tax contributions decreased. At the same time, spending on unemployment insurance and low-income assistance programs automatically increased to cover new beneficiaries, producing deficits. Automatic withholding of Social Security contributions further institutionalized this pattern. For the most part, these measures were off the table for party debate, including during recessionary periods. The debates that did arise were typically over length;

Congress's position in the postwar political and budgetary order are cited later in the chapter. Chapter 5 considers how and when congressional parties appear especially assertive and distinctive relative to the president.

[11] Kiewiet and McCubbins also find that Congress makes consistent and predictable adjustments to the presidential figures based on, for instance, economic conditions and which party is in the majority.

for instance, should we extend unemployment insurance coverage another ten weeks? These debates were not trivial, but the automatic nature of the spending dampened the ability of the parties to distinguish themselves on policy. Indexation of spending programs automatically adjusted spending to match changes in inflation. Although not economically countercyclical like the automatic stabilizers, indexation produced similar political results by removing issues from partisan debate. Discretionary spending or taxing, on the other hand, would force party distinctions—if any—to the surface.

The divided control between monetary and fiscal policy was a third limit on parties in the fiscal state. Fiscal policy was clearly in the purview of the executive and legislative branches; monetary policy was constructed by the Federal Reserve Board and was formally independent of ongoing presidential and congressional control. Although the level of Federal Reserve Board independence is a matter of some contention, Congress and the president did not have the same *direct* control that they possessed in fiscal policy. Congressional parties could shift the blame for economic problems, but blame shifting had costs—the parties would be hard-pressed to claim credit when economic news was good. Moreover, if control of the money supply became more significant in determining the health of the economy than was fiscal policy (Peterson and Rom 1989), then congressional parties had weak access to the more important policy tool. Perceptions of the relevance of congressional parties were bound to decline under such circumstances. Even if monetary and fiscal policy were equally important, the structural problem is that in the fiscal state party access to the monetary tool was restricted.[12] For example, one comparative study of the economic effect of partisan control of government and the autonomy of the central bank after 1971 shows that generally one must consider these variables in conjunction (Way 1994). Inflation will be lower and unemployment higher in a left government/independent central bank mix than in a left/dependent combination. For the United States, however, an independent central bank leaves party without a significant impact on inflation and unemployment from 1971 through 1992. Kane (1987, 1988) depicts a "fedbashing" relationship between Congress, the president, and the Fed—the president and Congress attack Fed performance but have no real interest in expropriating the Fed's power, and the Fed goes along with this "abuse" to protect its political perks. This depiction seems to fit the basic contours of the rise and fall of the Fed issue in the post–New Deal recessions (Kettl 1986). These institutions placed some loose outer limits on acceptable Fed behavior, but their control over

[12] Again, one can contrast this situation with the period before 1900. Not only were parties clearly the primary locus for control over trade policy, the gold versus silver versus greenback controversy was centered in the parties as well.

daily Fed decision making was less direct than was their control over fiscal policy (Woolley 1993: 19–25).

A fourth problem for parties in the fiscal state arose from the plebiscitary nature of macroeconomic goals. Politics oriented around Keynesian macroeconomic management methods tended to focus most strongly on issues most amenable to this type of management—inflation, unemployment, and economic growth. Presidential administrations of different parties tended to favor different mixes of these ingredients (Hibbs 1977). But did voters focus on partisan policy loyalties and policy intentions? Apparently not. Retrospective voting models suggest that for most voters the voting choice indicated approval or disapproval of the *results* of incumbent administration policy more than it indicated approval or disapproval of any particular economic policy (Fiorina 1981).[13] This is a dramatic change from the period before the 1930s. Voters then could not easily flip between free trade and protectionist demands, but they did flip frequently between alternative promises of macroeconomic growth after the 1930s.[14] The postwar "plebiscitary" voting for president also shows up in aggregate party identification and presidential approval, both of which fluctuated in response to economic conditions (MacKuen, Erikson, and Stimson 1989; cf. Jensen 1981a). Voting at the congressional level, in contrast, did not appear to be plebiscitary in the same way and proceeded on other cues, including incumbency and constituency service (Jacobson 1992; Abramson, Aldrich, and Rohde 1990: ch.10). This split-level view of the president and Congress helps explain why scholars have had more success linking economic and personal financial conditions with presidential voting than with congressional voting (Kuklinski and West 1981; Kiewiet 1983; Chappell and Keech 1985; Lewis-Beck 1988), and why incumbent-based elections and ombudsman services have become staples of the Congress literature (Mayhew 1974; Burnham 1975; Fiorina 1977; Cain, Ferejohn, and Fiorina 1987; Alford and Brady 1989; Parker 1989; cf. McAdams and Johannes 1988). The influence of the economy on congressional elections has been much more contentious than on the presidential side, with scholarly interpretations covering a wide range. It is probably fair to say that the rough consensus is that economics do not directly affect congressional elections to the same degree as presidential elections, that economics is not the predominant determinant of congressional election outcomes, and that to the extent congressional elections *are* driven by economics they represent punishment of the incumbent pres-

---

[13] Whether voters tend toward retrospective or prospective behavior has been a matter of contention in recent literature. See Haller and Norpoth (1994) for an overview of the debate.

[14] That is, if one's industry was protected but still suffering, one would demand additional protection rather than open trade.

ident rather than any particular evaluation of the economic performance of congressional parties themselves (Tufte 1975; Abramowitz, Cover, and Norpoth 1986; Radcliff 1988; Erikson 1988, 1990; Jacobson 1989; Born 1990; Waterman, Oppenheimer, and Stimson 1991; Lewis-Beck and Rice 1992; Campbell 1993; Alesina and Rosenthal 1995).

This analysis might appear to contradict public opinion data. Survey respondents are almost reflexively critical of Congress as an institution, if more gentle on their own representatives and senators. When comparing an abstract "Congress" to an individual president, respondents tend to blame the abstract institution. But digging a little deeper shows that public opinion is more complicated than this statement implies. For example, Louis Harris (studies 7580, 7583, 7588) asked respondents during the recession in March 1975 how much they would blame various institutions for the recession. Just over 35 percent said they blamed "Congress" "very much," with 17 percent blaming "the Ford Administration" very much. But 35 percent blamed the more abstract "Republican Administration in Washington" very much. And 57 percent blamed "a lack of leadership in the country." Earlier, I noted that 70 percent of the public feels that the *president* can make a significant difference in economic conditions, that is, the president can be a leader.

A survey in January 1975 showed that 43 percent thought "lack of action by President Ford to halt the recession" was a major cause of rising unemployment and recession, while 59 percent thought Congress's lack of action was a major cause, thus again casting Congress in a more negative light. Yet, respondents overwhelmingly believed that the Democrats, who heavily controlled Congress, could do a better job bringing the country out of recession (48 percent said Democrats, 16 percent Republicans) and handling inflation (42 percent, 15 percent). The party on which the public's criticism stuck was not the Democrats, controllers of Congress, but on Republicans, controllers of the presidency. In their behavior, voters clearly punish the president and his party, whether this party controls Congress or not. And the ability to punish even the president's party diminished after the 1940s given the perfectly sensible—in the fiscal state context—candidate-centered strategy adopted both by candidates and voters.[15]

[15] Reviewing the dispute over whether marginal seats were really diminishing in the postwar period, Garand, Wink, and Vincent (1993) find that in every category—winners receiving 50–55 percent of the vote, 55–60 percent, 60–65 percent, 65–70 percent, over 70 percent—incumbents are decreasingly likely to lose as one moves across American history. Eubank (1985) argues that some estimates of the proportion of voters defecting from their party identification to vote for incumbents have been overstated. Still, he calculates the following sizable and growing defection rates toward incumbents in House elections from 1956 through 1980 (excluding 1962): 15 percent, 16, 19, 25, 34, 32, 33, 37, 32, 41, 38–39, 35–36. (The final two entries, for 1978 and 1980, are estimates.) Defection away

By looking beyond the reflexive public tendency to criticize Congress as an institution, then, there are many suggestions that public opinion (and certainly voting behavior) holds the president accountable and believes he has the ability to lead the economy. A further example is provided by a comparison of presidential and congressional approval ratings with retrospective and prospective evaluations of personal and national economic conditions. Utililizing national survey data of 13,000 respondents collected monthly at the University of Wisconsin from September 1988 through April 1994, I found that for each economic measure (nine in all), presidential approval ratings were more strongly related to perceptions of the economy than were congressional approval ratings.[16] The pattern holds for the divided government period as well as the unified government period beginning in January 1993.

This bifurcation that renders presidential elections plebiscitary is a reasonable reaction by voters. Partisan rhetoric focuses on economic management, but parties in practice are restricted in their control of such policy. It is sensible for voters to discount parties and elevate candidates, to discount Congress and elevate the president. Within this environment, it is also sensible for members of Congress to present themselves increasingly in candidate-centered campaigns and to provide the institutional resources helpful in conducting such campaigns (Jacobson 1992). In surveys, the public is certainly willing to criticize Congress along with the president (and many others, such as large corporations and labor unions) when the economy goes bad. But in their actions, voters consistently pin economic responsibility and credit on the president, not on Congress.

One final question relating to this plebiscitary pattern is whether voting behavior was any different after the onset of the fiscal state than before. Certainly it would be insupportable to argue that economic conditions had no effect on voting before the 1930s. As the previous chapter indicates, economic issues were keenly interwoven with cultural, social, and identity concerns in nineteenth-century political parties. Even historians who emphasize ethnocultural influences in nineteenth-century politics acknowledge that economics also influenced voters (see Formisano 1993; Silbey 1991). Holt (1992) has made the strongest statements linking voting behavior to economic conditions, particularly for the 1840 election. Holt is correct to point out that ethnocultural analysts should avoid conflating economic and class voting: The two are not the same. But Holt makes a dubious assumption that social science findings about economic voting in the post–World War II period can be transferred to pre–Civil

---

from incumbents was more level during this period: 6 percent, 7, 8, 11, 9, 13, 6, 10, 12, 8, 7–8, 10.

[16] This data was collected and kindly provided by Diana C. Mutz.

War America; indeed, by resorting to one portion of the political science literature he ignores the growing portion of the literature that emphasizes how institutional arrangements and expectations influence behavior. More important, he does not acknowledge that the postwar studies argue that even minor economic changes in rather "ordinary" election years can influence voter behavior. Even if 1840 voting behavior were as Holt describes it, one cannot assume the same behavior applies in years that lack the catalyst of tremendous depression (see Kleppner 1987: 106–9, 137, 196). By suggesting systemic collapse, certainly a depression might be expected to force many voters to reevaluate their economic policy preference and the stances taken by political parties. But the stability of voting patterns in the nineteenth century suggests that such behavior would be atypical (Silbey 1991: 152–53). In "ordinary" times, voters belief in their party orientation toward economic policy encouraged party voting and discouraged party switching in response to economic conditions.[17] Some voters in the nineteenth century might have behaved in the party-switching fashion, but it would appear to be a comparatively smaller group than after World War II. And with turnout generally higher in the nineteenth century, the potential mobilization of nonvoters on the basis of economic conditions would be more limited than in the postwar period.

Unfortunately, the systematic social science explorations of voting behavior do not provide much direct leverage in understanding these earlier periods. Most studies focus only on the postwar period, or on shorter periods within that era. Those studies that push their time series analysis further back generally go back to the 1890s. The most important studies (Kramer 1971; Arcelus and Meltzer 1975; Goodman and Kramer 1975; Bloom and Price 1975; Alesina and Rosenthal 1989; Erikson 1990; Campbell 1991; Alesina and Rosenthal 1995) are generally not concerned with voting patterns in different subperiods and thus do not directly compare voting behavior in different historical periods. Kleppner argues that

[17] Holt, along with critics of realignment theory in particular, suggests that voter behavior in the nineteenth century might not be as consistent over time as once thought. One chief argument is that correlating the vote over time at the county level is subject to the ecological fallacy—significant numbers of voters could switch parties between elections, many old voters could drop out while new voters could be mobilized, and yet the support for a particular party, measured by percentage of the vote, might have changed little. Of course, one must be careful when using such data and attempt as best as possible to account for these contradicting trends. But the risk of ecological fallacy does not prove that it exists in the historical voting data. Clearly, earlier interpretations of rock-like solidity in voting behavior were overstated (see Reynolds 1988 and Argersinger 1992 for compelling accounts of party defections), but the variety and quantity of the data suggesting substantially more stability in voting in earlier historical eras than in the recent period remain compelling. And while it is not conclusive, the overwhelming chorus from contemporary observers appears to validate such a view (Burnham 1994).

in the time period covered by these studies, voters had begun to become more responsive to current events, though not to the extent they would after the 1930s (1987: 106–9, 137, 196). This behavior is consistent with changes in the state that were altering the position of party—the erosion of the currency issue, some incipient moves toward presidential initiative in budgeting and trade, statutory reform of elections and parties, and bureaucratic restructuring as described by Skowronek (1982). Although voting was moving more toward the fiscal state plebiscitary pattern, there was nothing inevitable about this progression. Not until the government could, through both structure and supporting policy, credibly monitor and adjust the business cycle would voters hold government, particularly the president, strictly accountable for fluctuation in that cycle.[18]

If the first four constraints tilt more toward policy-making structure, the fifth limit on the parties concerns the substance and outcomes of state policy. The role of the state after the 1930s was to undergird the economy. Undergirding affects, or was widely perceived to affect, the business cycle. This new policy role of the state threatened parties—a relatively stable or growing economy took away or minimized the public significance of the very issues around which the party system was formulated. And in economic downturns, when public attention to politics was high, the widespread diffusion of Keynesian ideas led to similar sets of solutions by the parties—the congressional parties converged in recessions.[19] Instead of choices, voters heard echoes.

As the politics of growth studies suggested, the convergence on policy substance, particularly during hard times, narrowed the parameters of debate. At the same time, the structural constraints of the fiscal state restricted the policy-making control of parties in several ways. Only with the breakdown of Keynesian economic management at the end of the 1970s would the parties begin to pose distinct alternatives to the electorate and set the foundation for party revival. What is important, then, is *not* a simple notion of government becoming larger and thereby injuring political parties. Rather, what is important is the manner in which government structure and predominant policy concerns interacted to influence the settings within which political parties operated. In sum, the fiscal state limits on parties contributed to declining party allegiance and declining focus on parties in the *public,* placed the *systemic* locus of policy initiation and control away from party hands, encouraged declining *congressional* party differences at periods of peak public interest, and when removed or revised *changed* the status of party.

[18] Walter Dean Burnham (personal communication) indicates that his analysis shows that election-year changes in personal disposable income explain much more of the variance in incumbent-party presidential vote from 1948 to 1980 than from 1900 to 1932.

[19] I discuss changes in intraparty cohesion and interparty conflict in chapter 3.

From the Old to the New Deal:
The Rise of the Politics of Economic Management

Building the fiscal state affected congressional parties in two dramatically different ways. For the short term, members could feel satisfied that they retained a role for Congress and built New Deal programs in a way that rewarded fellow party members on the state and local level (Karl 1983; Wallis 1987).[20] In the crisis atmosphere of the Great Depression, with threats from the left and right both domestically and internationally, members demonstrated a willingness to delegate authority to executive branch agencies in remarkable quantities. But delegation did not mean abdication: "The Congress of 1933 was no more the rubber stamp of presidential control than it had ever been. Roosevelt was pushing to its limits a legislative body that was far less radical than he was willing to be. It was unwilling to give up any more authority than the emergency required, and that only for so long as the emergency lasted" (Karl 1983: 124; cf. Chamberlain 1940; Conkin 1975: 86 ff.).

In the long term, the view is less favorable. The case studies below show that members of Congress placed a premium on maintaining distributional control over the budget. Establishing control over macroeconomic policy was less important. The president became the actual and symbolic manager of the macroeconomy. Maintaining control over budget shares is not inconsequential, but postwar politics revolved more centrally around preventing recessions, dampening inflation, and restoring growth. In short, the macroeconomic impact of the budget was the underlying axis of division in the emerging party system. By focusing on microbudgeting and neglecting macrobudgeting, party leaders placed congressional parties on the periphery of the central policy area of the New Deal party system.[21] On this central issue, voters would come to view the president and not congressional parties as in control.

The debates discussed below indicate how these short-term and long-term perspectives influenced the construction of the fiscal state. They illustrate

[20] Weir and Skocpol note that "the strength of local bases of power and congressional determination to block the institutionalization of stronger federal executive controls were the essential barriers to constructing a permanent, nationally coordinated system of social spending in the late 1930s" (1985: 135).

[21] These terms are borrowed from LeLoup's (1988) description of the Congressional Budget and Impoundment Control Act of 1974. Macrobudgeting refers to setting overall limits on spending and revenue as the first step, and subsequently working out the distribution among programs and departments. Microbudgeting works from the agency spending requests to formulate the budget totals. As Gilmour (1990) suggests, the 1974 reforms are probably better thought of as introducing "iterative budgeting," where macro- and micro-goals are determined simultaneously rather than allowing one goal to subordinate the other.

how the constraints indicated in the previous section were embedded in the process of redefining the state-economy relationship. Some of these constraints were seen as problematic at the time, and in these debates, members of Congress try to redress these problems. Other constraints, such as automatic fiscal policy, were seen as solutions to other problems. Either way, the concerns reflected and addressed in the debates from 1937 to 1946 gradually created a new set of state settings within which political parties would operate in subsequent decades.

The Recession of 1937: The Partial Legitimation of Fiscal Policy

The recession of 1937 confronted Congress squarely with the realities of the changing political order in the United States. The debate over responding to the recession shows the congressional parties grappling with the causes of recessions, administrative centralization, and delegation of authority.

Following his 1936 reelection, Roosevelt had turned to the old-time religion of budget balancing, promising in his 1937 budget message a balanced budget for 1938 and 1939. But in August 1937, the economy speedily collapsed into recession. Unemployment increased from about seven million to eleven million in less than six months. The stock market fell 43 percent. Industrial production fell by one-third, erasing one-half of the gain since 1932. Profits fell over 80 percent. Income fell by 12 percent. In less than one-fifth the time, the 1937 economy declined half as badly as the 1929 economy (Conkin 1975: 92–93).

The recession of 1937 triggered a deep debate in the administration (Stein 1969). Treasury Secretary Henry Morganthau argued that the best path was to balance the budget and let business take the initiative—fears of deficits, inflation, and taxes were, he believed, suppressing business investment. Others in the administration, including Roosevelt confidant and relief administrator Harry Hopkins, Secretary of the Interior Harold Ickes, and Federal Reserve chair Lauchlin Currie, challenged Morganthau's views. They agreed with Mariner Eccles's sentiment that "the government must be the compensatory agent in th[e] economy" (Leuchtenburg 1963: 245). Roosevelt agreed on April 2, 1938, one week after another stock market crash, that deficit spending was necessary for economic recovery (Leuchtenburg 1963: 256; Freidel 1990: 249–57).[22] Apparently waiting until after the House vote on the executive reorganization bill

---

[22] It seems fairly certain that the New Dealers were influenced by Keynes in a peripheral way; many of the ideas that came to be known as Keynesian had in fact been circulating in different guises over the course of the 1920s and 1930s (Hall 1989; Lee 1989; Stein 1969; Karl 1983: 158–59).

(April 8), Roosevelt asked Congress in mid-April for $3.75 billion in new spending. The request was approved within two months (Stein 1969: 100–23; Burk 1990: 267).

In the interval between the budget message and Roosevelt's policy shift, Congress engaged in a wide-ranging debate concerning the appropriate fiscal policy for the United States. Rep. Maury Maverick (D-Texas) declared that the recession of 1937 could be directly linked to the government pullback on spending. "It is almost impossible," he continued, "to believe that this is the same administration, presided over by the same President, with the same Congress, representing the same constituency that I knew a short time ago. Have [the American people] decided they didn't mean what they said a short time ago [in the election]? Of course they haven't" (*Congressional Record* [hereafter *CR*], Appendix, November 16, 1937, p. 49). Maverick voiced his displeasure at his party reneging on "solemn promises" and "party pledges" and urged more party responsibility.

Maverick placed budget balancing at the core of his explanation of the 1937 recession. Other members of Congress were not so sure. The rallying cry of the Republicans and conservative Democrats placed the onus of the recession on the New Deal itself.[23] Roosevelt cooked up the recession, they charged in speech after speech, with a recipe of overtaxing, overspending, arbitrary power, fearmongering, and business bashing. Some Democrats suggested that the private control of the money supply through the Federal Reserve was the root of the problem. As would become common in recessions, democratization of the Fed emerged as a political issue and just as quickly faded away. Other Democrats argued that business withheld investment to force repeal of the tax laws and prevent wage and hour bills (*CR*, February 14, 1938, p. 1901). Business clearly desired these changes.[24] Evidence for a capital strike, however, is scanty.

Maverick issued his complaints about his party's wavering on economic policy after a year of listening to political rhetoric extolling the political,

[23] Indeed, Roosevelt's difficulties were bipartisan: "In January 1937, for the first time in more than a century, one party controlled three fourths of the votes in House and Senate. And yet this Congress killed or brutally emasculated almost every Administration effort to expand the New Deal" (Polenberg 1966: 41; 1975). Still, even in this environment, even with the conservative coalition of Republicans and southern Democrats joining forces, the "first allegiance [of Congressmen] was to party, not coalition. In the months to come, partisan warfare would negate coalition efforts time and again" (Patterson 1967: 210).

[24] A petition from several Rhode Island business associations asked for: (1) repeal of capital gains and undistributed profits tax; (2) a balanced budget via lower spending; (3) preservation of free enterprise; (4) no government competition with private industry; (5) no attacking business, small or large; (6) the right to strike and work; (7) no government control of prices; (8) no new controls, such as wage and hour legislation; (9) no government reorganization or regional planning (*CR*, March 10, 1938, p. 3151).

economic, and moral virtue of budget balancing. These calls for budget balancing opened the window toward serious reform of the budgetary process, reform that might regain for congressional parties responsibilities lost in the Budget and Accounting Act of 1921 and the early years of the New Deal.[25] In January, Sen. Millard Tydings (D-Maryland) introduced a bill (S.J.R. 36) calling for an automatic balanced budget. One of Tydings's underlying goals was to move toward macrobudgeting and away from microbudgeting, that is, toward a more comprehensive view of the budget and away from a piecemeal approach. In Tydings's plan, Congress would approve an overall budget and then approve the separate appropriations. Under the plan, every provision for more spending would have to be offset by spending cuts, taxes, or taxes to pay off the debt. Referring to the 1974 budget reforms, Sundquist (1981: 200) described this procedure as the distinction between having a fiscal *policy* instead of a fiscal *result*.

In the debate on Tydings's proposal, senators voiced reservations about the procedures of the bill and its potential for *decreasing* congressional power. This position was ironic given the arguments in 1974 that macrobudgeting reforms would *increase* congressional power. One complaint was that the plan ignored spending needs in favor of budgetary procedures. As one senator put it, "How can you determine the needs of the Army by determining first the needs of the farmer?" (CR, January 12, 1937, p. 182).[26] To Tydings, though, the key issues were depression and fiscal responsibility. With depression "as sure to come again as the sun is to rise and set," the government needed to be free from any charges that it had caused the recession through deficit spending. Only then would the government have the legitimacy to respond to the recession with fiscal measures. Fiscal policy was not a partisan matter, and "whether Democrats or Republicans run the Government for the next 100 years" made little difference in what was correct policy (CR, January 12, 1937, p. 186). Balanced budgets were correct. Both parties voiced this idea frequently over the next forty years. In practice, both parties tolerated a little deficit as acceptable fiscal policy (Savage 1988: ch. 6). The "correct policy" that both parties converged on, particularly during recessions, was Keynesian in its essence. This tendency toward convergence on fiscal policy would become a hallmark weakness of the party system in the fiscal state.

A more serious challenge to Tydings's plan was that it usurped the role

[25] Among other things, the act made the president formally responsible for gathering agency requests into some kind of overall budget and presenting a revenue and spending package to Congress (Stewart 1989: 197–215).

[26] In the House, Rep. John Murdock (D-Arizona) argued that Congress should examine what the economy needed before indulging in "bookkeeper's economy" (CR, Appendix, May 20, 1937, p. 1230).

of Congress and the ability of congressional parties to put their distinctive stamps on budgetary distribution. Sen. James Byrnes (D-South Carolina) pointed out that unless Congress did its budgeting department-by-department with hearings and study, it would be dependent on the president's recommendation for the total size of the budget. It was Congress's duty to balance the budget, and it should not shift its responsibility to the president (CR, May 16, 1937, p. 1077). Sen. Thomas Connally (D-Texas) charged that the Tydings bill would make it more difficult for Congress to use its power of the purse in any manner it saw fit. In effect, he argued, other departments in the government would become proportionately stronger in controlling the purse (CR, January 12, 1937, pp. 181, 182, 185). Republicans voiced these complaints generally, and not only in relation to the Tydings bill (CR, May 4, 1937, p. 1073). To critics like Sen. Carter Glass (D-Virginia), the main fear was a shift away from Congress's traditional functions into uncharted lands of responsibilities. Tydings, he suggested, "wants Congress to go into the budgetary business," which was more properly the purview of the Bureau of the Budget.

By threatening traditional roles in Congress, Tydings's bill was not likely to pass. The Appropriations Committee was not anxious to lose the power it wielded by threatening program cuts. But the bill served as a warning shot that Congress and the parties needed to think carefully about their role in the new political order. Most members of Congress were concerned with controlling resource distribution and were not prepared to focus on the question of institutional control of macroeconomic management. They were content to delegate leadership to the president in this area. Some members of Congress did see a threat in the forthcoming fiscal arrangements and the increased power of the presidency. Despite this concern, Congress typically deferred budget coordination to the executive. Many congressional committees refused to consider legislation that had not been cleared by the Bureau of the Budget, relying instead on the administration for initial policy proposals and on administrative personnel for staff assistance (Dodd and Schott 1979: 81).

The committee system in Congress was one cause of this poor organization for purposes of directing fiscal policy. If, "on the one hand, committee government provided a rational, intelligent mechanism through which members of Congress could develop personal expertise and specialize in the creation and oversight of policies and agencies in specific jurisdictional areas; . . . [and] From the perspective of the member of Congress, committee government served his or her immediate interest," it was no less true that "the failure of committee government came in its impact on the interests and external power of Congress as an institution" (Dodd and Schott 1979: 84–85). Through committees, members of Congress protected themselves against a party or leader usurping the power of the purse, but not the executive.[27] So while the response to the recession of 1937 partially legitimized fiscal policy in the United States, it also consolidated the president-led view of fiscal management. The public reaction was similarly to associate economic well-being with the president while Congress became more closely linked to constituency service (Conkin 1975: 84; Brinkley 1989: 94–100).

The response to the recession marks the partial revolution of fiscal policy, and the revolution occurred both in policy and structure. Roosevelt's spending cuts from November 1937 to January 1938 were the last a president would make in the midst of a recession until 1980. Attempting strong expansionary budget measures in a recession was by 1938 a de facto national policy on which the parties converged, even if balanced budgets retained a moral allure during noncrisis periods.[28] Concerning structure, some members of Congress worried that the macroeconomic power of the president minimized the importance of congressional parties. But most members were less concerned about presidential leadership in this area than they were concerned that Congress retain flexibility in resource distribution.

On Controlling the Budget

Although the response to the 1937 recession confirmed the centrality of the president in fiscal policy, the confirmation was tentative: The institutional implications of this ascendancy for Congress and congressional parties remained a concern to many members. Was Congress "at the mercy of the departments in their demand for money," with no way to know if their requests were reasonable (CR, April 28, 1937, p. 3897)? Should Congress enhance the oversight role of the General Accounting Office and the comptroller? Should the House Appropriations Committee staff be enlarged to allow more investigations of government spending? Should not Congress have more access to the Bureau of the Budget's papers, files, data, and the testimony of agencies? Was too much legislation—90 percent or more—being drafted "downtown" (either as statutes or administrative rules)? Did Congress need to be more active fiscally and less reactive? Would Congress "degenerate to merely a body of harping criticism without having a real effect on legislation" (CR, December 15, 1944, p. 9537)?

[27] Even if the normal pattern was for the committee to do the work of the party, the committee had the capability to act as a check on party power.

[28] However, it was not yet national policy to achieve full employment by permanent fiscal policy or to even think seriously about the budget as a tool to meet a specific national income target (Stein 1969: 115–16).

I take up three of these disputes briefly here. The first of these concerns the role of the comptroller (Polenberg 1966: 23–25). Treasury Secretary Morganthau complained in 1938 that the acting comptroller general, Richard N. Elliott, was too aggressive. In a fifteen-page letter to Executive Expenditures Committee chair John J. Cochran (D-Missouri), Morganthau complained that Elliott wanted the power to block expenditures in those departments failing to follow his accounting regulations. To Morganthau, that would make Elliott "the most powerful administrative officer of the government, but without any responsibility to the Chief Executive elected by the people and with only such supervision of his acts as the Congress might be able to supply through occasional investigations." Echoing this argument, Roosevelt proposed eliminating the position of comptroller general in his executive reorganization plan. Congress rejected this proposal. Indeed, the prevailing view in Congress was that the comptroller general and the General Accounting Office should be even more aggressive. How, after all, was Congress to ascertain whether executive agencies were making reasonable demands in their funding requests (*CR*, April 28, 1937, p. 3897)?

The second dispute concerned whether increased oversight required a more activist role for Congress in fiscal policy formation. In January 1940, Sen. James Davis (R-Pennsylvania) proposed the formation of a Budget Service that would be an arm of and accountable to Congress (S. 3140). The Budget Service was intended to shift some fiscal power back to Congress. It would assume the Budget Bureau's task of creating the budget and would create budget oversight agencies to investigate expenditures, provide budgetary information to Congress, and serve as a budget process liaison with the executive branch. The liaison role involved cooperation with both the Treasury Department and the General Accounting Office and called for congressional liaisons to be installed in all government agencies as employees of the Budget Service. Davis's assertion here was stark: Congress, in particular the majority party in Congress, needed to control economic management by placing its personnel throughout the government.

After this bill died in the Finance Committee, Davis tried a more moderate approach. In April 1940, he called for the formation of a joint committee of Appropriations Committee members to establish a Congressional Budget Service (S. 3715). This bill did not call for the virtual elimination of the Bureau of the Budget but instead included the Budget Bureau in the Budget Service-Treasury-General Accounting Office liaison network. Davis also deleted the liaisons located directly in the executive agencies. After its referral to the Executive Expenditures Committee, the bill fared no better than Davis's first bill. In May, the Expenditures Committee passed Senate Resolution 271 in lieu of the Davis bill, but this resolution simply added more personnel to the staff of the Expenditures Committee. To the committee, the issue was oversight of executive agencies' spending proclivities, not the locus of fiscal policy formation. To improve oversight, one must increase staff on the committee (*CR*, May 22, 1940, pp. 6581–82).

Beyond the aggressive use of the comptroller and the monitoring of executive accounts, a third approach to reenergize Congress's role in fiscal management stressed the need to coordinate the taxing and spending functions. I discussed above Tydings's automatic balanced budget plan of 1937. Tydings reintroduced the measure in 1940 in somewhat different form. Here, instead of presenting a bill with a full-blown system for automatically balancing the budget, Tydings proposed that a special three-member committee be formed to "find the ways and means" to reach an automatically balanced budget (S.Res. 314). Introduced late in the session in an election year, the measure had little chance of passage and died in committee. Tydings reintroduced the legislation yet again in January 1941 (S.Res. 22) and it was adopted by the Senate in mid-February.[29] A week later, the three-person committee (including Tydings) began work. The committee's preferred plan would have had the tax schedule automatically kick in to provide revenues to meet appropriations. Consistent with Tydings's earlier proposal, this procedure would take budget balancing out of the arena of party politics. Exceptions for depressions and peacetime preparedness would have to be paid off in twenty years (*CR*, April 29, 1941, p. 3377).[30]

Despite the failure of this effort, the urge to automate economic policy—but not the distribution of resources within the budget—remained strong. The fiscal state integrated automation through features such as automatic stabilizers, uncontrollable expenditures, indexation, automatic budget caps, and, more arguably, incremental and predictable increases in spending categories. In some respects, the automation approach is good policy because it guarantees action regardless of the level of division and bitterness in Congress and it protects programs from frequent political attack.[31] But by divorcing party from policy, this proclivity for automatic policy weakened Congress and congressional parties and changed the way

[29] Members of Congress in both chambers in the early 1940s proposed plans similar in intent to the Tydings proposal. The Special Committee on Fiscal Planning brought together powerful members from the House Appropriations and Ways and Means Committees. Other such plans included the Joint Committee on the Budget (*CR*, January 21, 1943, p. 269) and the Joint Committee on Budgetary Control (*CR*, January 18, 1943, p. 212).

[30] Tydings, as part of the general movement in Congress stressing the need for independent information, also proposed the formation of a Joint Committee to Study, Analyze, and Evaluate Requests for Appropriations.

[31] This latter point about insulation from attack can also be a problem, as the boom in entitlement spending after 1970 suggests.

citizens viewed the responsibilities of the major political institutions. If economic policy is in many respects automatic and congressional parties see such policy as more desirable than discretionary policy, then party campaign pronouncements about fiscal management issues are decreasingly relevant to the public.[32] Why should a voter be swayed by fiscal management distinctions that the congressional parties minimize in practice? Why worry about these distinctions when with each passing year less and less of the budget is "controllable"? Perhaps incumbency would be a more meaningful guide to voting.[33]

Executive Reorganization and the Power of Congress

Reorganization of the executive branch produced a bitter conflict. To members of Congress, executive reorganization that centralized powers in the presidency, especially powers of economic planning, threatened the traditional ability of Congress to disburse resources and threatened a flexible party system that encouraged creative logrolling and unholy coalitions. Roosevelt longed for a more integrated party system; his fellow partisans in Congress were just as strongly determined to retain their policy flexibility and resource control. In their concern over the damage an executive-led planning state might do to Congress and the parties, members of Congress underestimated similar threats in the emerging fiscal state.

Although the reorganization literature stresses Roosevelt's efforts, Congress was involved early on. In October 1935, John J. Cochran (D-Missouri), chair of the Committee on Expenditures in the Executive Departments, requested organizational, personnel, and financial data from each executive department, along with suggestions for cutting spending. From this information, his committee was to formulate reorganization plans.[34] Cochran later established a committee of seven to investigate the

[32] The sense of congressional weakness was not limited to those within the Capitol or the administration's enemies; the *New York Times* (March 15, 1943) editorialized that Congress was disorganized and impotent. The *Washington Post* (January 23, 1944) echoed these sentiments, contrasting the choices as modernization of Congress or abdication of power.

[33] It is clear that many voters make precisely this decision. In the 1988 House congressional elections, 47 percent of self-identified Democrats defected to support a Republican incumbent while 52 percent of Republicans defected to support an incumbent Democrat (Abramson, Aldrich, and Rohde 1990: 270).

[34] Congressional involvement was more inadvertent than crusade. The proposal to look into reorganization was apparently part of an attempt by William Whittington (D-Mississippi) to prevent the reporting out of another bill from the committee. Indeed, Cochran had a difficult time getting members to agree to work over this issue during the November and December recess, which was critical if Congress was to be the first to place a reorganization plan on the table. Only one of eighteen committee members responded affirmatively and

existing organization of all executive and administrative agencies. The subcommittee was to determine how to reduce expenditures, increase the efficiency of operations through jurisdictional redefinition, and reduce the number of agencies through consolidation or elimination. Perhaps a greater potential incursion on presidential power was Cochran's desire to group, coordinate, and consolidate executive and administrative agencies of government according to major purpose and to segregate regulatory agencies and functions from those of an administrative or executive character. Cochran also wanted his committee to decide if Congress should pass acts for the regrouping, consolidation, and abolition of executive agencies, or if the president should be authorized to do so subject to congressional approval.[35]

Before the committee's work progressed far, Sen. Harry F. Byrd (D-Virginia) introduced Senate Resolution 217 in early January, 1936. The Byrd bill proposed the establishment of a five-person committee to investigate the overlap of executive functions. The bill to create the Special Committee to Investigate Executive Agencies of the Government was passed by voice vote in late February. Byrd rebuffed Cochran's attempt to form a joint committee (CR, April 29, 1936, pp. 6376, 6378). Quickly thereafter, the president announced that he was creating a commission to study government reorganization. With little partisan disagreement, Cochran and the committee decided that moving forward at that point to bring in a bill would be a waste of time and effort given that the Senate committee was not expected to report until the following session.

Although the Cochran committee lost a chance to lead the congressional reorganization effort, the House was not quiet. To keep the House and the Republicans in the reorganization picture, Harold R. Knutson (R-Minnesota) introduced House Resolution 436 on March 4, 1936. Knutson's proposal called for Cochran's Expenditures Committee to study the activities of all agencies of the executive branch to see where activities overlapped. On April 2 and 6, another Republican, Carl E. Mapes (R-Michigan), introduced two bills calling for a study of reorganization—the first a joint committee and the second a House committee.

The Republican efforts were upstaged by a bill (H.Res. 460) introduced

---

without qualification to Cochran's request (Committee on Expenditures in the Executive Departments, Tray HR74A-F13.4, 13998, Whittington Resolution, National Archives). Although it is not clear why the committee, particularly the Democrats, went along with a recommendation that they had little interest in, most probably saw this as a valence issue: How could you explain a vote against investigating ways to save money and cut down on bureaucracy? The standard works on executive reorganization (Karl 1963; Polenberg 1966; Milkis 1993) ignore the early congressional effort.

[35] Committee on Expenditures in the Executive Departments, Tray HR 74A-F13.4 13997, Whittington Resolution, National Archives.

by Majority Leader William B. Bankhead (D-Alabama) on March 23, 1936. Roosevelt's suggestion to Speaker Joseph Byrns that the House join the administration and the Senate in studying executive reorganization (though not in any truly "joint" sense) led to the introduction of the bill. Bankhead's bill, calling for the formation of a five-person Committee to Investigate the Executive Agencies of the Government, emerged from the Rules Committee in late April. It was the only congressionally initiated reorganization proposal to reach the House floor. On a 269–44 vote all but one Democrat joined with just under half the Republicans to support the Bankhead legislation, and a House committee was established in early May 1936.

The debate over the bill provided each party a chance to grab the popular mantle of reorganization and cost cutting while shaping the new state in a manner friendly to traditional congressional and party structures (*CR,* April 29, 1936, pp. 6375–87). Bertrand Snell (R-New York) argued that Roosevelt's motives were transparent: Fearing that the Byrd committee would recommend significant cuts in the executive branch, Roosevelt wanted a House committee available to counterbalance the more conservative Senate committee. By playing off the two congressional committees with his own, Snell suggested, Roosevelt could get the reorganization recommendations he desired. Democrats, including Whittington and Cochran, responded that Roosevelt had been serious about reorganization since 1933. Under the provisions of the Economy Act of 1933, Roosevelt had the authority to propose reorganization of executive agencies subject to a vote of rejection by Congress. In the two years that Roosevelt had this authority, he sent up seventeen separate reorganization suggestions and none were challenged.

Whether Roosevelt had shrewdly hoped to play off the congressional committees or not, the executive branch did dominate the drafting of the reorganization plan. If Cochran had a bill ready by February 1936, as he originally hoped, Congress might have shaped the reorganization agenda with its more modest ideas of cost cutting. But even within Congress there was doubt regarding Congress's ability to lead. In the debate over the Bankhead bill, Mapes argued with some hyperbole that everyone inside and outside the Capitol agreed that the best way to reorganize was to let the president do it by executive order and avoid legislation. Mapes asserted that "Logrolling, bickerings, jealousies, ambitions, prejudices, and play for party advantage combined have been powerful enough to block all legislative attempts at reorganization in the past, and there is no reason to believe that conditions in that respect will be any different in the future. The President is the only one who can do the job" (*CR,* April 29, 1936, p. 6379). Mapes's view that the president needed to lead in the reorganization process encountered no serious opposition in the House.

With no bill ready by February, Cochran's committee (and Congress) took a backseat to the newly appointed President's Committee on Administrative Management, led by Louis Brownlow. Unlike the congressional effort, the Brownlow committee focused not on cost reduction but on ways to improve the integration of government programs and the ability of government to intervene effectively in the economy, under the direction of the president. The administration's 1937 reorganization bill, which closely mirrored the Brownlow committee report issued after the 1936 election, consisted of five elements (Polenberg 1966: 21). First, the president was to be provided with six executive assistants. Second, the merit system would be expanded, government salaries would be increased, and a more powerful civil service administrator would be established. Third, fiscal management would be improved through budget planning, restoring control of accounts to the executive branch, and providing Congress with independent audits of transactions.[36] Fourth, planning activities and policy coordination were to be concentrated in a National Resources Planning Board. And fifth, two new cabinet posts would be created and all agencies, including the independent regulatory commissions, would be brought within the twelve major departments.

Each of these elements, particularly the last four, struck directly at cherished congressional prerogatives. Unlike the consensus over cost cutting that had dominated the congressional reorganization discussions, Roosevelt's plan provoked sharp reactions in Congress.[37] Opponents argued that the bill did not commit to reduce the size of government. Opponents also criticized the provisions for centralized control over long-range goals for public works, resource development, economic management, and social policies that later became strongly identified with the National Resources Planning Board. Uneasiness about planning—which threatened to remove the power over distribution of resources and federal funds from congressional hands—was palpable in Congress. The entire bill raised hackles, with the fifth item especially fiercely resisted: The Brownlow

[36] The Roosevelt administration had a long history of differences with the incumbent Republican auditor, John R. McCarl. Therefore, the issue of audit versus control was a live one. In particular, the administration was upset that McCarl used a general policy guideline of pre-audits, which meant that he was involved in the business of preventing government transactions from taking place. The administration felt that the comptroller's proper role was to provide Congress with analysis of executive actions that would help revise programs where needed. Aside from the frustration of having program content affected by the comptroller's actions, the administration also had some constitutional difficulties with the comptroller's role: Was the comptroller involving the legislative branch in the administration of laws? This provision in the reorganization bill was intended to prevent the comptroller from pre-auditing programs.

[37] Holt (1975) discusses the "dictatorial" notions opponents saw behind much of the Roosevelt program.

committee "proposed taking the more than 100 independent agencies, boards, commissions, and administrations and placing them by executive order in twelve major executive departments, several of which were to be new creations. Reaction was swift" (Dodd and Schott 1979: 338–39). Under the proposal, the president and the bureaucrats and intellectuals populating New Deal agencies—not Congress—would determine how to reorganize these agencies.

After some weakening, the reorganization bill won narrowly in the Senate (42–40) in March 1938. Following more weakening, the House narrowly defeated (204–196) the bill in early April, as about a third of the Democrats defected and joined the unanimous Republican opposition to the bill. Writing of the reorganization effort, Karl argues that "Roosevelt had tried to bring off a genuine revolution and had failed to do so" (1983: 157; see also Milkis 1993). Following the defeat, the administration proposed a reduced bill containing simply a provision delegating reorganization powers to the president subject to a concurrent resolution veto. The bill exempted several agencies and commissions from reorganization, allowed no new departments, and included some noncontroversial proposals from 1938. Later that year, Roosevelt submitted five reorganization plans and all were approved. Most significant was the creation of a five-division Executive Office of the President (Sundquist 1981: 52–54) and the transfer of the Budget Bureau from the Treasury Department to the Executive Office. The Budget Bureau would later subsume tasks of the National Resources Planning Board when Congress eliminated that agency. Members of Congress again displayed a willingness to centralize macroeconomic policy decisions in the presidency if Congress retained influence over the distribution of resources. Believing they were protecting traditional prerogatives of congressional parties, members underestimated the impact the new power relations would have on the future salience and power of Congress and the parties. If members' individual interest is solely reelection, this may not matter very much. But if having parties control key policy areas, differ in these areas, and convince voters that these differences matter enhances policy making, governmental responsiveness, and representation, then this concession to presidential power matters.

Indeed, Milkis argues that the executive reorganization bill represented a conscious plan by Roosevelt to restructure party politics by accentuating the role of the president and diminishing the role of other branches of government. Arguing that many in the administration considered party government impractical in the United States, Milkis suggests that "New Dealers disavowed any long run party strategy and instead sought to translate modern liberalism into state action by a reorganized—a more integrated—form of Presidential administration. Whereas a more responsible party system might have established more palpable linkages between the Executive and Legislature, the administrative strategy pursued by Roosevelt endeavored to implement New Deal policies and by-pass the inertia built into the America party system by reconstituting the Executive Department as a more autonomous policy-maker" (1981: 4; see also Milkis 1993). If the fiscal and welfare state could not be reliably advanced and defended by future congressional Democrats, then Roosevelt would institutionalize as much of the New Deal as possible in state structures that would be less subject to political eradication (cf. Shefter 1994: ch. 3). To Milkis, Roosevelt viewed the Democratic party as a "waystation" on the road to administrative government.[38] Roosevelt's was a partisan leadership directed at the Democratic party becoming "the party to end all parties" (Milkis 1993: 5). Ultimately, "focusing on the personal responsibility of the Chief Executive and neglecting the party system attenuated the link between parties and the policy process" (Milkis 1981: 31; see also Milkis 1993: 9–10). The less central position of parties in the process leads to less focus on the parties by the public and to the emergence of a candidate-centered politics (Wattenberg 1990).

Milkis does not satisfactorily demonstrate the remarkable prescience and foresight he attributes to the administration's party plans. The reorganization plan, after all, was conceived before the infamous court-packing and electoral purge episodes and should be considered along with them; Roosevelt's actions reflect a desire for more cohesive parties and for institutional entrenchment of the New Deal, not simply a system of presidential aggrandizement. In this way, as Skowronek (1993) suggests, Roosevelt was a reconstructive president intent on recasting the party system, not discarding it. Milkis's argument about motives would be more convincing if he could show that Roosevelt was particularly wedded to a planning model and not to a fiscal alternative. But studies of the New Deal and Roosevelt agree that his weight was not firmly behind either camp. The distinction matters, because as Katznelson and Pietrykowski (1991) note, congressional Democratic support was far broader for the fiscal than the planning alternative. Unless Roosevelt was prepared to place all his political weight with the planners, it is difficult to understand the utility of displacing the role of a party that was tolerating developments toward a fiscal state. But whatever Roosevelt's intent, Milkis's conclusions about the *impact* of executive reorganization in a loose-party state are sound. Institutionalizing New Deal reforms in the state would not build a "party state" but would lead instead to a diminished stature for party over time.

[38] Milkis (1984) extends the argument to Lyndon Johnson and sees in him much the same disbelief in the practicality of the responsible party model and a desire to institutionalize his changes in American politics.

Postwar Planning

Postwar planning posed the dilemma of the congressional parties starkly: How could Congress preserve its power while also accommodating a revised relationship between state and economy? What would happen to the parties in the bargain? Voices from all sections of the political spectrum agreed that the threat of depression loomed over the postwar economy (*CR*, February 24, 1941, p. 1337; April 29, 1941, p. 3378). As early as 1941, serious discussion and debate began over how best to smooth the transition from war to peace. The case for planning was stated succinctly by Sen. Sheridan Downey (D-California) in a radio address: "If we are not able at that time to meet economic disaster with an economic plan, we shall go under" (*CR*, November 5, 1941, p. 8513).

Given Congress's accommodation to a presidentially led fiscal state, Roosevelt pressed Congress to concede further. With a proposal that Rep. Alfred Beiter (D-New York) labeled "insurance against a postwar collapse," Roosevelt suggested that the government develop shelves of public works projects that the president could start quickly (*CR*, February 19, 1942, p. 1487). His 1942 Budget Message requested authority to use a flexible tax in emergencies. But Republican members of Congress saw any administration involvement in economic planning as potentially dangerous to their institutional role. To Rep. Everett Dirksen (R-Illinois), who agreeed that postwar planning was needed, "when it is stated . . . that an overall, endless, limitless, permanent authority be vested in the hands of the president of the United States without a single guide line, then I say it is time for the Congress to stop, look, and listen. Congress will have nothing to say about it. . . . [A program is necessary, but] let Congress keep its hands on it" (*CR*, February 19, 1942, pp. 1489–90). Senator Tydings and Sen. Robert M. LaFollette Jr. (Progressive-Wisconsin) also expressed concern about Congress's seemingly small role in Roosevelt's vision of postwar planning.

The National Resources Planning Board (NRPB) formed the center of the debate between the two branches. Much of the dispute concerned NRPB publications regarding the postwar order, particularly "After the War: Full Employment." In "After the War," Alvin Hansen argued that fiscal policy could produce economic stability.[39] Particularly upsetting to budget balancers was his belief that "A public debt is an instrument of public policy." More hysterical commentary saw the NRPB as a manifestation of a New Deal desire to overthrow the American Way of Life. More

---

[39] Hansen was one of the most prominent American advocates of a version of Keynesianism that argued that capitalist economies had reached a permanent stagnation point. See Jeffries (1990) on Hansen and the NRPB.

moderate, and preponderant, commentary criticized the activist fiscal action implied by the plan. The battle came to a head in early 1943 when the House Independent Offices Subcommittee deleted appropriations for the NRPB. Roosevelt sought to put the onus on Congress, declaring in a press conference on March 12, 1943, that the responsibility for postwar planning now rested entirely with the members of Congress (*CR,* March 12, 1943, p. 1977). Despite some congressional information gathering regarding the postwar economy, from this point on the planning vision became localized in plans for a Full Employment Act (Norton 1977: 235–41).[40]

Reorganizing the Legislature

The debates discussed above suggest that concern over institutional changes in American politics was widespread in the 1930s and 1940s. Many members of Congress believed that the House and Senate required fundamental changes. Even staunch supporters of Franklin Roosevelt and the New Deal voiced concerns about the perceived weakening of Congress relative to the executive branch and the declining significance of congressional parties in controlling the direction and content of public policy—especially in the critical area of economic management. But to Roosevelt supporters, the problem was not executive branch aggrandizement of power but instead legislative branch abdication of responsibility. Rep. Jerry Voorhis (D-California), a strong Roosevelt supporter, argued that Congress lacked initiative to assume its rightful place in American politics. Voorhis, outlining five key areas for congressional involvement, complained that Congress was performing poorly in all areas except providing for the national defense through authorizations and appropriations. It was lax in watching over the expenditure of appropriated funds. It had done little to streamline and improve executive agencies on its own. Power over the supply of credit was outside congressional hands. And the body as a whole had not taken credible action to guard against future depressions. Inaction, Voorhis summed up, put Congress "in a position of seeming to be an unimportant part of the machinery of the national life of American today" (*CR,* February 24, 1941, pp. 1335–38). This image of unimportance, he would later argue, was surely reinforced by the administration's impoundment of congressionally appropriated funds (*CR,* April 2, 1942, pp. 3296–97).

[40] A fascinating body of literature has emerged since the mid-1980s assessing the formation and limits of America's welfare state and social Keynesianism. See, for example, Katznelson (1986) and the essays by Weir, Orloff, and Skocpol; Orloff; Amenta and Skocpol; Weir; Finegold; and Quadagno in Weir, Orloff, and Skocpol (1988).

From the other side of the aisle, Dirksen was perhaps the most vocal member of Congress on the question of Congress's place in the political system. According to Dirksen, three weaknesses hampered Congress: a weakened power of the purse; a lack of control over appointments to much-enlarged executive agencies; and the increasing complexity of congressional work. More areas of policy concern and more hours lost to administrative routine were both the evidence and the result of this greater complexity. In short, Congress was simply not equipped to compete with the Executive in the new age of administration and bureaucracy: "I have not heard one but a thousand lamentations in the well of this House over the years, relative to the growing power of the Executive and the growing power of the governmental bureaus, but is it not a fact that we are slavishly dependent upon those bureaus today for information, for data, for advice, for guidance, for the very good reason that the Congress has no instrumentality or weapon of its own for such information?" (CR, October 1, 1942, p. 7696). Charging that legislators had willingly become "supplicants" to the Executive branch, Dirksen proposed that Congress could emerge from its dependent status only if it could obtain an independent set of facts. To do so, Congress needed to equip and staff itself to put it on an even level with the Executive branch.

Although concerned about the position of Congress relative to the president, many members of Congress equally feared sacrificing any of their independence from party discipline. To members growing increasingly independent, the fear of increased party power permeated the debate over legislative reorganization, especially Dirksen's call for party policy committees (Dodd and Schott 1979: 66–71; MacNeil 1982: 76). In their deliberations, members of Congress sought to find some way to balance the often competing demands for a strong Congress, independent members, and disciplined and responsible parties.[41] While members depended on fellow partisans to get things done, they did not want to be beholden or obedient.

The budget-making process emerged again as an arena in which to air

[41] A small firestorm was touched off in early 1946 when former Vice President Henry Wallace issued his own version of legislative reorganization. Wallace wrote in Colliers that he was upset to see President Harry S Truman's bills "killed, shelved, or emasculated by Democratic Congressmen," and argued that party discipline, though not a purge, needed to be enforced. In his vision, majority leaders and the president would pick the test issues against which members would be measured. His call, which amounted to a call to oust party members who deviated on the big issues, drew a hail of criticism on Capitol Hill. Sen. Alexander Wiley (R-Wisconsin) was not alone in dragging out the specter of Hitler, Himmler, and Stalin. Sen. Bourke Hickenlooper (R-Iowa) declared that Wallace's "strange and unusual political pronouncement . . . is not reflective of our general political attitudes or our determination to maintain freedom of thought and freedom of action in both political parties in our state" (CR, March 19, 1946, pp. 2400–1).

these concerns. One idea was to have a joint committee on the budget that would consider both revenue and spending questions. In the House floor debate, Rep. Wright Patman (D-Texas) argued that combining the spending and taxing committees concentrated power in too few members and violated the checks and balances between the chambers. Others feared that the idea had the "effect of putting our stamp of approval on the deficit spending." And Rep. Emmett O'Neal (D-Kentucky) charged that it made little sense to talk about budget totals before considering each specific agency bill. But that of course is the burden of fiscal policy—managing the economy via fiscal techniques and meeting the wide range of public needs are not equivalent. Indeed, asked Rep. Albert Gore (D-Tennessee), "Does the Congress have a fiscal policy? . . . Is there anything which will loom before the Congress within the next decade more important than fiscal affairs? Under the present system, we have no formal way of developing a fiscal policy, and what is more, we have no way of sensibly following a policy if we had one" (CR, July 25, 1946, p. 10079).

Dozens of budget reform ideas were floated during this period. Some, such as requiring open hearings on appropriations bills, requiring the entire appropriations committees to consider all bills, providing more time to consider the bills before they reached the floor, and limiting "permanent" appropriations, saw the independence of the appropriations committees as problematic. The president's powers were targeted in suggestions that Congress eliminate executive transfers between appropriations categories, direct the comptroller to analyze the competency of each egency's management, and establish annual budget revenue and expenditure totals by joint action of the revenue and appropriations committees of both houses. On the other hand, some members sought to increase the president's autonomy while making Congress more accountable for its rhetoric. For example, one suggestion was that recorded votes to increase the debt limit be made mandatory, while another proposal allowed the president to cut appropriations by a uniform percentage in midyear to meet budgetary goals.

As Dirksen's remarks suggest, budget reform was not the only issue. Thirty-two reorganization bills were proposed in 1944 to deal with Congress's weaknesses, and by the end of the year Congress created the Joint Committee on the Organization of Congress to pursue options (CR, December 15, 1944, p. 9536). The debate led in the Senate by LaFollette (co-chair of the committee along with Rep. Mike Monroney [D-Oklahoma]) indicates the wide scope of the changes being contemplated. Among the reforms discussed to improve congressional access to information were reducing the number of committees, adding more expert committee staff, strengthening the Legislative Reference Service, and adding more in-office nonlegislative staff. Items intended to increase the efficiency of Congress included prohibiting legislative riders on appropriations bills, confining conferences to issues in dispute, prohibiting special committees, registering lobbyists, prohibiting private claims legislation, and increasing salary 50 percent. Provisions restructuring party power promised a more centralized, somewhat more hierarchical initiation, formulation, and deliberation of legislation. These reforms included the establishment of party policy committees in each house "as an offset to organized pressure groups"; establishing a Joint Legislative-Executive Council consisting of the majority policy committees, the president, and the Cabinet; and strengthening oversight of executive branch administration of laws.

The burden of LaFollette's argument in the Senate was that Congress faced a new state and a new world and that it must either become effective through reorganization or become obsolete. Despite this dramatic painting of the problem, and despite the long list of reforms proposed, the preponderance of debate on the floor of the Senate concerned a proposal to establish a director of personnel in each chamber. Most senators opposed the new position because they feared that the director would take the hiring function away from members of Congress. Members of Congress were not willing to abdicate their control of a rare outpost of patronage hiring (CR, June 10, 1946, pp. 6344–6549).

To the Speaker of the House, the key issue in the reforms was party power. Sam Rayburn (D-Texas) opposed reforms that would strengthen the political parties and strengthen Congress's fiscal policy role. During the six weeks he held the reorganization bill before referring it to committee, he arranged the cancellation of party policy committees, the Joint Legislative-Executive Council, and the enforcement provisions for a legislative budget. He considered the policy committees both unnecessary and a possible threat to his leadership. Particularly upsetting was that the Democratic policy committee would have scheduled legislation and disciplined members—two of the Speaker's key powers. Complaining that "I don't want any debating societies around me," Rayburn also feared that a legislative-executive council left him out of the loop. If the White House and the majority congressional party were to meet, Rayburn wanted himself and not a council to be the key representative from the congressional side. Rayburn's actions appear to have been motivated not simply by concern for his own power but by concern for the immediate future of his party: By rejecting the committees and the council, and by refusing to convene Democratic party caucuses to work out party policy positions, he believed that he was holding a faction-ridden party together. Any new kind of party body would, he feared, expose those rifts in the party that had been papered over during the Roosevelt years (Hardeman and Bacon 1987: 346; see also O'Neill 1987: 131).

As Rayburn steered the reorganization bill away from stronger parties,

House members tried to minimize the loss of congressional autonomy by eliminating the two provisions most directly curtailing that autonomy: requiring members of Congress to be on the record when voting for higher debt and granting the president authority to reduce expenditures independently. So although the bill would include important changes in the way Congress did business, the House actions stripped the bill of its most innovative elements.[42] In particular, the House abandoned those elements that reshaped the interaction between president and Congress and those that enhanced the parties' role in Congress.

The Senate passed its version of the legislative reorganization bill on June 10, 1946, by a 49 to 16 vote. On July 25, the House approved its version (229–61). On the following day, the Senate agreed to the House version, and the president signed the bill on August 2. In the area of modernization and streamlining, the final bill reduced the number of standing committees by over one-half in each chamber, redefined committee jurisdiction, and reduced the number of committees on which a member could serve from ten to two in the Senate, and from five to one in the House. Each standing committee could hire four professional staff members, except for Appropriations, which had no limit on staff hirings. The bill reduced arbitrary committee chair power by regularizing committee procedures regarding periodic meeting days, keeping of records, reporting of approved measures, quorums, and the conduct of hearings.

Reorganization also promised greater oversight of the executive branch. Committees were for the first time given explicit responsibility to watch agencies: Appropriations exercised financial control before the fact, expenditures committees (later Government Operations) reviewed administrative structure and procedure, and authorizations committees scrutinized implementation and operation of programs. Congress also attempted to challenge the president in budgetary policy by establishing a Joint Committee on the Budget. This committee was expected to develop overall spending and revenue figures that would be approved early in the legislative session. But there was no real enforcement mechanism and the relationship between the legislative and executive versions of the budget was unclear. Once in practice, it suffered a quick death.

Finally, the bill provided for additional assistance for congressional research by increasing staff assistance, adding money for the Legislative Research Service and for salaries. As mentioned above, the proposed party policy committees, which were to consist of all committee chairs or ranking members, were omitted. The Senate later created its own version of the committees; the House parties continued informal, unstaffed steering committees.

---

[42] According to one opponent: "We can refute the thesis of the managerial revolution (hierarchy, organization, streamline, etc.) and maintain the instrument of representative government" (CR, July 25, 1946, p. 10055).

With the Legislative Reorganization Act, Congress addressed several areas of weakness identified in the preceding ten years. The reluctance to build party government, however, and to assert more control over the fiscal policy process (Dodd and Schott 1979: 89–90) meant that Congress did not fundamentally change its operation. The steps taken forward were hesitant. The Joint Committee on the Budget, composed of members of each chamber's appropriations and revenues committees, proved to be short-lived. The committee was responsible for creating the "legislative budget," including overall limits on taxing and spending. For the first time, Congress had the institutional capability to conduct fiscal policy. But the legislative budget quickly ran into difficulties. Members complained that the bill was unsatisfactory because it forced (or tried to force) Congress to adhere to overall limits before the appropriations committees had any chance to look at department budgets. Ensuring a salient role for parties and Congress in the fiscal state meant breaking the mold of established congressional procedure, but breaking congressional molds proved to be difficult. Power continued to decentralize as subcommittees flourished and chairmanships were distributed widely. Congress excised from the final bill pivotal reorganization proposals. The most significant innovation in the bill, the legislative budget, came under quick attack. By 1949, the legislative budget and the joint committee were defunct, and Congress was out of the fiscal policy game or on its far periphery (Harris 1964: 107–8).

The Employment Act of 1946 and the Establishment of the Fiscal State

Ten years of debate had led to remarkable changes in fiscal and budgetary policy, executive reorganization, and the organization of Congress. Yet at the end, the position of Congress had diminished in the national political spotlight and efforts to ensure salience for congressional parties in the new state—and thus in the minds of citizens—were sidetracked. Too few politicians noted the discrepancy between building a party competition based on economic management and then tying congressional parties only loosely to responsibility for that management. Voters were not attracted by specific means of macroeconomic policy the way voters in the past held fast to protectionism or free trade. In the fiscal era, voting became plebiscitary—results more than policy techniques were what mattered. Unlike trade policy in the past, fiscal policy was technical and confusing and did not fit well into established sectional or cultural worldviews. Given these differences between trade and fiscal policy, it is understandable that congressional parties would focus more on controlling budget shares than on controlling fiscal policy. With the president clearly the central figure in economic management, voting for Congress followed other cues, such as incumbency (cf. Karl 1983: 181). On the revenue side, the story was much the same: Postwar tax politics were for the most part consensual (Witte 1985). Such a system worked well for incumbent members of Congress; at the same time, it weakened the connecting glue that party provides throughout a political system. If people believe the parties are discussing issues that matter and issues that the parties control, they are less likely to abandon political participation or to withdraw into cynicism.

Indeed, while the loss of control over macroeconomic matters was the most damaging for the parties, Sundquist notes that the problem extended to other areas as well: "The Council of Economic Advisers (CEA), in particular, became a model. For groups dissatisfied with the way in which government policies were being formulated, the solution seemed clear: create a council in the Executive Office of the President to concern itself with the issue, and require the president to sign his name to a periodic report prepared by the council corresponding to the Economic Report of the President. . . . In seven broad policy fields—the budget, the economy, national security, manpower, the environment, housing, and urban growth— it had by statute directed or invited the president to be chief legislator" (1981: 143–44, 147). Congress had surely not yielded all its decision-making power, but it had just as surely "magnified the stature and importance of the presidency and the public dependence on presidential leadership" (1981: 63).

The Employment Act of 1946 institutionalized the changes of the preceding decade. The bill passed in 1946 differed markedly from the one originally proposed in 1945 as the Full Employment Act. In its earliest version, the bill placed Congress as the central policy initiator (Sundquist 1981: 63). Few outside witnesses or members of Congress testifying at committee hearings, however, argued that Congress should have the responsibility for coordinating agency funding and revenue requests (Sundquist 1981: 39–45). Gradually, the provision of information became the key point: The president could initiate policy, but Congress must receive information from the executive branch on economic policy and be able to generate and gather information on its own. The 1946 legislation accomplished this latter task by directing the new Joint Committee on the Economic Report of the President (later renamed the Joint Economic Committee) to conduct hearings on the annual report of the president's Council of Economic Advisers.

Although the bill moved down the road toward Keynesianism, "radical" versions of Keynesian ideas were removed between 1945 and 1946. Maximum employment, not full employment, was the policy goal, and no longer was the government legally obligated to achieve even that more limited target. Maximum employment would be balanced against other needs of national policy. There was no "right" to employment. The president could not independently vary the rate of expenditure of appropriated funds (Stein 1969).[43]

Despite some potential, the Great Depression, the New Deal, and World War II did not produce social democracy. As Gourevitch (1986: 162) puts it, the New Deal in the United States rested on a "complicated cross-class, cross-ethnic, cross-sectoral, cross-regional coalition" that could agree on a "commercial Keynesianism" (Collins 1981) but not a social Keynesianism. Commercial Keynesianism called for an arms-length government relationship with the economy, maximum reliance on automatic mechanisms, limited fine-tuning through taxes rather than spending, and a focus on growth and the business cycle rather than distribution of wealth. The "range of material circumstances, institutional structures, and ideas" (Hall 1989: 390) were favorable toward the *introduction* of Keynesian ideas in American economic policy; they were not well suited to the *consolidation* of social Keynesianism after World War II (Weir 1989). The Employment Act was an explicit confirmation of Keynesianism's limits in the United States. By blocking a transformation toward social Keynesianism, the congressional parties showed that American parties can be policy oriented and vital in defining the contours of state activity. From this act of strength came weakness: The parties ironically endorsed a system that accorded them few opportunities to control the economic management that would be at the core of American politics in the postwar decades. Fearing the planning state, their blinkered vision obscured the consequences of the fiscal state.

Changes in the State

Did changes in the fiscal state end the decline of parties by the 1990s? Certainly congressional parties became more vibrant with the collapse of Keynesianism in the late 1970s: When the Keynesian consensus unraveled, space opened for new partisan visions of political economy. But in other parts of the party system, particularly among voters, decline persisted. The reason is that the fiscal state had not been structurally overthrown and Keynesianism, though in disrepute, still awaited its successor.

The Congressional Budget and Impoundment Control Act of 1974 (CBICA) introduced the most significant structural change in the fiscal

[43] A similar idea, standby tax powers, was rejected in the generally more accommodating 1960s (Fisher 1972: 155–73). By these actions, members of Congress were not arguing that they should control economic management but rather were displaying their customary protective action regarding what are viewed as distributive benefits.

state.[44] Besides restricting the president's power to defer and rescind congressionally appropriated funds, CBICA transformed the making of budgets within Congress. New Budget Committees in each chamber developed a budget resolution that established total spending and revenue targets for the upcoming fiscal year and allocated funds into broad program areas. Reconciliation bills crafted by the Budget Committees could force spending and revenue committees in Congress to produce specific amounts of savings. Power once wielded by the traditional budget committees—Appropriations, Ways and Means, Finance—shifted to the new committees. The Budget Committee work was aided by new congressional institutions, including most importantly the Congressional Budget Office (CBO). CBO gave Congress access to the kind of expert analysis, advice, and information long available to the administration. But the era of Budget Committee dominance was short. After 1980, budget policy emerged from ad hoc, annually shifting coalitions pieced together by parties, leadership groups, and the president—in short, anyone who could forge an agreement tolerable to legislative majorities (Gilmour 1990; Palazzolo 1992).

Studies of the new budget procedures became a major growth industry in political science in the 1980s.[45] The consensus was that the budget procedures had not worked well. Although many blamed the process for huge deficits, habitually late appropriations, and the use of accounting gimmicks to keep the government afloat, the process was less to blame than were fundamental political conflicts and the vacuum of any guiding macroeconomic theory (White and Wildavsky 1989; Gilmour 1990). After the process failed to get any significant control on spending, Congress passed the Gramm-Rudman-Hollings budget reform in 1985. This reform threatened to implement automatic deficit reduction provisions if Congress failed to meet its deficit target. Disillusioned with Gramm-Rudman-Hollings and its revision by 1990, Congress reformed the process yet again. This time, Congress imposed nonfungible spending caps (for example, defense spending cuts could not be transferred to discretionary domestic spending) and pay-as-you-go procedures for additional spending. Late in 1991, dissatisfaction with the nonfungible nature of the caps raised the prospect of yet another revision in the budget-making law.[46] In Bill Clinton's first year in office, Congress agreed to a five-year process of cuts in discretionary spending as part of the president's economic program.

[44] In the mid-1970s the Humphrey-Hawkins full employment bill loomed as another possibly significant alteration in the state. By the time the bill passed, it had been watered down to the point where it was no threat to the basic fiscal state framework laid down over forty years before, and it was ignored soon after passage.

[45] Schick (1980) provides a comprehensive early assessment; see also Schick (1990).

[46] Testimony by three budget experts—Louis Fisher (1990), Rudolph Penner (1990), and Henry Aaron (1990)—before the House Committee on Rules, Subcommittee on the Legislative Process, illustrates most of these complaints.

For present purposes, whether these reforms created a salutary budget process is secondary to whether they profoundly changed the assumptions of the fiscal state. They did not. The reforms did not alter the bifurcation of monetary and fiscal policy, the plebiscitary nature of macroeconomic goals, the technical complexity of fiscal policy, or the reliance on automatic fiscal policy. Indeed, in some ways, these limits became even more constraining. Gramm-Rudman-Hollings and its descendants raised automatic fiscal policy to a higher plane, while monetary policy became even more ascendant as arguments about fiscal policy took place with little consideration of ongoing economic conditions. Did the fiscal state still place predominant responsibility for fiscal policy in the executive branch? Through the first two years of the Clinton presidency the answer was yes. The president's power was surely not what it was. Fisher (1990: 4; see also Jones 1991) notes that the president's budget did not define the process or retain the monopoly of attention as it once did. But the president's budget—unless utterly lacking in credibility because of overly optimistic estimates of economic growth—was still taken as an important starting point for the process. Differences between presidential and congressional fiscal plans were on average small (Peterson and Rom 1989). Although the allocation of funds sometimes differed importantly from the presidential to the congressional budget, the fiscal policy impact of the budgets was typically quite similar (cf. LeLoup 1983; Ellwood 1983; Schick 1983; Witte 1986; Hansen 1986; Kamlet and Mowery 1987; Kamlet, Mowery, and Su 1988; White and Wildavsky 1989). Congress still waited for the president to initiate major changes in fiscal policy. House Majority Leader Richard Gephardt (D-Missouri) reiterated this familiar sentiment in 1990: "It's much harder for us to be on offense. The Congress is not meant to be the leading force in the country. It's set up to be a check on presidential power. It can put an imprint on things. From time to time, it can set policy, but that's rare" (*The New Republic,* May 14, 1990, p. 20). The responsibility of each branch was more diffuse and obscure than before 1974, but both Congress and voters still placed the onus of responsibility on the president. Structural limits—president versus Congress, monetary versus fiscal policy, automatic stabilizers and uncontrollable spending, and plebiscitary voting—remained. The parties were not in control. In chapter 6, I consider whether state-building proposals by the Republican Congress in 1995 overcome these remaining limits.

Conclusion

During the building of the fiscal state, concerns about Congress's autonomy from the president and members' autonomy from party competed with arguments stressing the importance of party to institutional, personal, and policy goals. These multiple concerns, reflected in the debates and decisions over the response to recession, executive reorganization, the balance of power between the branches, postwar planning, and legislative reorganization, helped define the operational procedures of the fiscal state and the place of parties in that state. In a pitched political environment with pressures from left and right and from multiple sectors of American society, Congress made decisions that addressed both policy problems and institutional concerns. Not all the long-term consequences of these decisions were clear at the time, but the decision to focus on budgetary distribution more than macroeoncomic policy control had significant implications for the actual and perceived importance of parties in the political process. In the public, these new perceptions about the relevance of parties opened the door early in the postwar period to what the party decline literature shows to be more neutral and more negative assessments of parties and to voting behavior that was decreasingly linked to party. As the political system changed under the fiscal state, citizens were increasingly receiving media messages elevating the importance of the presidency and decreasingly focused on parties and policy, even when discussing Congress (Wattenberg 1990: ch. 6). At the same time, the greater one's media exposure to unemployment news, the stronger the impact of one's personal economic condition on presidential performance ratings (Mutz 1994). The combined result of these media effects is a placement of the president, not the parties, at the center of responsibility and control of the macroeconomic system. In the fiscal state period, such a "placement" by citizens makes great sense, as does an effort by congressional politicians to conduct candidate-centered campaigns. I turn next to the new state's implications for party cohesion and party conflict.

3

Party Cohesion and Party Conflict
in the House of Representatives

IF THE IMPORTANCE of managing the business cycle helps to define the general position of party in the United States, then the cohesion and distinctiveness of congressional parties should be affected by the business cycle and its management. To understand party cohesion and party conflict in Congress requires consideration of the state as a significant environmental context affecting the parties. Surprisingly, scholars have generally ignored the nonpolitical and noninstitutional environment when explaining aggregate party cohesion and party conflict.[1] This gap is curious because virtually all other parts of the political system intersecting with Congress, including elections, public approval ratings, the significance of constituency pressure, and policy outcomes, have been evaluated for their link to economic conditions. It is doubly surprising that parties advertising themselves as expressly interested in managing economic conditions would not be expected to exhibit regularized behavior in response to economic stimuli.

What explains this curious oversight? Technical methodological reasons might be adduced, but the overarching reason for the exclusion of economic conditions from these models is the lack of a theoretical structure within which their inclusion would make sense. The notion that parties are constrained by their environment has been largely limited in these other approaches to the electoral environment and the environment within the House. The wider environment, such as the structure and policy of the state, has not been considered directly relevant to understanding legislative voting behavior (cf. Harmel and Janda 1982). In this chapter, I show that this wider environment influences congressional parties in important and predictable ways.

Party Cohesion and Party Conflict, 1947–1990

To understand party cohesion and party conflict in the postwar period, I utilize all budget-related roll-call votes in the House of Representatives

---

[1] Attempts to pin down the dimensions underlying congressional voting are similarly constrained. See Clausen (1973); Sinclair (1981); Poole and Daniels (1985); Koford (1989); Poole and Rosenthal (1991); Koford (1991); and Clausen and Anderson (1994) for extensions of dimenional analysis.

from 1947 through 1990.[2] Budget-related means a vote involving: (1) an explicit expenditure, increase in expenditure, or decrease in expenditure via authorizations or appropriations; (2) changes in the debt ceiling; (3) taxes; (4) budget resolutions or reconciliation measures that establish spending and taxing targets; and (5) rules to take the various bills under consideration, including rules asking for immediate passage. Votes that define policy without explicit budgetary implications are excluded. For the postwar period, about 40 percent of all votes are budget related in a typical year (chapter 4 considers smaller slices of these budget votes). Budget-related votes do differ from those votes that are not budget related. The percentage of votes featuring opposing party majorities correlates at .39 for the two series, indicating patterns of party conflict that are roughly similar but still distinctive.[3] Looking at the entire set of budget-related votes provides a macrolevel sense of party cohesion and conflict and implicitly acknowledges that resources are limited and budget decisions are interconnected.[4] Over the period, "the budget" was increasingly seen as the central battleground in Congress; the collection, distribution, and transfer of dollars was a large part of political combat after 1947, and bargaining over the distribution of budget resources was seen as a method to solve disputes. The definition and solution of problems via the transfer of funds is part and parcel of the fiscal state approach to public policy.[5]

Roll-call analysis of this type has some obvious drawbacks. First, shifts in the political spectrum cannot be readily inferred from cohesion and conflict data. Thus, it is difficult to detect in this aggregate data that the political and fiscal debate became more conservative in the 1980s. Another shortcoming is that we cannot know from this data exactly why individual representatives voted the way they did; we see only the mass

[2] This chapter and the next focus on the House. Chapters 2 and 5 also discuss the Senate.

[3] The range runs from 28 to 56 percent of all votes. The proportion of votes that are budget-related began increasing around 1971. To see if this changing proportion may have affected the aggregate party cohesion and conflict levels, I included the percentage of votes that were budget-related as a variable in the estimations reported later in this chapter. In no case was this variable near significance. Comparing my budget votes to the total number of party votes and roll-call votes in Stanley and Niemi (1990: 192, 199) provides the data necessary to calculate and compare the budget and nonbudget series across the 1953 to 1988 period.

[4] Just as an understanding of elections cannot be gained solely by looking at critical elections, so, too, an understanding of party voting in Congress cannot rely solely on key votes.

[5] The ever-increasing scope of what actors believed could be accomplished with the budget is apparent in a comparison of Joint Economic Committee analyses in the 1960s (United States Congress, Joint Economic Committee 1963, 1969). The 1963 committee report provides detailed analysis on how to make the budget more intelligible as a reflection of national economic trends and as a causal agent of those trends. The tone is distinctly that of economic fine-tuning. The same committee's 1969 report reflects a much wider concern with the social and regulatory importance of the budget; the necessity of meeting social needs is the predominant tone.

shifts in party cohesion and party disputes (cf. MacKuen, Erikson, and Stimson 1989: 1129–30). Finally, an aggregate approach such as this does not reveal clusters of representatives that might override party lines in a consistent way on certain issues nor does it attempt to extract dimensions linking individual voting behavior on a series of votes.

With a focus on aggregate partisanship, these problems are secondary to the major question. Shifts in the policy agenda are not unimportant, but party strength can be traced without taking it explicitly into account. The second and third concerns effectively ask whether it is a problem if voting simply coincides with the party position but is not determined by it. To be certain, congressional studies based on interviews often find representatives rejecting the notion that party was an important reason for their vote.[6] But to the extent that these apparent "other influences" are consistent with party lines then parties send out a more consistent public message. If Congress is indeed the linchpin of the party system, as I argue earlier, then these messages are of great significance. The public is unlikely to be aware of subtle clustering or coalitions or dimensions of representatives, but it will be more likely to perceive (and hear in the media) that Democrats voted for x while Republicans preferred y (or non-x).[7] Even if the three drawbacks are valid, then, they are concerned with questions other those pursued here.[8]

A total of 5,331 roll-call votes were budget-related from 1947 to

[6] Often, the representative's objection is more to the suggestion (or his or her inference) that the party leadership is pressuring him or her to vote a particular way (Kingdon 1973). One promising approach is offered by Jackson and King (1989): Assume party to be significant from the outset. That is, Jackson and King suggest that interpretation improves when we ask what degree or type of, say, constituency pressure must exist in order to negate a Republican's "natural" tendency to vote a certain way on a bill.

[7] Dimensional analysis comprises a large proportion of the existing body of roll-call literature. Sinclair's (1981) study of the House over the 1925 to 1978 period discovers that government economic management, social welfare, and civil liberties emerge as dimensions from the New Deal period through 1968. Through 1952, international involvement appears as a dimension; foreign aid replaces it from 1953 to 1968. Sinclair further finds that from 1969 through 1976 government economic management is unsteady as a dimension. Perusal of the graphs of the dependent variables later in this chapter certainly support the idea that party conflict on these issues collapsed after 1968. Clausen's (1973) sophisticated application of dimensional analysis for the 1954 to 1963 period presages many of Sinclair's findings. Highly interesting discussions of roll-call analysis technique are in MacRae (1970) and Weisberg (1978).

[8] Another potential, but generally unnoted, problem with this approach is that the cohesion or conflict score might be biased by a large number of amendments on a single bill or high number of amendments on many bills. If the parties have few differences on twenty votes relating to nine different bills but have extreme differences on twenty-five votes relating to a single bill, the resulting average could be viewed as misleading. One way to control for this is to use not votes but bills as the unit of analysis. In this manner, each bill counts equally in the computation of a cohesion or conflict index, giving perhaps a better sense of party disagreement across a range of different types of legislation. This alternative measure is achieved by weighting each vote; if a bill had a single vote, that vote receives a weight of

Table 3.1
Classification of Budget-Related Roll-Call Votes, House of
Representatives, 1947–1990

Type	Percent of Votes[a]	Party Oppositions, Percent of Votes		
		50 vs. 50	75 vs. 75	90 vs. 90
Appropriations	35.6	57.1	19.3	2.5
Authorizations	49.6	54.2	18.6	1.9
Tax	5.5	57.9	26.0	7.2
Defense	12.6	42.9	11.2	1.3
Agriculture	6.1	59.4	24.6	2.8
Trade	1.3	50.8	20.9	3.0
Budget resolution	6.1	68.1	39.6	9.8
Debt limit	2.8	67.6	33.1	9.3
Rules	11.7	53.9	25.7	7.1

Note: Entries in the 50 vs. 50, 75 vs. 75, and 90 vs. 90 columns indicate the percent of votes of a given type (appropriations, authorizations, and so on) with a majority of one party opposing a majority of the other party, with 75 percent or more of one party opposing 75 percent or more of the other, and with 90 percent or more of one party opposing 90 percent or more of the other, respectively.

[a]Total N = 5,331.

1990.[9] Table 3.1 lists the different types of votes. Just under one-half of the votes over this period are authorization-related, while another third are appropriation-related votes. (The Appendix presents annual data on vote type.) Votes split the parties most often in budget resolutions and debt. Defense shows the fewest splits. Tax votes are slightly more divisive

one; if a bill has four votes, each vote has a weight of .25. Each bill, then, is weighted one, while the weight for the individual votes on the bill is determined by the number of votes relating to the bill. One then calculates a cohesion or conflict score across the number of bills rather than the number of votes. This procedure reduces the number of cases, but it does control for the problem above and compensates for the greater average number of votes per bill in the present era than in the early 1950s (due partly, at least, to the introduction of electronic voting in 1973 and enhanced amendment votes in the Committee of the Whole in 1970). As it happens, this alternative measure correlates very closely with the results of the unweighted indexes—over +.90 for Democratic and Republican cohesion and Democratic-Republican conflict. Because of this close correlation, I rely on the unweighted and more familiar vote-centered rather than bill-centered data.

[9] I obtained vote tallies from the annual *Congressional Quarterly Almanac* and *Congressional Quarterly Roll Call,* and corrected and recomputed where necessary. Votes of

Table 3.2
Party Conflict across Administrations, 1947–1990: Percent of Votes with Opposing Party Majorities

Type	Truman 1947–1952	Eisenhower 1953–1960	Kennedy Johnson 1961–1968	Nixon Ford 1969–1976	Carter 1977–1980	Reagan Bush 1981–1990
Appropriations	81.2	67.8	63.4	41.1	51.2	63.4
Authorizations	58.9	60.8	65.6	42.1	45.1	60.8
Tax	75.0	50.0	61.8	54.2	54.3	60.3
Defense	85.7	18.4	31.3	27.0	26.8	59.9
Agriculture	79.2	87.5	67.5	58.7	53.5	48.0
Budget resolution	na	na	na	92.6	71.9	60.3
Debt limit	na	40.0	92.0	50.0	78.8	66.7
Rules	65.5	57.1	60.5	27.2	42.0	65.4

Note: Entries indicate the percent of votes of a given type that featured opposing party majorities in a given adminis-tration. For example, 51.2 percent of the appropriations votes during the Carter administration featured a majority of Democrats opposing a majority of Republicans.

than authorizations and appropriations votes, but they are also much less frequent. For the Democrats, the party's northern and southern wings split least often over rules, debt limits, and agriculture, and most often over defense.[10]

Party polarization in these categories changes over time. One of the striking features of table 3.2 is the high level of party division across issue types in the Truman era despite a 26.8 point range between cate-gories. By the Reagan era, partisan divisions had become regularized across all these policy categories to a more consistent degree and the range between policy categories was narrower. Although the range is 18.7 points for the Reagan-Bush era, most of the issue categories are tightly clustered from 60 to 65. Partisan intensity was higher from 1947 through 1952 than from 1981 through 1990, but it was more consistent and predictable across categories by the 1980s. One possible explanation for this change is that with huge budget deficits and reconciliation procedures linking each part of the budget to other parts, general partisan policy predisposi-tions directed voting across the areas.

Despite the much-discussed regional stresses in the Democratic party, figure 3.1 shows that Democrats were typically more cohesive on budget-

---

questionable budget-related status were further checked by examining Congressional Quar-terly's account of the vote and including them in the database if appropriate. Along with much of the party cohesion literature, I omit "consensus" votes, that is, votes on which 90 percent or more of Democrats and 90 percent or more of Republicans agree on the vote (for example, 90 percent of each party opposes an amendment).

[10] These percentages are based on the entire forty-four-year period and are not average annual figures. "South" includes Alabama, Arkansas, Florida, Georgia, Louisiana, Missis-sippi, North Carolina, Oklahoma, South Carolina, Tennessee, Texas, and Virginia.

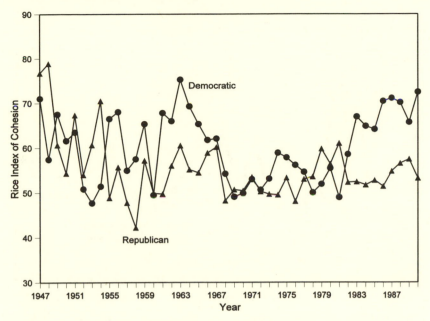

3.1 Democratic and Republican Cohesion on Budget-Related Roll Calls, House of Representatives, 1947–1990

related matters than were Republicans.[11] This difference likely reflects the strain of near-permanent minority party status for the Republicans. On well-publicized major votes, Republicans, especially with a Republican in the White House, were usually able to keep defections to a minimum while Democrats often lost votes to the Republican side. But on a day-to-day basis, the Democrats controlled the House and it was the Republicans who had to switch sides to make an impact.

Figures 3.2 and 3.3 show Republican and Democratic cohesion, respectively. Each figure has two lines: One shows the index for all budget-related votes, the other computes the index without defense, agriculture, tax, and trade votes, each of which has at one time or another generated postwar intraparty conflicts. Interestingly, they have roughly opposite effects for the two parties. Eliminating these policy area votes tends to inflate Republican cohesion in the early years and deflate it after 1968; for the Democrats the relationship is basically the reverse. Through 1976, the parties' cohesion levels share a weak, positive relationship (r = .27), but

---

[11] I use the Rice index to measure party cohesion. On any given vote, the Rice index for the Democrats is the absolute value of the difference between the percentage of Democrats voting yes and the percentage of Democrats voting no. The mean across individual votes produces the annual cohesion figure.

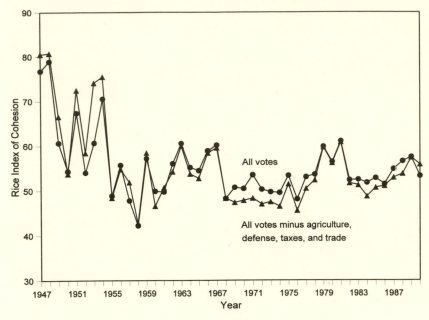

3.2 House Republican Cohesion on Budget-Related Roll-Call Votes

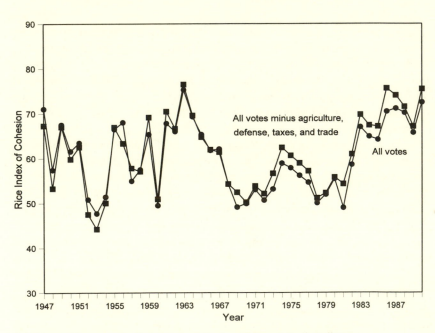

3.3 House Democratic Cohesion on Budget-Related Roll-Call Votes

the patterns diverge sharply after that (r = −.46), precisely the period the fiscal state comes under widespread criticism and skepticism regarding its performance. The Democratic cohesion decline through the 1950s and the sharp acceleration in the late 1950s and early 1960s tracks the increasing clout of northern liberal Democrats during the attempt to reconstitute the role of the state via Great Society programs (see chapter 6). The confusion of both parties after 1965 is evident in the collapse of cohesion.

To give voters a meaningful choice, parties need to be cohesive *and* distinctive. Indicators of party conflict show a clearer pattern of decline and resurgence than do the cohesion data. Figure 3.4 shows this pattern for party conflict as measured by the index of party dissimilarity.[12] This index focuses on the policy position distance between the two parties but does not necessarily indicate parties that are in opposition (that is, there is position distance but not opposition if a bare majority of one party favors bill x while 98 percent of the other party favors bill x). Particularly notable, of course, is the collapse of dissimilarity after 1966, the bottoming out in the early 1970s, and the steady increase in the later 1970s. Party dissimilarity was by 1983 approaching Great Society high points and in 1987 approached the highs of the late 1940s; the decline in the distinctiveness of the congressional parties had been nearly fully reversed.[13] Another measure of party conflict, the party vote, stresses not the distance between the party positions but the tendency of the parties to be in opposition. A party vote exists when a majority of one party votes "yea" while a majority of the other party votes "nay." For budget-related votes from 1947 through 1990, the party votes indicator suggests the same pattern as party dissimilarity (fig. 3.4).[14] Because each tells a different part of the story of party conflict, I will rely on both here. Figure 3.5 shows the percentage of party votes at different levels of party opposition. The patterns in the three series are consistent.

Although each of these indicators provides some insight into the strength

[12] For an individual vote, the index of party dissimilarity is the absolute value of the difference between the percentage of Democrats voting yes and the percentage of Republicans voting yes. These individual scores are then averaged to produce annual dissimilarity scores.

[13] Reversed, that is, from its postwar lows. It still remains the case that overall party cohesion and particularly dissimilarity (all votes) are at much lower levels than was common in the late nineteenth and early twentieth centuries. The improvement in partisanship is also present at the committee level. Unekis and Franke (1994) show that since 1971 universalism in committee voting—majorities of both parties on the same side of a vote—has been much less frequent than on the floor. As with floor voting, partisan voting in committees has been increasing, but at a steadier rate. Universalism is far more likely on votes to move bills to the floor than on amendments. On the prestige committees, universalism is rare on any kind of votes; on constituency and policy committees, universalism is low on amendments and high on moving bills to the floor.

[14] The dissimilarity and party votes series correlate at .83.

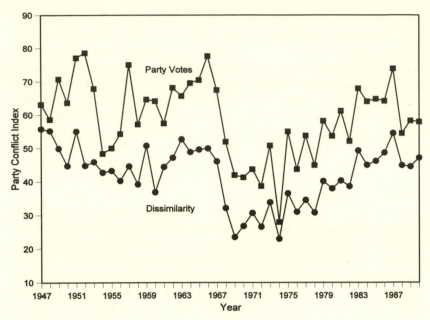

3.4 Measures of Party Conflict in the House, 1947–1990

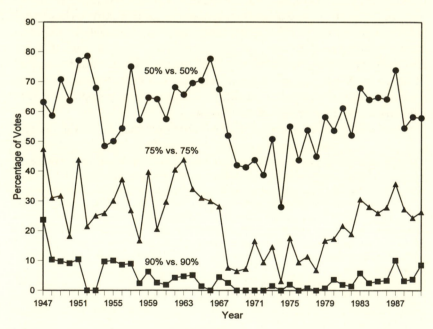

3.5 Party Votes in the House, 1947–1990

of party voting in the House, none is by itself a sufficient measure of the health of the party system. This is most obviously true in the limited nature of the indicators: They cannot tell us whether the cohesion and conflict manifest in the House matter to the public. But setting this problem aside—chapter 1 indicates a positive correlation between the level of party conflict and the public's favorable attitudes and attention toward the major parties—and narrowing attention to the status of party in the House, none of the individual measures explains enough. Party cohesion is surely important, but the parties can be cohesive yet not particularly different. Higher party cohesion may contribute to higher party conflict; it does not guarantee it.[15] And party conflict can increase in the face of decreasing party cohesion. Complicating matters further, a high percentage of party votes does not guarantee either very cohesive or very different parties. In theory, the parties could produce a party vote score of 100 while each party was divided 50.1 percent/49.9 percent (the correlation of annual party votes with Democratic and Republican cohesion, respectively, is .38 and .27).

Though these indicators fall short individually, multiplying them together produces a useful index of party salience in the House. The highest scores will be registered in those years when the parties are staking out polarized positions (dissimilarity), when they are both internally united (cohesion), and when they are on opposite sides of many votes (party votes). Multiplying the party conflict series (party votes and dissimilarity) and the party cohesion series (Republican and Democratic) produces the party salience time series of figure 3.6. The figure shows that the postwar congressional party system most met the responsible ideal in the period from 1947 to 1952. Another, lower peak arrived between 1962 and 1967. A third peak, but the lowest of the three, is the recent improvement in party status from 1983 to 1990. The period from 1968 through 1978 shows the party system in particular disrepair, with the Watergate, inflation, recession, and reform year of 1974 marking the ebb.[16] What this figure suggests is that congressional parties indeed revived after the early 1970s, but that the salience of the parties in the 1980s was neither unprecedented in postwar history nor especially high in comparison with earlier postwar peaks. The evaluation of developments in the 1980s should be favorable but cautious. And it is equally important to remember that

[15] Dissimilarity and party votes moved in opposite directions (one increased as the other decreased) in eleven of forty-three years, or about 25 percent of the time.

[16] The results are the same when the series is calculated additively instead of multiplicatively, when the series is either added or multiplied as a set of mean deviations, and if the component variables are normalized to have comparable variation (although in this latter case, 1969 becomes the low year). The results are unchanged if dissimilarity, which has the highest correlation with the various computed series, is omitted.

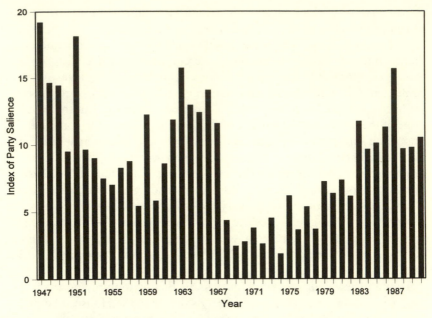

3.6 Party Salience in the House, 1947–1990
Note: The Index of Party Salience equals the product of party dissimilarity, party votes, Democratic cohesion, and Republican cohesion, divided by 1,000,000. Maximum = 100, minimum = 0.

this 1980s partisan music did not engender voters to get up and dance. Precisely as the congressional parties became more salient, the voters increasingly decided to sit this one out. Those who did participate were less inclined to dance with the party that brought them.

The high party vote scores for budget resolutions (see table 3.1) raises the possibility that the increase in party differences in the 1970s and 1980s may simply reflect the onset of budget resolutions after 1974 (they were created as part of the Budget and Impoundment Control Act of 1974).[17] In fact, this is not a problem. First of all, budget resolution votes contribute only 6.1 percent of the total number of roll-call votes. Their overall impact, then, is fairly small: The average annual percentage of party votes from 1947 to 1990 is 58.9 percent with budget resolution votes and 58.6 percent without them. The index of party dissimilarity changes from 42.1 with the budget resolution votes to 41.5 without them. The effect on party cohesion is also fairly small: Democratic cohesion was 60.2 with the votes included, 59.8 without; Republican cohesion was 55.4 with budget resolution votes included, 54.7 without. Even looking only at the period

[17] A legislative budget similar to the budget resolutions was in place in 1947–1948 before being dropped as unworkable.

since 1975, the largest annual differential is 1.5 points (for Republican cohesion) between indexes including budget resolution votes and indexes excluding these votes.

The new tendencies toward greater party conflict and greater party cohesion mask some curious subdevelopments. Interestingly, party voting was both more intense and less intense in the 1980s than in the 1960s. For instance, comparing the party dissimilarity of the mid-1980s to the dissimilarity of the early-to-mid 1960s (roughly similar levels overall) produces a mixed result. Considering solely party votes—those votes that actually pose party majorities on opposite sides—dissimilarity in the 1980s trails the level of the 1960s. Considering only non-party votes the 1980s dissimilarity level is higher than the 1960s level. The reason for this pattern is not clear. This dichotomy in the data can be seen as suggesting that a new wave of partisanship is pushing through, first making the votes without opposing majorities more contentious and then gradually polarizing the party votes as well. Or, the dichotomy could suggest that as the role of the government has expanded the parties might be finding more policy areas to be partisan issues but at the same time not dividing as fiercely on those issues because with a wider array of issues "partisan" it becomes increasingly difficult to make everyone in the party happy at all times.[18]

Explaining Party Cohesion and Party Conflict

Existing studies of aggregate party cohesion and party conflict in the House rely almost exclusively on internal and external political variables or internal structural variables.[19] Patterson and Caldeira (1988) utilize the most comprehensive battery of political and structual variables, many of which appear in other studies. Turnover, party platform conflict, divided government, and split districts constitute Patterson and Caldeira's electoral and party context. The size of the majority party, proportion of southern Democrats, proportion of eastern Republicans, presidential support scores, and the proportion of party votes in the previous year form the congressional party context. And the number of roll calls, number of bills passed, number of committee assignments per member, first or second session, and rules changes regarding recorded teller and computerized votes form the organizational context. Other studies add such political conditions as the popular vote for the president, changes in the controlling House party, Progressive anti-party reforms, the realignment process,

[18] I thank Joseph White for pointing out this possibility to me.
[19] Collie (1984, 1988b) and Patterson and Caldeira (1988) provide comprehensive reviews of the literature.

regional divisions, and bipartisan coalitions (Sinclair 1977; Clubb and Traugott 1977; Clubb, Flanigan, and Zingale 1980; Brady 1988; Deckard and Stanley 1974; Deckard 1976; Sinclair 1978, Bensel 1984; Collie 1988a, 1988b, 1989; Cover, Pinney, and Serra 1994).

The internal structure of Congress, for example, centralization of leadership or power of the caucus, has been the central focus elsewhere (Brady, Cooper, and Hurley 1979; Sinclair 1983; Hammond 1991). Some studies suggest that party leaders in the late 1970s and 1980s were able to lead primarily because they were dealing with more ideologically consistent party members (Shaffer 1980; Bensel 1984; Collie and Brady 1985; Aldrich 1995; Brady 1990).[20] Rohde (1991; see also Ornstein and Rohde 1978) argues that voters in the 1970s began sending more ideologically consistent parties to Congress. Tension from a perceived maldistribution of power within these "new" parties led to the congressional reforms in the 1970s that increased the strength of both the leadership and the caucus, and leaders were better able to lead more consistent parties. Cox and McCubbins (1993) agree that the reforms were an attempt to bring the institution, especially the committees, under firm party direction, but they dispute the notion that the parties ever really lost power in the institution (see also Kiewiet and McCubbins 1991). Whether believing leaders were leading or being led, most scholars agree that congressional party labels were more meaningful in the mid-1980s than they had been in the previous two decades.

Studies emphasizing political variables or internal structural variables have provided helpful insights into party cohesion and conflict, but both have proven problematic and inconsistent. In some cases, the analytical power of the politics-only models derives from their time span and the use of congress-by-congress data. (I examine one example below.) If we focus the data on, for example, the post–New Deal era and use yearly data, these models often become less satisfactory. Other problems are methodological. For example, internal structure has proven difficult to measure. It has traditionally been accommodated via dummy variables, but these variables tend to be blunt. Taking some of these shortcomings into account and reanalyzing shows the models to be less successful and historically encompassing than initially believed.

Even with these shortcomings addressed, the existing studies would be hampered by their narrow view of environment. The notion that parties are constrained by their environment has been limited in these other approaches to the electoral environment and the political-structural environment within the House, often within the context of reelection; the

[20] Brady (1990) makes a general argument along these lines for changes in party cohesion; however, he expresses skepticism about the significance of the cohesion improvements of the 1970s and 1980s.

wider historical setting, such as the structure of the state or the implications of specific types of public policy, has been omitted (cf. Harmel and Janda 1982). This chapter suggests all of these environments—including the state—are important and help explain party cohesion and conflict.

To illustrate these difficulties, consider the well-regarded model developed by Brady, Cooper, and Hurley (1979). This model seeks to explain party cohesion and party conflict over the period 1887 to 1968 by using sets of external and internal independent variables, the latter set in the form of dummy variables. The external variables are the percentage of House members serving their first term, an index of economic conflict between the parties (measured by content analysis of the previous presidential platform), a dummy variable representing whether the president and the majority party in the House were of the same party, and the size of the dominant regional faction within each party.[21] The internal dummy variables are the presence of a strong centralized leadership (1887 through 1910 = 1, else = 0) and the presence of a strong party caucus (1887 through 1938 = 1, else = 0). The 1939 to 1968 period (zeros on both internal variables) is, then, the baseline model to which the dummy intercepts are added. The hypothesis is that all these variables enhance cohesion and conflict.

Table 3.3 presents the results for the Brady, Cooper, and Hurley model for the entire 1887 to 1968 period.[22] Each of the models explains about one-third of the variance in the level of cohesion or party voting. Coefficients for two of the independent variables in the Democratic cohesion regression have the wrong sign, and serial correlation of the errors is marginally problematic, as indicated by the Durbin-Watson figure.[23] Two of

[21] This last variable compared the size of northeastern and midwestern Republicans against the rest of the party; the same comparison was made between southern and border Democrats and the rest of the Democratic party. Because this variable was consistently insignificant in the Brady, Cooper, and Hurley results, it has been dropped here.

[22] Brady, Cooper, and Hurley present the model in two stages: first with the internal variables alone, then with both sets of variables, although in the latter case they report only the coefficients for the external variables. Here, to save space, I present the reanalysis of the regression including both sets of variables.

[23] Serial correlation—in which consecutive prediction errors in an estimated model tend to be highly correlated—may indicate that a gradually changing variable has been left out of the estimation or that the functional form of the variables is incorrect. It can reflect, then, a kind of specification error. These errors should, if possible, be corrected by the analyst. In other cases, however, errors are autocorrelated even without specification error. Analysts can then turn to one of several standard techniques to correct the problem and reestimate the regression. Serial correlation can vary in type—errors can be correlated in an autoregressive or moving average process—and lag structure. The most common format in political science research is a first-order autoregressive correlation in which consecutive errors are correlated (one examines correlograms to confirm or refute this generalization). The Prais-Winsten estimation procedure, a nonlinear least squares procedure that is in most in-

Table 3.3
Brady, Cooper, and Hurley Model for Explaining House Party Cohesion and
Conflict, 1887–1968

Independent Variables	Democratic Cohesion	Republican Cohesion	Party Voting
Constant	66.18***	61.44***	38.84***
	(3.53)	(4.00)	(6.29)
First-term members	−0.21	0.16	0.21
	(0.14)	(0.15)	(0.24)
Platform conflict	15.45**	−3.66	23.99**
	(6.94)	(7.87)	(12.36)
Unified government	1.83	5.96**	6.76*
	(2.37)	(2.68)	(4.21)
Strong centralized leadership	8.03***	7.71***	6.57*
	(2.68)	(3.04)	(4.78)
Strong caucus	−1.77	0.77	1.70
	(2.41)	(2.73)	(4.28)
Standard error of regression	5.70	6.46	10.15
Corrected R^2	.31	.33	.37
F-statistic	4.64***	4.94***	5.76***
Durbin-Watson	1.42	1.92	1.91

Note: Entries are unstandardized regression coefficients. Standard errors in parentheses.
$^*p \le .10$; $^{**}p \le .05$; $^{***}p \le .01$, one-tailed.

the other three variables are significant. Platform conflict points the wrong
way in the Republican cohesion estimation, while two coefficients are significant. Three variables are significant in the party voting regression.

Brady, Cooper, and Hurley's aim is to show that the set of external variables are more important than the internal variables in determining party
cohesion and party conflict. Table 3.3 does not allow for any confident
statements either way about that particular issue. But more important
than the answer is the question: The authors seek to show that contemporary research about the motivations of representatives can be pushed
back in time. By showing that the structural internal variables are relatively less important than the external variables (first-termers, platform
conflict, unified government), one can mute the criticism that different political eras may have operated on different political principles or that the

stances asymptotically equivalent to maximum likelihood estimation, was used here to determine the size of the correlation between errors, known as rho (Ostrom 1990: 34–35). In
the case of Democratic cohesion reported in table 3.3, rho is 0.29, or just under the common rule-of-thumb of 0.30. If the serial correlation correction is made, thus producing a
form of generalized least squares, platform conflict is no longer significant.

same principles may have resulted in different behavior, because these external variables are assumed to have the same impact on congressional behavior across time. The underlying approach of the Brady, Cooper, and
Hurley analysis runs counter to the view that historical periods present
substantive and theoretically important limits and opportunities on institutions such as parties.

Table 3.4 indicates that, for Democratic cohesion and party voting, a
reanalysis of the Brady, Cooper, and Hurley model is more successful for
the period from 1887 to 1938 than for 1939 to 1968. These dates coincide with those given by Brady, Cooper, and Hurley for the end of the
strong central leadership, strong party caucus era. The second column for
each dependent variable shows whether the model predicts fluctuations in
an era (1939–1968) when the internal structural variables do not change.
For Democrats and party voting, the model provides a weak fit to the post-
1938 data.[24] The negligible performance of the model regarding party
voting indicates that understanding what increases party distinctiveness
in the fiscal state era requires an alternative or additional set of variables.
For Republican cohesion, the model is actually more effective in the post-
1938 period. The variance explained is over 50 percent, the F-statistic is
high, and all the coefficients are in the expected direction with two (other
than the intercept) significant. (It is interesting to note that each party fits
the model best when it is typically the minority party.) For present purposes, the important point is that the Brady, Cooper, and Hurley data suggest that attention to historical eras is prudent.[25]

Economics, Politics, and Parties: Building an Alternative Model of Cohesion and Conflict

In the fiscal state, one might expect to find important relationships between economic conditions, party cohesion, and party conflict because
managing the economy is at the core of this state and party competition.
Economic conditions could be an important determinant of how "strong"
and relevant the parties appear. Ideally, the parties would become more
cohesive and more distinctive as the economy turns down, offering voters a choice instead of an echo. If this were indeed the relationship between economic conditions and the parties, one would have to conclude

[24] I also tried a cutpoint of 1946–1947, which is where the data is cut in the present analysis. No appreciable differences resulted.

[25] I certainly do not mean to suggest that the Brady, Cooper, and Hurley model is somehow unusually afflicted by the problem of historical periods. Instead, it is representative of
studies that exhibit similar problems. I isolate it here because it is well-known and in many
respects seminal.

Table 3.4
Reanalysis of Brady, Cooper, and Hurley Model for Two Eras

Independent Variables	Cohesion				Party Voting	
	Democratic		Republican			
	1887–1938	1939–1968	1887–1938	1939–1968	1887–1938	1939–1968
Constant	64.19***	71.08***	64.77***	52.63***	36.44***	34.08***
	(6.22)	(4.41)	(7.54)	(4.33)	(11.22)	(10.06)
First-term members	−0.23	−0.16	0.05	0.81***	0.26	0.54
	(0.17)	(0.24)	(0.21)	(0.23)	(0.31)	(0.54)
Platform conflict	19.30***	−53.63**	−2.65	3.91	21.60*	54.49
	(7.75)	(20.47)	(9.38)	(20.07)	(13.96)	(46.65)
Unified government	1.45	2.43	5.52	4.15**	10.97	1.76
	(3.81)	(2.27)	(4.62)	(2.23)	(6.88)	(5.18)
Strong centralized leadership	7.70***		8.67**		6.49	
	(3.01)		(3.64)		(5.42)	
Strong caucus[a]						
Standard error of regression	6.17	3.83	7.47	3.76	11.12	8.74
Corrected R^2	.37	.27	.20	.53	.25	.00
F-statistic	4.73***	2.76	2.60	6.16**	3.11**	0.96
Durbin-Watson	1.52	1.82	2.00	2.03	1.95	2.12

Note: Entries are unstandardized regression coefficients. Standard errors in parentheses.
[a]There are no entries for caucus because the value of caucus is 1 for every Congress from 1887 to 1938 and 0 for every Congress from 1939 to 1968.
$^*p \leq .10$; $^{**}p \leq .05$; $^{***}p \leq .01$, one-tailed.

that the party system might be more responsive to public needs than is usually recognized. Clearly, if parties become more cohesive and more distinctive at a time when public attention to and demands on parties are heightened, then one must conclude that parties in some respects perform the "responsible" role so often demanded of them by critics. Unfortunately, the constraints on fiscal state parties distort this ideal relationship between economic conditions and party response.[26]

Postwar parties operated within the constraints of the fiscal state. They also operated within the constraints of congressional coalition building. Party cohesion and party conflict, the dependent variables, cannot be understood without considering both these sets of constraints. In this section, I suggest how the fiscal state matters for party behavior, and I develop an alternative model of party cohesion and conflict.

The parties actively competed on their ability to provide growth, avert recession, and induce recovery. Campaign rhetoric touted each party's ability to produce economic prosperity. But this competition was limited by features of the fiscal state. Monetary policy was not subject to congressional voting. Automatic stabilizers defused and often removed from the agenda key issues of economic policy. The power of Keynesian ideas, even if a conservative Keynesianism, encouraged members to rally around the Keynesian flag during recessions.

To tap into the effects of these constraints on party behavior, the economic portion of the model includes variables that might be expected to spur party cohesion and distinctiveness. The economic variables are the unemployment rate and the rate of inflation. Unemployment and inflation are advantageous because they are widely disseminated and discussed,

---

[26] Because the fiscal state exists in a particular time and place, it would not be appropriate to expect the same kind of relationship between the state and parties to exist before and after the onset of the fiscal state. Even scholars who employ historical approaches to political science sometimes overlook this point. Skowronek's (1982, see also 1993; cf. Orren and Skowronek 1994) basic sympathies are surely consistent with this idea that historical periods pose important conditions on politics. In execution, however, Skowronek projects forward all party decline from one institutional episode around the turn of the century. Because he allows no room for policy and policy outcomes and because he does not consider New Deal structural changes to rival those of the Progressive era, he misses the important contributors to party decline that emerge only after the New Deal. Bringing policy back in lets us see that the institutional changes of the New Deal were indeed as significant for the health of parties as the reforms of the Progressive period. Of course, scholars also need to avoid downplaying too excessively the party-weakening developments of the period before the New Deal (see Eden 1993; Brand 1993). The point is that while there is a relationship between the state and parties across history, the particular configuration of this relationship changes. With different configurations come different expectations about the reaction of congressional parties to changes in the environment. This does not mean comparisons cannot be made across historical periods; it does mean one needs to be certain the comparisons are appropriate.

they are salient to both voters and representatives, and they have been used with some success in modeling other political-economic interactions. They are also the most theoretically compelling variables available because they loom so large in the Keynesian analysis at the heart of fiscal state macroeconomic policy.[27] To capture the effects of simultaneous high inflation and high unemployment, a combination fundamentally challenging to the Keynesian approach, an unemployment-inflation interaction term is employed.

Because perceptions of the seriousness of these problems may change over time, I also use an adjusted form of these variables. Specifically, the adjusted form of unemployment is the unemployment gap. Introduced by Hibbs (1987), the unemployment gap measures the distance between the official unemployment rate and the "natural" rate of unemployment (the natural rate is not a constant but instead gradually increases from 5 to 6 percent across the 1947–1990 period). Economists suggest that pushing unemployment below the natural rate will accelerate inflation; it is akin to the notion of "full employment." The gap suggests that unemployment will be politically important when the official rate exceeds the natural rate and becomes increasingly important as the gap widens. I employ a similar gap for the adjusted form of inflation: the amount by which the actual inflation rate exceeds a 3 percent "desirable" rate. This rate has resonance in recent history. In the low-inflation era of the late 1950s through the late 1960s, inflation largely stayed under this threshold. Concerns about Lyndon Johnson's failure to finance the Vietnam War in an economically prudent manner grew when the inflation rate neared and exceeded 3 percent in the late 1960s and early 1970s. Ronald Reagan's administration marked its economic policy as successful when the inflation rate dipped to that level. In 1992 and 1993, inflation was absent as a major issue as it hovered around 3 percent, and in 1994, the Federal Reserve Board embarked on a series of interest rate increases to keep inflation below that figure. Like unemployment, inflation becomes an important political issue as the inflation gap grows. My expectations for the impact of these variables on party cohesion and party conflict are explained below.

Inclusion of economic variables does not preclude inclusion of the kind of political variables featured in existing aggregate party voting models. Indeed, research employing political indicators indicates that these variables matter for congressional coalition building and that they can make a contribution toward explaining party cohesion and conflict. And theo-

---

[27] King and Plosser (1989) and Stock and Watson (1989) provide useful discussions of alternative business cycle indicators. Summers (1990) discusses alternative measures of unemployment. Over the 1947 to 1990 period, the consumer price inflation and unemployment rates correlate at .16.

retically, including political variables makes sense. In chapter 2, I suggest that, in the formation of the fiscal state, members of Congress were influenced by several different incentives and opportunities, some of which were clearly political or institutional. The idea here is to widen what is considered the environment within which the parties in the House work. This means considering both the fiscal state (reflected in economic variables) and the political-structural atmosphere to be parts of that environment.

Based on findings in other party voting studies, I incorporate the following variables: the number of first-term representatives, the size of the majority party (or simply the number of party members for individual party cohesion estimations), and a dummy variable for congressional election years. Because other studies show that unified government leads to higher party cohesion and, particularly, more party conflict, I employ a modified version of this variable. Normally, analysts include a dummy variable to denote whether government is unified or divided. Sometimes a dummy is included to denote the party of the president. If the default conditions were unified Democratic control, one could then compare the coefficients for any set of desired properties: divided Republican control, for example. Unfortunately it is usually difficult to tell whether these alternatives are significantly different from the default condition, particularly if one of the dummies is statistically significant and the other is not. To deal with this problem, I utilize a simple if inelegant dummy variable scheme. The default condition is unified Democratic control (sixteen years). I include a dummy for each alternative scenario that actually occurred during 1947 to 1990: unified Republican control (two years); divided Republican control (eighteen years); divided Democratic control (two years); divided Republican control with the chambers of Congress also in split party control (six years). If nothing else, this format reminds us just how infrequently some of these alternatives appear. Separating out these infrequent combinations reaffirms that caution is in order when speculating on or interpreting the coefficients that are produced using the more common one or two dummy-variable format.[28]

Another important question is how to treat southern Democrats. Past studies have used the size of the southern contingent within the party as a key determinant of internal party dissonance. The idea was that the more evenly the party was split between North and South the greater the strains on party cohesion. The party should be more cohesive, according to this argument, when one of the sections grows in size relative to the other. I use a variable that measures the size of the dominant faction (either South or non-South) in the Democratic party as a way to examine

---

[28] I thank Charles Franklin for assistance on this matter.

this problem.[29] But this variable does assume that the party sections are different. More recently, however, scholars have emphasized how southern Democrats are looking more and more like northern Democrats (Rohde 1991). If this is the case, then variables measuring solely the size of the southern contingent in the party or the size of the dominant faction may be misleading and overlook slow-moving changes occurring in southern politics. Therefore, I have included a measure of the ideological leaning of southern House Democrats.

Unfortunately, standard measures of the ideological leaning of members of Congress are built from the same data that create the cohesion and conflict indexes, namely, roll-call votes. Key votes tabulated by the Americans for Democratic Action, for example, fall in this category. So do Conservative Coalition votes, which are defined as votes in which a majority of southern Democrats join Republicans in opposition to northern Democrats. My measure of southern ideology relies on Conservative Coalition votes. Specifically, the measure used here indicates the average percentage of southern Democrats who voted with the coalition on Conservative Coalition votes. Clearly, the percentage has a minimum of 50 taking the conservative position (or there would be no Conservative Coalition vote) and a maximum of 100.[30] This use of the data is preferable to simply using the percentage of votes that are Conservative Coalition votes because it is not so clearly linked with the dependent variables examined in this chapter. For example, since the appearance of the Conservative Coalition means by definition lower Democratic party cohesion, it is more nearly a substitute measure for cohesion than an explanation of it. Focusing instead on the changing strength of the conservative position among southerners when this position clearly asserts itself in a Conservative Coalition vote is, I think, a reasonable indication of conservative predisposition that does not mimic the dependent variables of party cohesion and party conflict.[31]

Three additional variables round out the set of political indicators. Because of the dramatic effects of the Vietnam War on American politics and the possibility that the effects of the war might be absorbed by other vari-

[29] The South is the majority faction in only two terms: 1947–1948 and 1953–1954. These were also the terms in which Republicans held a majority in the House. As a practical matter, then, this variable indicates what happens as the South becomes a smaller proportion of the party over time.

[30] For estimation purposes, I subtract 50 from the percentage; the highest conservatism level is therefore 50 (100 percent voting conservative minus 50 percent equals 50).

[31] The southern conservatism index correlates with Democratic cohesion at $-.30$; the percentage of votes where the Conservative Coalition appears, by contrast, correlates with Democratic cohesion at $-.69$. The southern conservatism index correlates with party dissimilarity at $-.34$; Conservative Coalition appearance correlates with party dissimilarity at $-.48$.

ables in the model, I included the number of American battle deaths in Vietnam as a measure of the war's political intensity.[32] Next, a dummy variable notes the year following the midterm congressional election. If the midterm election is truly an electoral corrective device, as history and previous studies suggest (Tufte 1975; Alesina, Londregan, and Rosenthal 1993), then one might expect partisanship to be highly pitched in the year following that election. This dummy variable tests that possibility. Finally, I include a dummy variable to tap into the postreform congressional era, in particular the latter part of that era.[33] This variable is "on" for the years 1980 to 1990, the era of the reconciliation process in budget politics. It was in this period that the centralizing aspects of the congressional reforms were fully in effect, largely because of the conflict over budgetary policy. Though not ideal, the dummy variable format for structual variables is consistent with existing studies.

This battery of independent variables adds the fiscal state environment to the major influences cited in the literature. Incorporating these influences should prevent falsely attributing explanatory effects to the economic variables. In sum, the independent variables are:

Economic:

Unemployment:	Unemployment rate and unemployment gap (expect positive relationship to Democratic cohesion, negative relationship to Republican cohesion, negative relationship to party conflict)
Inflation:	Inflation rate and inflation gap; percent change in consumer price index $(+,-,-)$
Unemployment∗Inflation:	Unemployment/inflation interaction term and gap interaction term $(-,+,+)$

Political:

New members:	Number of first-term members in House elected in most recent election for party conflict estimations, percentage of first-term party members for party cohesion estimations $(+,+,+)$
R president, D Congress:	= 1 if divided government with Republican president, 0 otherwise $(-,-,-)$
R president, R Congress:	= 1 if unified government with Republican president, 0 otherwise (neither cohesion nor conflict

[32] I thank anonymous reviewers for this suggestion and for pointing out the problem of changing southern Democratic ideology.

[33] Rohde (1991) suggests that the reforms should have had gradual and not immediate impacts on congressional behavior. I did test a dummy variable for the entire 1975 to 1990 period that proved insignificant.

should differ from unified Democratic government baseline; expect coefficient values of 0)

R president, D House: = 1 if divided government with Republican pres-
                          ident, Senate controlled by Republicans, 0 other-
                          wise $(-,-,-)$

D president, R Congress: = 1 if divided government with Democratic pres-
                          ident, 0 otherwise $(-,-,-)$

Vietnam: American battle deaths in Vietnam, divided by
                          1,000 $(-,-,-)$

Party size: Number of Democrats or Republicans, respec-
                          tively, for individual party cohesion estimations
                          $(-,-,$ not applicable$)$

Election: = 1 if congressional election year, 0 otherwise
                          $(-,-,-)$

After midterm: = 1 for year following midterm election, 0 other-
                          wise $(+,+,+)$

Majority size: Majority party members as a percent of all mem-
                          bers, minus 50 percent (na,na,$+$)

Southern conservatism: Average southern conservative vote on Conserva-
                          tive Coalition votes, minus 50 percent (higher
                          scores indicate higher conservatism) $(-,$ na,$-)$

Dominant faction: Dominant regional group (South, non-South) in
                          Democratic party as a percent of all Democrats,
                          minus 50 percent $(+,$ na,$+)$

Structural:

Reconciliation: = 1 for 1980–1990, 0 otherwise $(+,+,+)$

How might these variables affect party cohesion and party conflict?
Considering the political variables first, a high percentage of *newcomers*
indicates several things that might tend to promote both cohesion and
conflict: Committee turnover and the removal of at least some committee
chairs, a concern in Congress with a changing public mood, a perceived
pro- or anti-administration mandate from the voters, and the traditional
precedent for freshmen members to be the most party loyal (cf. Brady
1988). Under *unified government,* parties understand that their unity is
tantamount to control of the legislative process, while the minority party
realizes it can to some extent remain "above the fray" while shifting blame
to the party controlling both the executive and legislative branches: Cohesion and conflict should increase. A similar logic may work in the case
of the *size of the majority party:* A larger majority party, though unwieldy,
realizes it possesses the capability to push through policies; a smaller minority party has some incentive to avoid "me-tooism" in voicing its message. Together, these incentives increase conflict. On the other hand, large

may simply become too large to maintain growing levels of cohesion. This problem of scale would affect the parties individually in the *party size* measures. *Vietnam* presented searing divisions in American politics; as the war intensified, I would expect less party cohesion and less party conflict. *Congressional elections* may lead to a focus on constituency that weakens both cohesion and conflict. And a very simple Downsian premise would be that, given a unimodal preference structure among the populace, parties will tend to move closer together as an election approaches in order to capture a greater share of the median voter pool. The *post–midterm year*, on the other hand, tends to boost both cohesion and conflict as the opposition party reads the midterm election results as a negative evaluation of the administration and the president's party circles the wagons to protect the president and the party. As for Democratic factionalism, cohesion should improve as one of the factions becomes larger. Because this *dominant faction* was almost always northern, party conflict should also rise. As *southern conservatism* decreases, Democratic party cohesion should increase and differences between the two parties should increase. Finally, *reconciliation* should increase both cohesion and conflict as it (and other reforms) placed new tools in the hands of party leadership and to some degree established alternative party–influenced power bases outside the committees (Sinclair 1983; Shepsle 1989; White and Wildavsky 1989; Rohde 1991; Davidson 1992). Since the reconciliation process becomes prominent during and *because* of the breakdown of fiscal state macroeconomic management, this variable is useful not only as a test of structural reforms but as a test of fiscal state influence on the parties. That is, the reconciliation process provides another measure, along with economic conditions, of what happens to party cohesion and conflict when the operating assumptions of fiscal state macroeconomic management collapse. With fiscal state constraints reduced, reconciliation should allow parties to be cohesive and distinctive.

Studies of party development make a convincing case that parties prefer to focus and compete on the issues that arose during their formative era (Lipset and Rokkan 1967; Burnham 1970; Shefter 1984; Shafer 1991b). Other issues are disorienting and may disrupt existing patterns of power, while these familiar issues can be easily integrated into existing party competition (Baer and Bositis 1988, 1993). The shift from, as Sundquist (1973) describes it, one major issue overlay to another is a wrenching process completed historically only by deeply destabilizing political and economic events. For the fiscal state period, those familiar issues revolve around the nature and scope of governmental management of the business cycle. Ideally, periods of economic stress would provide the impetus for parties based on economic management issues to coalesce and distinguish themselves from their rivals (congressional level of party), mobilize and perhaps convert voters in a particularly steep downturn (voter level of party), and take a more assertive role in policy initiation (system level of party). Every recession poses anew the questions about the nature of the state and economic management that are central to the postwar parties.

But does party behavior take this course in the fiscal state environment? I expect not. While the parties may behave predictably to the onset of economic stresses, especially recession (combatting recession has been the central though not the only driving force of the Keynesian approach), it is likely a response that *weakens* rather than enhances the role and image of parties. Part of that weakness derives from constraints discussed earlier: "automatic" policy making and comparatively less control over monetary than fiscal policy. Weakness also results from party behavior that reduces party conflict. Given that the Democrats were the "founders" of the fiscal state and somewhat more disposed to active government, I expect that Democratic cohesion will increase when faced with increasing unemployment and inflation. Either of these problems can, in effect, be dealt with by Keynesian formulas. For the Republicans, however, decreased cohesion is likely as party members move away from their initially less enthusiastic embrace of Keynes and toward a more supportive Keynesian outlook. Because of the strength of the Keynesian consensus, the automaticity of stabilizing policies and uncontrollable expenditures, and the effective absence of major monetary policy disputes, I expect party conflict to decline, not increase, when unemployment or inflation are solitary economic problems. Conflict should decrease but not disappear. Basic party differences in philosophy can still create conflict in the postwar period. Differences in policy details will remain, but the debates over details are fought in largely Keynesian terms. When *both* unemployment and inflation are high, the Keynesian policy prescriptions are scattered and the party response should reverse: Democrats should become less cohesive as they abandon Keynesian dictums and Republicans more cohesive as they rally around the opportunity to build a new defining political economy. Party conflict should increase as the Keynesian consensus loses its grip and the agenda potentially opens up to long-neglected or entirely new concerns. Different non-Keynesian assumptions about economic management can become credible alternatives. Supply-side economics and industrial policy would be two examples of these alternatives in the 1980s. Both started with different assumptions about the operation of the economy and individual behavior than did Keynesian fiscal policy, and both had different goals. When one of the major tenets of the fiscal state begins to weaken, legislative parties have an opening to rebuild their strength and relevance.

Therefore, I expect economic conditions to have significant effects on party behavior. The null model here is that presented in existing political models of aggregate party voting. That null model allows for no impact of economic conditions on party voting. My expectations about the behavior of congressional party members require no heroic assumptions. They suggest only that members will normally be cautious about crawling out far on a policy limb, particularly in an area in which the winning electoral policy *appears* clear, and that members will be opportunistic when it comes to replacing this policy system.[34] Voting dominated by plebiscites on the presidential level and a political system that places the president at the center of responsibility for the macroeconomy reinforce this caution. It is also not surprising that there is some comfort to be found in numbers, especially if politicians perceive the electoral environment to be unstable (Schlesinger 1991; Pomper 1992: 39–40; Malbin 1993).

Nor do these expectations deny the connection between parties and macroeconomic policy outcomes. Beginning with Hibbs (1977, 1987; see also Weatherford 1988; Woolley 1988; Alesina 1987, 1988; Alesina and Sachs 1988; Williams 1990, among others) empirical studies confirm the presence of a partisan political business cycle. The president's party, in particular, has a modest but significant impact on economic outcomes: Democrats tend to reduce unemployment while Republicans tend to reduce inflation.[35] Democrats also are associated with reductions in income disparity between rich and poor. Hibbs suggests that these differences arise from the contrasting core constituencies and elite coalitions of the parties.

Although the specific partisan tools used to achieve these different outcomes have been less convincingly demonstrated, Spiliotes (1993) shows that fiscal state expectations describe these tools well and that party coalitions cannot be the whole explanation. Spiliotes finds that in twenty-four of thirty-one years from 1954 to 1984, presidential policy choices were consistent with the partisan differences highlighted by Hibbs. Of the seven exceptions, six are recession years: precisely what one would expect in the fiscal state. And while some in the public view the Democrats as better solvers of unemployment and the Republicans best in mastering inflation,

[34] Opportunities for entrepreneurship are no doubt greater in areas that are not widely considered the main axis of party competition, and individual members can build enterprises around these issues. As the building of the fiscal state demonstrated, members of Congress have, since the founding of the state, been protective of their individual autonomy. The strategic considerations mentioned in the text are consistent with one of the possible explanations for universalism given by Collie (1988a, 1988b, 1989; see also Unekis and Franke 1994). See also Shafer and Claggett (1994) on the ordering of party identifiers on economic/welfare and cultural national dimensions for a discussion of apparent winning strategies for the major parties.

[35] Over an eight-year term, the difference between having a Democratic and Republican president is about 2 percentage points of unemployment. The partisan effect reduces substantially if either the Johnson or Reagan administration is omitted from the analysis (Hibbs 1987: ch. 7).

over half the electorate from 1976 to 1982—when these issues dominated politics—saw no difference in the parties' ability to solve these problems (Parker 1986: 394). In short, my expectations concerning party cohesion and party conflict during economic stress are not incompatible with central findings in the partisan political business cycle literature, but my focus differs: I am concerned with the consistency of partisan messages and the distinctiveness of partisan policy alternatives.

Economics, Politics, and Parties: Estimating the Economic-Political Model

To examine how well these economic and political variables explain party cohesion and conflict, I estimate models with both the unadjusted and adjusted economic variables. For cohesion, the dependent variables are the Rice indexes for each party; for party conflict, I use the index of party dissimilarity and the percentage of party votes. Each estimation also employs the one-year lagged value of the dependent variable as an independent variable. This dynamic specification suggests that there is likely to be some continuity in party conflict from year to year as issues reappear on the agenda. In both authorizations and appropriations, for example, substantial portions of the budget process cover the same ground annually: issues return, party positions do not usually change radically from one year to the next, the preferences of returning members tend to be consistent, and institutional norms about how budget-related items are to be processed evolve slowly. More generally, if we suspect that there are at least some broad principled differences between Democrats and Republicans, these also should return annually. By not allowing the economic variables to absorb these underlying continuities, this dynamic specification avoids inappropriately overestimating the strength of the economic variables.[36]

Party Cohesion

Table 3.5 shows that for Democrats all the political variables except the congressional election year are in the expected direction. Three of the political measures are also statistically significant. The coefficients on gov-

---

[36] I should note that a plausible countercase could be made. Unlike the case of budgeting, for example, representatives do not begin each session with a concrete baseline of cohesion or dissimilarity from the preceding session from which they can simply choose to add or subtract.

Table 3.5
Party Cohesion in the House, 1947–1990

Independent Variables	Democrats		Republicans	
	Unadjusted Economic Variables	Adjusted Economic Variables	Unadjusted Economic Variables	Adjusted Economic Variables
Constant	3.7860***	3.8130***	4.0048***	3.9736***
Economic:				
Unemployment	.0408**	.0345**	−.0230*	−.0288**
Inflation	.0113	−.0136	.0056	.0028
Unemployment*Inflation	−.0050*	−.0074*	.0001	.0020
Political:				
New members	.0023	.0026	−.0015	−.0016
R president, D Congress	−.0541*	−.0543	−.1132***	−.1179***
R president, R Congress	−.1711*	−.1518	.1346	.1214
R president, D House	−.1653**	−.1650**	−.0441	−.0501
D president, R Congress	−.1663	−.1775	.2683	.3041
Vietnam	−.0050	−.0038	−.0051	−.0065*
Party size	−.0025*	−.0023	−.0002	.0000
Election	.0084	.0031	−.0031	−.0016
After midterm	.0788**	.0735**	.0816***	.0862***
Southern conservatism	−.0077**	−.0081**		
Dominant faction	.0078	.0067		
Structural:				
Reconciliation	.1300**	.1313**	.0573*	.0561*
Party cohesion$_{t-1}$	.2917**	.3254**	.0435	.0157
Standard error of regression	.0837	.0897	.0655†	.0647†
Corrected R^2	.587	.527	.653	.660
F-statistic	4.732***	3.920***	6.265***	6.438***

Note: Entries are unstandardized regression coefficients. For ease of presentation, standard errors have been omitted.

*$p \leq .10$; ** $p \leq .05$; ***$p \leq .01$, one-tailed test except for "R president, R Congress."

†This model was reestimated as generalized least squares, Prais-Winsten method, due to high values of the Breusch-Godfrey test for serial correlation with a lagged dependent variable.

ernment control are as expected in three cases, two significantly in the unadjusted model. The various forms of divided government show lower cohesion than does the baseline Democratic unified government. Unified Republican government unexpectedly depresses Democratic cohesion by 14 to 16 percent across the two models. (Because the dependent variable is in log form to reduce nonstationarity, the coefficients can be transformed and read as percentage changes in the dependent variable given a one-unit change in the independent variable. The untransformed coefficients are provided in the table; the percentage change figures are emphasized in the discussion below.)[37] This suggests that it is necessary to consider the partisan composition of divided and unified government and not simply the presence of one of these types. The coefficients suggest that, for the Democrats at least, loss of congressional control was a bigger blow to party cohesion than was loss of the presidency. But caution is still in order because two of these alternatives—divided Democratic government and unified Republican government—existed for only two years each. In the more common cases of divided Republican government and divided Republican government with split control of Congress, the coefficients are as expected and mostly significant.

As expected, the year following the midterm election increases party cohesion by about 8 percent. And party cohesion also suffers as the Democrats get larger, with a loss of about .3 percent for each additional party member. Internal changes in the Democratic party also have the expected results. In particular, for each additional percent of southern opposition to the Conservative Coalition position, party cohesion increases about .8 percent. This supports Rohde's (1991) general argument about increasing similarity between southern and northern Democrats, but it provides no direct support for his claim that the *constituencies* of northern and southern Democrats have become more similar. Fiscal state expectations and Rohde's structural argument are both supported by the reconciliation and reform period: This period adds about 14 percent to party cohesion. Prior-year Democratic cohesion also has a significant impact on current-year levels. Because the lagged terms are significant, the other variables in the model have both an immediate and a gradually decreasing, longer-term impact on cohesion; the lagged endogenous variable can be interpreted as a form of a conventional distributed lag model (Ostrom 1990: 72–74). A bout of unemployment, inflation, or both has a lasting impact on party politics. Both the immediate and long-term impacts are important; for clarity, my discussion focuses on the immediate impact.

For Republicans, the political variables also perform largely as expected, with reconciliation, the post-midterm year, and Vietnam (in the adjusted model) significant.[38] The post-midterm year has about the same

---

[37] To calculate, take the antilog of the estimated coefficient in the table, subtract 1.0 from that figure, and multiply the result by 100 to get the percentage change per unit increase. The untransformed coefficients are in any case good ballpark estimates of the actual percentage change figure (a coefficient of 0.1153 becomes about .122 after transforming; that is, a 12.2 percent change after multiplying by 100).

[38] The Republican estimations, and the party dissimilarity and party vote estimations discussed below, displayed signs of serial correlation. Because the standard Durbin-Watson

effect as it does on Democrats; in contrast, the reconciliation period increase of 6 percent is less fruitful for the Republicans. Vietnam dampened party cohesion by about .6 percent for each additional one thousand American battle deaths. The new members coefficient is unexpectedly negative, but it does not near significance. Probably the most notable difference between the Democrats and the Republicans, however, is that the lagged term for the Republicans is small and not significant. This difference may reflect the generally greater levels of turnover among Republicans than Democrats.[39] Perhaps it is a sign of the problems facing a long-term minority party that has to decide continually whether to be the loyal opposition or to go along to get along.

As with the Democrats, the Republican results on government control indicate that partisan composition as well as unified government needs to be taken into account. Both forms of divided Republican control are correctly signed, with the more common Republican president and Democratic Congress combination significantly less cohesive than unified Democratic government. On the other hand, unified Republican control adds about 13 to 14 pecent to Republican cohesion and is significantly higher than unified Democratic government. Exceptionally high Republican cohesion also occurred during the two years in which Harry Truman faced a Republican Congress. Republican cohesion was boosted by about 35 percent by this divided Democratic control. Although this coefficient is highly significant (in a two-tailed test), it is difficult to know how much to generalize based on a two-year period. Nonetheless, there is some support here for the idea that control of Congress has a larger influence on party cohesion than does control of the presidency. Both instances of Republican control of Congress display higher cohesion than the three

---

measure of serial correlation does not apply to estimations with lagged dependent variables, I used the Breusch-Godfrey test (which is similar to Durbin's m test) to check for correlation. My first response was to employ additional variables—the budget deficit, changes in personal income, presidential election years, the Democratic percentage of the presidential vote, among others—and to estimate alternative polynomial forms of the variables. None of these proved useful. (Other aggregate studies of roll-call voting run into the same problem. Patterson and Caldeira [1988], for example, employ an especially large set of independent variables, including many that would seem to change slowly over time, but are still forced to correct for serial correlation.) To correct for the serial correlation, I used a two-step procedure described by Ostrom (1990: 34–35, 67–71). The first step involves running instrumental variables regression to estimate the autoregressive parameter. The second involves estimating the model under a Prais-Winsten form of generalized least squares to produce consistent estimates.

[39] The average annual percentage of newcomers in each party was about the same during the 1950s (Democrats 13.2 percent, Republicans 14.2 percent) and 1970s (Democrats 16.3 percent, Republicans 16.5 percent). But in the 1960s (Democrats 11.4 percent, Republicans 19.0 percent) and 1980s (Democrats 10.5 percent, Republican 16.1 percent), the Republican newcomer contingent exceeded the Democratic.

instances of Democratic control. But in two of the three situations where Republicans control the presidency, their cohesion falls below that of the unified Democratic period. In sum, it appears that for both parties the ideal situation is unified control by that party. Beyond that, controlling Congress provides a bigger cohesion boost than controlling the presidency.

Unadjusted unemployment and inflation affect Democratic cohesion as expected—Democratic cohesion improves when either of these are individually problematic and declines when unemployment and inflation are both high. These results conform to fiscal state expectations. The adjusted model, however, presents a different pattern. Here, the unemployment gap and the gap interaction term perform as expected, but the inflation term is incorrectly signed (and near significance in the "wrong" direction). Except for inflation, these results are consistent with expectations. The inflation result in the adjusted model might be explained by a party coalition interpretation of party behavior. That is, Democratic constituencies push the party to respond to unemployment (Hibbs 1987; Alvarez, Garrett, and Lange 1991). In this case, the party becomes more cohesive. But these constituencies do not push the party in any particular direction to combat inflation, and party cohesion suffers. The party coalition explanation, however, does not explain why Democrats would not unify when unemployment and inflation are high if this is a constituency especially concerned about unemployment. Here, fiscal state expectations perform better.

The Republican results are mixed. For the unadjusted model, unemployment weakens cohesion as anticipated. Inflation, however, increases cohesion as a party coalition approach might suggest (though it is not near significance). And the interaction term, expected to be positive, is effectively zero. In the adjusted model, unemployment again weakens Republican cohesion and inflation remains positively signed. But the interaction term is now correctly signed—simultaneously high unemployment and inflation increase Republican cohesion as the Keynesian logic of the fiscal state becomes less compelling. To some degree, then, the Republican results support both the fiscal state expectations of party behavior I have proposed and the more conventional party coalition expectations. It is notable, however, that Republican cohesion (like Democratic cohesion) responds more strongly to unemployment than to inflation, a relationship more in accordance with fiscal state expectations than party coalitions.

Because the interaction term joins two continuous variables, conditional coefficients express the relationship between the variables.[40] Specifically, the conditional coefficient for unemployment would be:

[40] For all practical purposes they are continuous, although unemployment is of course bounded at zero percent and 100 percent.

$$(\beta_{\text{unemployment}} + \beta_{\text{interaction}} * \text{Inflation}_t)\text{Unemployment}_t$$

while the conditional coefficient for inflation would be

$$(\beta_{\text{inflation}} + \beta_{\text{interaction}} * \text{Unemployment}_t)\text{Inflation}_t$$

The conditional coefficient simply says, in the first case, that the effect of unemployment on cohesion depends on the level of inflation. (Similarly, in the second case, the effect of inflation on cohesion depends on the level of unemployment.) Because of its primary emphasis in Keynesian history and the Keynesian framework, I focus on how unemployment affects cohesion, given the inflation rate.

As the inflation rate increases, unemployment is increasingly less productive for Democratic cohesion. An unadjusted inflation rate of about 8 percent is the break-even point for Democrats (see table 3.6). With inflation less than 8 percent, increases in unemployment tend to increase Democratic cohesion; with an inflation rate over 8 percent, increases in unemployment decrease Democratic cohesion. With zero inflation, 1 percent of unemployment increases Democratic cohesion about 4 percent. A 6 percent unemployment rate would result in about a 28 percent increase in Democratic cohesion if there was no inflation.[41] In a more realistic scenario, with both variables at 6 percent, Democratic cohesion improves by about 7 percent. With unemployment at 8 percent and inflation at 10, Democratic cohesion declines by about 7 percent.

The relationships in the adjusted model are the same. One percentage point of the unemployment gap increases Democratic cohesion by 3.5 percent if there is no inflation gap. A 3 percentage point unemployment gap produces an 11 percent increase in Democratic cohesion. The break-even point here is an inflation gap of 4.7 percentage points. After that point, additional unemployment hurts Democratic cohesion.

As indicated above, the findings are not as supportive for the Republicans, particularly in the unadjusted model. In that model, unemployment consistently hurts Republican cohesion, regardless of the inflation rate. For example, 1 percent of unemployment at an inflation rate of 0 drops Republican cohesion by 2.3 percent, but a 20 percent inflation rate hardly differs: cohesion drops 2.6 percent. Eight percent unemployment decreases Republican cohesion by 17 to 18 percent across all inflation levels. An incorrectly signed interaction term and a small coefficient for

[41] Using the formula for conditional coefficients shown earlier: $(.04081 + (-.00498*0))$ creates a conditional coefficient of .0408. Multiplying this by an unemployment rate of 6 results in .2448. Using the antilog formula for calculating percentage changes given in footnote 37 produces a change of 27.7 percent.

Table 3.6
The Conditional Effect of Unemployment on Democratic Cohesion

	Unadjusted Cohesion Model		Adjusted Cohesion Model	
Inflation Rate or Gap	Conditional Coefficient	Change	Conditional Coefficient	Change
0	0.0408	13.02%	0.0345	10.92%
2	0.0309	9.70	0.0197	6.09
4	0.0209	6.47	0.0049	1.48
6	0.0109	3.34	−0.0099	−2.93
8	0.0010	0.30	−0.0247	−7.16
10	−0.0090	−2.65	−0.0396	−11.19
12	−0.0189	−5.52	−0.0544	−15.06
14	−0.0289	−8.30	−0.0692	−18.75

Notes: Entries in the "change" columns indicate the percent change in party cohesion for three percentage points of the unemployment rate or gap at the given inflation rate or gap, respectively. Three points of the unemployment gap equates to an official unemployment rate of about 8 to 9 percent (gradually increasing over time). Unadjusted and adjusted indicate whether the estimated model employs inflation and unemployment rates, or inflation and unemployment gaps, respectively.

inflation produce this pattern. These results may indicate that since it was largely economic management in the 1930s that pushed the Republicans into their minority position, the desire not to be caught on the "wrong" side of these issues remains very strong. (The support by congressional Republicans for extending unemployment insurance benefits during the 1991 recession, despite White House opposition, is a case in point.)

In the adjusted model, the fiscal state expectations are more nearly met. As inflation increases, unemployment becomes less damaging to Republican cohesion. If the unemployment gap is 4 percentage points and the inflation gap is 0, Republican cohesion drops by 11 percent. An inflation gap of 8 points cuts this Republican loss to about 5 percent. Although the break-even point occurs at an unlikely inflation gap of 15 percentage points, the model works as expected: Republican cohesion suffers less when inflation and unemployment are simultaneously high.

Party Conflict

The cohesion results provide some support for fiscal state/Keynesian consensus expectations of how parties respond to economic stress. Certainly Democratic behavior fits more neatly into these expectations than does Republican behavior. But cohesion is only one piece of the party voting puzzle. The other important piece is party conflict—cohesive parties voicing similar views clearly do not offer voters a significant choice. Recall from chapter 1 that party strength requires parties to offer clear differences to voters. To understand party decline and resurgence in the American polity, the distinctiveness of parties is more telling than their internal level of cohesion, though both matter and the two are related. For party conflict, the economic-political model in both the adjusted and unadjusted form works well. Taking account of the twin fiscal state constraints of Keynesianism and items being left off the agenda makes the level of party conflict explicable.

Turning first to the political variables, the results for party dissimilarity in table 3.7 show that the parties move toward each other in election years: Dissimilarity declines by 8.5 percent. After the midterm, party dissimilarity increases about 14 percent. Every one thousand battle deaths, the intensification of the war, decreases dissimilarity by 1.5 percent. The reconciliation period pushes the parties apart by over 20 percent. As expected, large majority parties tend to increase dissimilarity. Large numbers of first-termers, however, do not. Finally, changing Democratic party composition works as expected in one respect: As southern conservatism declines, party dissimilarity increases. On the other hand, a larger dominant faction does not make for more party dissimilarity. Given less conservatism of the southern faction, this finding simply indicates that with the factions becoming more alike, the relative size of either the majority or minority is not terribly important.[42]

Both forms of divided Republican government decrease party dissimilarity, as expected, but with split control of Congress, the decrease is not significant. Divided Republican government without split congressional control leads to over 7 percent less party dissimilarity. Dissimilarity under unified Republican government is virtually identical to that under unified Democratic government. Harry Truman again provides the only unexpected result: Dissimilarity during divided Democratic control was unusually high (though not significant). Again, the results are a mixed lot: Unified government generally features more dissimilarity than does divided government, but Democratic presidents also tend to be associated with greater dissimilarity.

Like dissimilarity, the only unexpected results for party votes were the

[42] Additionally, as a regional faction grows, it may grow beyond its "natural" boundaries. For instance, greater success by Democrats in the North may come partially by taking formerly Republican or competitive seats. If this is so, then one would expect the ideological diversity of a regional section to increase as it becomes a larger portion of its party (or, strictly speaking, a larger part of Congress). For northern Democrats, this seems to be the case. Comparing the northern share of the Democratic House contingent with the northern Democratic support for the Conservative Coalition (as tallied by Congressional Quarterly) produces a correlation of .77. As it became larger, the northern contingent became more ideologically mixed as conservatism grew.

Table 3.7
Party Conflict in the House, 1947–1990

Independent Variables	Party Dissimilarity		Party Votes	
	Unadjusted Economic Variables	Adjusted Economic Variables	Unadjusted Economic Variables	Adjusted Economic Variables
Constant	2.6722**	2.4270***	1.9966**	1.6209**
Economic				
Unemployment	−.0237	−.0229*	−.0666**	−.0611***
Inflation	−.0241	−.0170**	−.0386*	−.0118*
Unemployment*Inflation	.0021	.0060*	.0063*	.0128**
Political:				
New members	−.0002	−.0003	−.0003	−.0002
R president, D Congress	−.0768**	−.0880**	−.0396	−.0557
R president, R Congress	.0009	−.0090	−.1949*	−.2187**
R president, D House	−.0200	−.0373	.1357	.1151
D president, R Congress	.1988	.2737	.1785	.2112
Vietnam	−.0140***	−.0160***	−.0078	−.0108*
Majority size	.0082*	.0085*	.0192***	.0189***
Election	−.0891*	−.0880*	−.1262	−.1246
After midterm	.1286***	.1332***	.0570	.0619*
Southern conservatism	−.0103**	−.0087**	−.0057	−.0035
Dominant faction	−.0054	−.0076	−.0149	−.0176
Structural:				
Reconciliation	.1999**	.1965**	.1424**	.1432**
Party conflict$_{t-1}$	.4109**	.4125***	.4739***	.4539***
Standard error of regression	.0947†	.0919†	.1186†	.1099†
Corrected R²	.820	.830	.701	.744
F-statistic	11.984***	12.784***	6.667***	8.002***

Note: Entries are unstandardized regression coefficients. For ease of presentation, standard errors have been omitted.

*$p \leq .10$; **$p \leq .05$; ***$p \leq .01$, one-tailed test except for "R president, R Congress."

†This model was reestimated as generalized least squares, Prais-Winsten method, due to high values of the Breusch-Godfrey test for serial correlation with a lagged dependent variable.

signs on the Democratic dominant faction and the number of first-term members. Despite some differences regarding which variables are significant, the two conflict measures produce comparable results. The major discrepancies are in the government control variables. Unified Republican control did not much affect party dissimilarity, but it significantly decreases party votes by nearly 18 percent. And divided Republican government with split congressional control now increases party votes (near the two-tailed significance level). In short, the relationship between government control and party conflict is not nearly as neat and orderly for party votes.

Adding the economic variables introduces policy-related substantive variables that can be expected to move the parties together or apart, depending on the situation. In the unadjusted model of party dissimilarity, all the economic variables are correctly signed, though none reach significance. In the adjusted form model, the model is well supported. One percentage point of the unemployment gap lowers dissimilarity by 2.3 percent at zero inflation. A 3 point unemployment gap weakens dissimilarity by over 6.5 percent. The break-even point is a 3.8 percentage point inflation gap. Moving from an inflation gap of zero to 3.8 points weakens the negative impact of unemployment on party dissimilarity. Beyond the break-even point, an increased inflation gap boosts dissimilarity. Four points of the unemployment gap and 8 points of the inflation gap help dissimilarity by over 10.5 percent. In sum, inflation and unemployment as isolated problems reduce party dissimilarity. When both are problems, party dissimilarity rises. The economic portion of the model works well with party dissimilarity. Table 3.8 shows the effects of the unemployment gap on party conflict at different levels of the inflation gap.

As tables 3.7 and 3.8 suggest, economic conditions have a strong impact on party votes. Both forms of the party votes model display economic coefficients that are significant and in the expected direction. Unemployment or inflation reduce party votes when they are isolated problems; in

Table 3.8
The Conditional Effect of the Unemployment Gap on Party Conflict

Inflation Gap	Party Dissimilarity		Party Votes	
	Conditional Coefficient	Change	Conditional Coefficient	Change
0	−0.0229	−6.63%	−0.0611	−16.74%
2	−0.0108	−3.18	−0.0355	−10.11
4	0.0013	0.39	−0.0100	−2.95
6	0.0134	4.10	0.0156	4.78
8	0.0255	7.94	0.0411	13.12
10	0.0375	11.92	0.0666	22.13
12	0.0496	16.05	0.0922	31.85

Note: Entries in the "change" columns indicate the percent change in party conflict for three percentage points of the unemployment gap at the given inflation gap. Three points of the unemployment gap equates to an official unemployment rate of about 8 to 9 percent (gradually increasing over time).

tandem, they increase party votes. With zero inflation, 1 percent of unemployment reduces party votes by just under 6.5 percent. Six percent unemployment with zero inflation depresses the percentage of party votes by
fully one-third. The negative effects of unemployment are reduced until
the inflation break-even point of just over 10 percent is reached. In the adjusted form model, one point of the unemployment gap reduces party
votes by about 6 percent at the zero level of the inflation gap. Four points
of the unemployment gap depress party votes by more than 21 percent.
An inflation gap of 4.8 marks the break-even point. For a stagflation-type
year in which the unemployment gap is 3 percentage points and the inflation gap is 7 percentage points, a little more than half the 17 percent
boost in party voting is felt immediately; the remaining half affects party
voting over the following decade. This boost is a bit more than the increase
caused by reconciliation. Lagged party votes and lagged dissimilarity
("party conflict$_{t-1}$" in table 3.7) were positively and significantly related
to current levels of party votes and dissimilarity, respectively, supporting
the notion that underlying continuities in budget politics—for example, a
set of authorization and appropriation issues that returns to the agenda
annually—produce a consistency over time in party conflict. This year's
party conflict resembles last year's party conflict. Like budgets themselves,
party conflict does not begin entirely anew in succeeding years.

Figure 3.7 indicates that the level of party conflict produced by various
combinations of the inflation and unemployment gaps are as expected in
the fiscal state. If there is low unemployment, additional inflation creates
less conflict. At higher levels of unemployment, more inflation produces
more conflict. For lower levels of inflation (inflation gaps of 0 and 3), more
unemployment produces less party conflict. For higher levels of inflation
(inflation gaps of 6 and 9), more unemployment produces more party conflict. Party conflict is highest when both the inflation and unemployment
gaps are high.

Conclusion

Party voting behavior is influenced by several environments—economic,
political, and structural. On the whole, the data presented in this chapter
support the fiscal state expectations underlying the economic-political
model, particularly with regard to the economic variables. To reiterate,
the economic variables allow tests of the notion that party voting behavior follows patterns expected in a system dominated by a Keynesian
policy consensus. As I have noted, this policy consensus existed within
the structural parameters of a system that restricted direct party control
over monetary policy and "automatic" fiscal policy and where presidents,

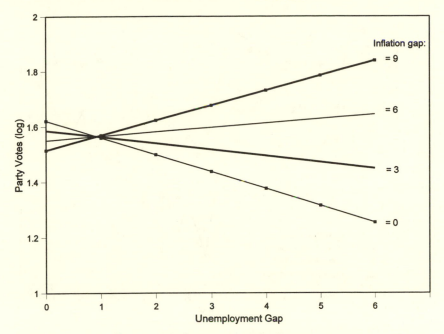

3.7 Party Votes at Alternative Inflation and Unemployment Gaps
Note: Each line represents the value of the intercept term plus the economic coefficients. All other independent variables are set to zero.

not congressional parties, set the essential outlines of fiscal policy. Voters received muted party distinctions precisely when they looked to the political system for alternatives. This is not to say there were no party distinctions, but rather that distinctions softened during critical periods of economic stress. I have noted where the model does less well, but, generally, the relationships work as expected. At minimum, the results suggest that party behavior depended on more than the political and institutional environments emphasized in the aggregate party voting behavior literature. I have also presented two forms of the economic portion of the model, not to argue on behalf of either but to examine whether the fiscal state expectations generally hold across the models. They do. The reader can decide which form of the variables more sensibly measures unemployment and inflation. Figure 3.8 provides a longitudinal look at the fit of the economic-political model for dissimilarity and party votes.

Having been the founders of and, for most of its duration, the main beneficiaries of the fiscal state, the Democrats displayed a particular attachment to a main premise of the economic management exercised by that state: There is a trade-off between unemployment and inflation, and the fiscal apparatus of the state provides the tools with which to structure

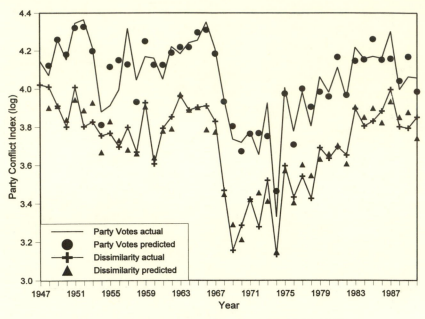

3.8 Party Conflict and the Economic-Political Model, 1947–1990

this trade-off. Democrats, then, became more cohesive under either inflation or unemployment because the solitary occurrence of either one of
these problems had, in a sense, a built-in budgetary solution in Keynesian
theory. Conversely, the simultaneous existence of high inflation and high
unemployment—stagflation—destroyed the idea that one can make a
trade-off between the two. For the Democrats, the conflation of the two
problems scattered party cohesion.

For the Republicans, in the adjusted form model, this conflation reduced the normally damaging effects of unemployment on Republican cohesion and provided an opportunity to attack the governing model put in
place by Democrats. Although Republicans predominantly accepted the
trade-off between unemployment and inflation, factions in the party argued that the trade-off could be managed by other means, particularly
monetary policy, and that the government's taxing and spending could be
streamlined. Simultaneous high inflation and unemployment provided a
way for Republicans to overcome the fear of being on the wrong side of
high unemployment history again. For both Democrats and Republicans
the fiscalization of politics in the 1980s, a direct result of the breakdown
of the Keynesian model, provided an opportunity to explore and promote
new relations of state and economy.

The business cycle does affect the parties: The parties offered a more distinctive message when the dominant assumptions of fiscal management broke down in the mid to late 1970s. The weakening of the Keynesian consensus provided room for party movement. In one sense, there is a positive message here: With the economy in particularly poor stagflationist condition, the parties responded by supporting different packages of policy choices. But the parties' strategy of convergence when high unemployment or high inflation were lone threats left voters with increasingly similar policy packages precisely when they were searching for answers. Stagflation was hardly desirable, but it did encourage parties to diverge while voters' attention was peaked.[43] The irony for the parties may be that their increased conflict on economic management issues in the 1970s and 1980s did not much matter. As long as the public thought about economic issues in a plebiscitary manner and did not perceive the congressional parties to be *controlling* key policy areas, nicely divergent policies on economic management would not gain stable support for a party or generate beliefs that parties matter. Reviving political parties beyond Congress requires fundamental changes in state-economy relations.

[43] Note that voters' attention to politics increases during election years but that these are also times when party conflict is reduced.

4

A Dime's Worth of Difference?
North and South,
Appropriations and Authorizations

POLITICAL PARTIES are often viewed as dichotomies. They are either weak or strong, principled or pragmatic, united or divided, motivated by office holding or motivated by other purposes. Probably no dichotomy is as common as the sectional dichotomy that, historically, portrayed the two major parties as representing separate regions or, more recently, saw the Democratic party as divided between North and South.[1] As I indicated in chapter 3, scholars have pointed to this split in the Democratic party as a major strain on that party's internal cohesion. And the data shows that this is not a mistaken impression: The ideological tendencies of the party sections have affected intraparty cohesion and interparty conflict. If this is so, is the party behavior predicted by the economic-political model more common among Democrats from one region than the other? If the Democratic sectional dichotomy is as powerful as is sometimes suggested, can we really contend that the fiscal state affected "the Democratic party" and that "the party" responded to the economy in a singular manner?

Scholars also often focus on dichotomies in macroeconomic management. Budgets are either in deficit or surplus. Policy is either fiscal or monetary. Authorization does not ensure appropriation. These last two dichotomies have each produced two literatures, one on each part of the budgetary process. With direct partisan control of monetary policy highly unlikely in the fiscal state, the dichotomy between authorizations and appropriations is particularly important. Does the predicted fiscal-state party behavior appear more often in one of these areas than another? If so, how does this dichotomy affect more general conclusions about parties and the fiscal state?

In this chapter, I probe these two dichotomies more closely by extending the analysis of chapter 3. Are the behaviors suggested by the economic-political model found in the North and the South, in authorizations and appropriations? Since scholars often consider these dichotomies to be fundamental to postwar politics, it is important to consider whether party voting behavior in the fiscal state transcends or honors these boundaries.

---

[1] Technically, the division is usually South and non-South.

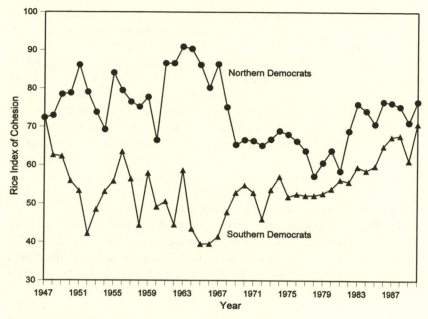

4.1 Intraregional Democratic Cohesion, 1947–1990

Democrats North and South: The Great Divide?

One major theme in American political and economic history has been the regional split between the interests of the North and those of the South. From the devastating events of the mid-nineteenth century to the bitter battles over civil rights in the 1950s and 1960s, sectional divisions have often leapt to the fore in American politics. At the same time, and often deeply intertwined with these more dramatic events, basic structural economic differences have pushed the regions toward dramatically different policy positions (Chase-Dunn 1980; Bensel 1984, 1990). These differences have of course been amply pursued by scholars. As noted in chapter 1, some analysts have argued that the partisan split over trade was merely the reflection of sectional differences. I contend that such an argument is not convincing, but it is important to see whether a similar problem could plague an analysis based on the parties' place in the fiscal state.

Figure 4.1 shows the cohesion level on budget-related roll-call votes for the two regional wings of the Democratic party. Northerners were more cohesive as a group than were southerners for every year from 1948 through 1990, while in 1947, the regions were equally united. Although these different cohesion levels are striking, the more remarkable pattern in figure 4.1 is the change in the trajectories of southern and northern cohesion. From 1947 to 1963, the cohesion level of the two wings was weakly correlated at $-.10$. For the next seventeen years, through 1980, the cohesion trends were virtual opposites ($r = -.81$). Then, from 1981 to 1990, both regions displayed improving cohesion ($r = .68$). During the Great Society, the two wings were at their furthest polarity, with the north in the 85 to 90 range of the cohesion index and the south registering at 40 to 45. The northern figure during that period is truly striking: It indicates that, on average, 95 percent of northern Democrats voted together on budget-related votes. Over time, the gap between the regional cohesion levels gradually decreased. But it is clear that this did not happen solely on the basis of changes among southern Democrats. The figure shows that scholars are correct to note that changes among southern Democrats have had important implications for parties and politics. But figure 4.1 shows that an equally important change occurred in the North as cohesion declined for fifteen years. Thus, at the very time that analysts suggest that the South started to look more like the North, the North started to look less like itself. If the constituency-based views of parties are correct—that is, if the behavior of the party in government reflects the composition of its constituency—then northern Democrats became more rather than less heterogeneous over time.

Ideological change in the two wings reinforces this point. Figures 4.2 and 4.3 present common measurements of party ideology by the Americans for Democratic Action (ADA) and by Congressional Quarterly's analysis of Conservative Coalition support. (These data are not based on the roll-call sample from fig. 4.1.) The ADA score calculates how often individual members of Congress support the ADA "liberal" position on key votes. Conservative Coalition support refers to the percentage of time a member votes with the Conservative Coalition. Both figures tell the same story: Conservatism increased among northerners and decreased among southerners. Important change was occurring in both sections, not the South alone.

Despite Sundquist's (1973) view that the New Deal was spreading slowly to all parts of the Democratic coalition and unifying the party's policy views, for much of the postwar period the two wings of the party did not make progress toward greater internal unity. Indeed, for much of the 1960s, internal party conflict grew. Turning again to the budget-related votes, figure 4.4 shows that the tension between the regions showed no signs of abating until 1969.[2] During the later 1960s, the divi-

---

[2] Party votes and party dissimilarity are measured the same as previously, except that I now compare the conflict between northern and southern Democrats rather than Democrats and Republicans.

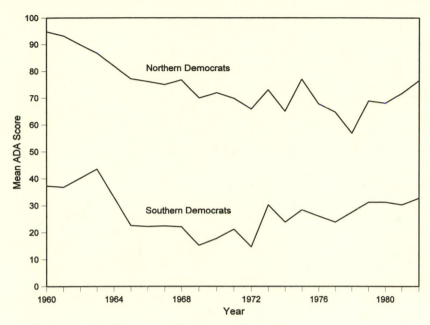

4.2 Support for ADA Liberal Policy Positions
Note: Figures for 1962 and 1964 interpolated.

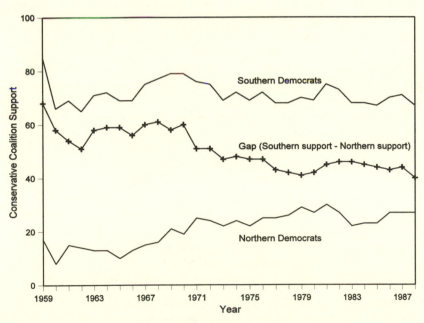

4.3 Support for Conservative Coalition Policy Positions

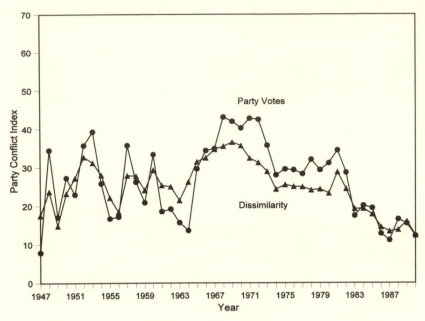

4.4 Intraparty Conflict: Northern and Southern Democrats, 1947–1990

sion was particularly intense, with over 40 percent of the votes posing North and South on opposite sides. By 1986, the two groups were back at the relatively low conflict level of the 1947 to 1949 period. Within the otherwise declining pattern of intraparty conflict during the 1970s and 1980s, the year 1981 stands out. This was the year of President Reagan's most aggressive push toward implementing his new vision of state-economy relations, a vision based on a new macroeconomic management model and a commitment to raising defense spending while lowering social spending and tax revenues. The two sections were as far apart as they had been in nearly a decade.

A final way to examine intraparty conflict is by noting the disagreements between each Democratic section and the Republican party. Figures 4.5 and 4.6 indicate that the two regions share a similar pattern of conflict with Republicans over the postwar period. Not surprisingly, northern Democrats find themselves at odds with Republicans more often than do southerners. But what is striking about these figures is that each region shares a comparable decline and resurgence of interparty conflict.[3] After sustained decline, party conflict had reached minute pro-

[3] The decline is clearly interrupted by a spurt of party conflict during the Great Society period. This spurt is particularly evident for the northern Democrats. There is also a difference in the resurgence of conflict. Northern conflict with the Republicans begins moving up

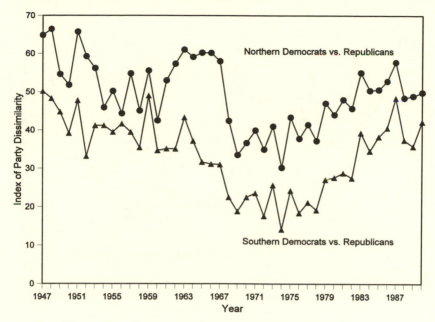

4.5 Party Dissimilarity between Democratic Sections and Republicans

portions by the late 1960s. The tensions between southerners and Republicans were so slight between 1968 and 1978 that the *intraparty* dissimilarity between northern and southern Democrats exceeded that between the South and Republicans.[4] (Party votes were also more prevalent between northern and southern Democrats than between southern Democrats and Republicans from 1968 to 1974.) The more important point, however, is that with all their differences, Democrats from the North and South are enough alike that their historical pattern of conflict with Republicans looks similar—even in the period *before* the intraparty changes in Democratic ideology and composition discussed in chapter 3 had fully taken effect. This suggests that the economic-political model may be applicable to both sections of the Democratic party. It also suggests that it is incorrect to place too great a weight on the transformation of southern

---

after 1969; Southern conflict remains steady for a decade and accelerates after 1978. But the difference is slight. For both sections, a fair summary is that decline bottomed out by 1969 and that sharp increases in interparty polarization begin in earnest after 1978.

[4] Even northern Democrats and Republicans found they had more in common than did southern and northern Democrats in 1969, as measured by party dissimilarity. Democrats in this period (average annual dissimilarity about 30) were most intensely divided over defense issues (average annual dissimilarity about 36), particularly defense authorizations (average about 39). Defense did not directly constitute a large proportion of the budget-related votes in this period.

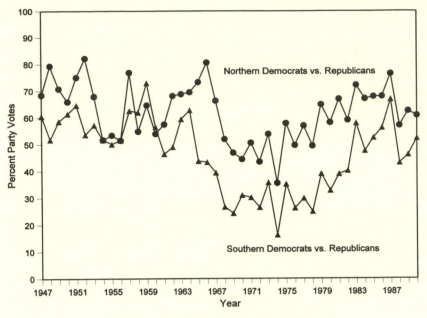

4.6 Party Votes between Democratic Sections and Republicans

Democrats when explaining the changes in party voting since 1970. This transformation matters. But the decline and resurgence of interparty conflict exists even when the South is ignored entirely in figures 4.5 and 4.6.

The Economic-Political Model and North-South Conflict

The internal cohesion of each party segment is interesting in its own right. Of primary interest here, however, is how these segments interacted with each other and with the Republican party. How might intraparty regionalism among the Democrats affect party voting behavior? Studies indicate that southern Democrats were generally less accepting than northerners of the expanded economic functions of the state during the New Deal (see, for example, Weir, Orloff, and Skocpol 1988; Weir 1989), especially aspects of welfare and labor policy. On the notion that the government should act to minimize the dislocation of economic slowdowns, however, northerners and southerners were in rough agreement. Indeed, the "conservative Keynesianism" that dominates the fiscal state was part of the price of southern acquiescence to that state. I anticipate a general similarity between the regional sections in their conflict with Republicans, with expectations for the effects of the independent variables the same as in chapter 3. Still, there are reasons to expect the model to better capture northern Democratic conflict with the Republicans, including the greater activist leanings of the northerners and the lack of any significant challenges to the tenure of southern Democrats for most of the period studied here. In other words, looking at northern Democratic and Republican conflict entails looking at actual competitors, competitors that could at least theoretically capture each others' seats and thus might face more pressures toward convergence. But for much of the postwar period, that is not the reality in the South, where Republicans were not serious or in many cases even theoretical challengers.

North-South tensions within the party are obviously another way of talking about party cohesion. The regressions of intraparty dissimilarity or "party" votes on the independent variables of the economic-political model should resemble the party cohesion regressions presented in chapter 3.[5] There, I suggested that unemployment should increase party cohesion; here, I argue effectively the same thing: Unemployment should reduce intraparty conflict. Because the intraparty conflict measures increase as the party becomes less unified, the signs will be the reverse of those expected for Democratic party cohesion in the previous chapter, but the substantive meaning will be the same.[6]

Intraparty Cohesion and Conflict

Table 4.1 shows the results for the estimations of northern-southern conflict measured by party votes and party dissimilarity. (As in chapter 3, the party votes and party dissimilarity are in natural log form to reduce nonstationarity.) The results are largely as expected. Looking first at dissimilarity, unemployment and the inflation-unemployment interaction are correctly signed and significant in both estimations. Inflation is not significant in either case; it is correctly signed in one instance and incorrectly in the other. (As in the previous chapter, when the adjusted economic variables are employed, inflation is signed consistently with a coalition view of party voting behavior.) In each instance, however, the interaction term works as expected in the economic-political model. Reconciliation also

---

[5] There is a difference: The party cohesion measure makes no assumptions about the source of internal party splits, whereas in this chapter I look specifically at sectionalism as the cause of internal stress.

[6] Unemployment, inflation, new members, post-midterm election, dominant faction, and reconciliation are expected to be negative. The unemployment-inflation interaction, divided government of any form, Vietnam, congressional election year, southern conservatism, and the lagged dependent variable are expected to be positive. Unified Republican government is expected to be zero.

Table 4.1
House Democratic North-South Conflict, 1947–1990

Independent Variables	Party Dissimilarity		Party Votes	
	Unadjusted Economic Variables	Adjusted Economic Variables	Unadjusted Economic Variables	Adjusted Economic Variables
Constant	2.1210***	1.6009**	2.1867***	0.9223
Economic:				
Unemployment	−.0680**	−.0555**	−.1565**	−.1373***
Inflation	−.0407	.0060	−.0809	.0109
Unemployment*Inflation	.0101*	.0179**	.0200**	.0334***
Political:				
New members	−.0021	−.0031	.0058	.0048
R president, D Congress	−.0077	−.0137	.0611	.0433
R president, R Congress	−.0156	−.0406	.0131	−.0667
R president, D House	.2124*	.1998*	.3596**	.3190*
D president, R Congress	.0465	.0855	.5233*	.6874**
Vietnam	.0145	.0104	.0220	.0113
Election	−.0113	−.0072	−.0204	−.0062
After midterm	−.0574	−.0463	−.1738*	−.1498*
Southern conservatism	.0013	.0036	.0085	.0122
Dominant faction	−.0022	−.0018	.0031	.0026
Structural:				
Reconciliation	−.3492**	−.3519**	−.4236**	−.3887**
Party conflict$_{t-1}$	.4388***	.4561***	.3446**	.4338**
Standard error of regression	.1610	.1632	.2388	.2475
Corrected R^2	.676	.667	.617	.589
F-statistic	6.833***	6.609***	5.513***	5.009***

Note: Entries are unstandardized regression coefficients. For ease of presentation, standard errors have been omitted.

*$p \leq .10$; **$p \leq .05$; ***$p \leq .01$, one-tailed test except for "R president, R Congress."

has the expected effect on internal party division. Among the remaining political variables, the only significant relationship is for divided government under a Republican president and Senate. Unified Republican government is, as expected, effectively zero. Divided Republican government and the congressional election year are incorrectly signed, but neither is significant.

Party votes between northerners and southerners behave in largely the same manner as party dissimilarity. Unemployment and the interaction term are more strongly significant in the party votes estimations. Reconciliation retains its substantial and significant effects. Signs change on the percentage of newcomers and dominant faction variables, but neither variable is significant. The post-midterm year is significantly related to party votes. And divided government performs as expected in all instances: It increases internal party conflict. Unified Republican control is, again, effectively zero as expected. Four of the six divided government variables are statistically significant. In sum, intraparty conflict is captured well by the economic-political model, especially by the measures of economic conditions and the reconciliation process. The North-South divide does not prevent a convergence toward Keynesian remedies as unemployment worsens, nor the loss of policy direction when Keynesianism falters.

Conflict between Democratic Regional Sections and Republicans

Given the generally greater support among northerners for the tenets of the New Deal and its dominant position in the Democratic party for much of this period, I suggested above that one might expect that the model would fit particularly well for northern Democrats. The results in table 4.2 confirm this expectation. Three variables in both dissimilarity estimations—the percentage of freshmen, unified Republican government, and divided Democratic government—are incorrectly signed, while the size of the majority party is incorrectly signed in the revised estimation. The remaining coefficients are as expected and mostly significant. Unemployment, inflation, and reconciliation are of particular importance, and all are properly signed and significant. The interaction term is correctly signed in both dissimilarity estimations and significant in the adjusted form estimation. This pattern carries to the party votes estimation, where only unified Republican government and divided Democratic government are incorrectly signed.[7] The key variables for testing the impact of the fiscal state have the expected significant effects (again, the unadjusted interaction term nears but does not reach significance). Poor economic conditions produce a convergence between northern Democrats and Republicans, while high unemployment and inflation boost party conflict. By giving congressional parties a more significant role in the macroeconomic policy process, reconciliation also boosts party differences. When the parties increase their control of a policy area, they increase their intraparty cohesion, interparty differences, and systemic strength.

These key variables are less effective in explaining conflict between southern Democrats and Republicans. Estimation results in table 4.3 are

[7] These incorrect signs result from the unexpectedly high Republican cohesion during these periods.

Table 4.2
Conflict between Northern Democrats and Republicans, 1947–1990

Independent Variables	Party Dissimilarity		Party Votes	
	Unadjusted Economic Variables	Adjusted Economic Variables	Unadjusted Economic Variables	Adjusted Economic Variables
Constant	3.0321***	2.9102***	3.5062***	3.3879***
Economic:				
Unemployment	−.0523**	−.0444**	−.0788***	−.0686***
Inflation	−.0387*	−.0275***	−.0473*	−.0285***
Unemployment*Inflation	.0037	.0087**	.0057	.0123**
Political:				
New members	−.0004	−.0000	.0005	.0010
R president, D Congress	−.1613***	−.1773***	−.1476***	−.1689***
R president, R Congress	−.1458	−.1543*	−.2020*	−.2161**
R president, D House	−.0361	−.0783	.0442	−.0081
D president, R Congress	.2730	.2880	.2617	.2894
Vietnam	−.0178***	−.0211***	−.0173***	−.0214***
Majority size	.0020	−.0013	.0060	.0017
Election	−.0632*	−.0689**	−.0954**	−.0993**
After midterm	.1362***	.1367***	.0731*	.0750*
Structural:				
Reconciliation	.1199*	.1048*	.1476*	.1364*
Party conflict$_{t-1}$	.3047**	.3053**	.1904	.1693
Standard error of regression	.0951	.0915	.1188	.1122
Corrected R^2	.740	.760	.592	.636
F-statistic	9.549***	10.479***	5.346***	6.234***

Note: Entries are unstandardized regression coefficients. For ease of presentation, standard errors have been omitted.

*$p \leq .10$; **$p \leq .05$; ***$p \leq .01$, one-tailed test except for "R president, R Congress."

weak. On the plus side, nine out of twelve of the economic coefficients are correctly signed. But in only one instance does the entire triad of unemployment, inflation, and the interaction of unemployment and inflation affect partisan voting in the predicted manner. The unemployment gap is incorrectly signed in both of its estimations. And the remaining estimation produces a coefficient that is virtually zero for the interaction term. Only one of the twelve economic indicators is significantly related to southern Democratic and Republican party conflict. Finally, as expected, the reconciliation process increases party conflict, but it does not do so significantly.

Table 4.3
Conflict between Southern Democrats and Republicans, 1947–1990

Independent Variables	Party Dissimilarity		Party Votes	
	Unadjusted Economic Variables	Adjusted Economic Variables	Unadjusted Economic Variables	Adjusted Economic Variables
Constant	1.5529*	2.0529**	3.0187**	2.7565**
Economic:				
Unemployment	−.0041	.0330	−.0108	.0129
Inflation	−.0067	−.0185*	−.0318	−.0203
Unemployment*Inflation	−.0000	.0023	.0022	.0043
Political:				
New members	−.0011	−.0015	−.0002	−.0005
R president, D Congress	−.0316	−.1157**	−.0136	−.0337
R president, R Congress	.1609	.0734	.0000	.0100
R president, D House	.0309	−.1256	.0604	−.0000
D president, R Congress	.3480	.2942	.3023	.3546
Vietnam	−.0141**	−.0130*	−.0202**	−.0187*
Majority size	.0010	−.0082	−.0047	−.0069
Election	−.1018	−.0971**	−.0938	−.1036
After midterm	.1897***	.2428***	.1607**	.1567**
Southern conservatism	−.0076	−.0055	−.0142*	−.0127
Structural:				
Reconciliation	.1028	.1140	.1038	.0779
Party conflict$_{t-1}$	.7166***	.7011***	.5702***	.6298***
Standard error of regression	.1459†	.1341†	.1981†	.1982†
Corrected R^2	.778	.816	.665	.665
F-statistic	9.987***	12.658***	6.089***	6.083***

Note: Entries are unstandardized regression coefficients. For ease of presentation, standard errors have been omitted.

*p ≤ .10; ** p ≤ .05; ***p ≤ .01, one-tailed test except for "R president, R Congress."

†This model was reestimated as generalized least squares, Prais-Winsten method, due to high values of the Breusch-Godfrey test for serial correlation with a lagged dependent variable.

Two political variables are consistently significant predictors of conflict between southern Democrats and Republicans. As for the northern Democratic relationship with the Republicans, in all four estimations the intensification of the Vietnam conflict reduced partisan disagreement. Similarly, the year after the midterm election features a high level of partisan conflict between southern Democrats and Republicans. One area of difference between the northern and southern relationships with the Republicans is the lagged impact of conflict. The size of these coefficients are more than twice as large for southern Democrats as for northerners.[8] Most likely this difference reflects the very steady return to office of southern Democrats who faced little or no Republican competition.

Again, this finding suggests the possibility that as southern politics becomes more competitive and more like northern politics, the economic-political model will better explain southern Democratic interparty conflict. To test this possibility very crudely, I regressed southern Democratic and Republican conflict on the set of variables shown in table 4.3 for the period from 1970 to 1990. Two divided government dummy variables were inapplicable, and they were dropped from the estimation. On the notion that southern politics became over time more like the north, I included a simple trend variable that increased by a value of one for each year. Obviously, southern politics did not increasingly come to resemble northern politics in even portions over a twenty-year period. I use the measure more to control roughly for this change than to create a definitive measure of "change." In each case—that is, two estimations each of party dissimilarity and party votes—the three economic variables and reconciliation are correctly signed; seven of the twelve economic variables are significant as are all four coefficients for reconciliation. One cannot read too much into these results—by starting in 1970 the model examines a period with no sustained decline in the dependent variables—but they do suggest that there is reason to believe that interparty conflict with the Republicans became increasingly similar for the two Democratic sections.

As it stands, the model provides at least a rough approximation of interparty conflict for southern Democrats and a strong approximation of that conflict for northerners. With northerners a continually growing segment of the party, their behavior increasingly determined the overall shape of Democratic voting behavior.

Authorizations and Appropriations: Separate Tracks, Same Destination?

Studies of aggregate party cohesion and conflict in Congress do not normally distinguish between votes intended to authorize or reauthorize programs and votes intended to appropriate funds for programs already approved. Studies of the policy process and the budgetary process often observe whether partisanship was "high" or "low" in a particular year or a particular policy area, but they do not generalize about what partisan-

---

[8] Dropping southern conservatism from the southern Democratic interparty conflict estimations produced no substantive change in the coefficients or their interpretation.

ship should look like on authorizations versus appropriations votes. Most often the focus is on *either* the authorizations committees or the appropriations committees. Rubin, however, suggests that "it makes little sense to look at congressional budgeting without looking at the relationship between authorizations and appropriations" (1988: 124). Does party behavior on appropriations and authorizations votes run on parallel or perpendicular tracks?

One major approach to understanding this relationship between authorizations and appropriations argues that the interest of authorizations committees in specific budget levels varies over time; it tends to increase when stirred by some particularly important issues or set of environmental circumstances. The flip side is that the work of appropriations committees is more "incremental, focusing on changes between years, ignoring the base, and not comparing major policy alternatives. . . . The authorizing committees orchestrate a variety of interest groups, consider a range of policy alternatives, arrive at compromises, and then feed the budgetary implications back into the appropriations process" (Rubin 1988: 125). Other studies are not so sure that the processes are in such contrast. Like authorizations, the appropriations process of the 1980s was highly influenced by economic circumstances, and the notion that the appropriations process worked under a "guardian of the treasury" ethos that insulated the Appropriations Committees from authorization demands has been strongly challenged (White and Wildavsky 1989; Schick 1990; Kiewiet and McCubbins 1991). Even the traditional incremental changes were likely to reflect at least partly the economic environment—the great budget battle of 1957, with the Democratic Congress cutting Eisenhower's spending plan in the face of expected high inflation, is a case in point.

It would be too strong to say that the literatures on authorizations and appropriations are always distinct. We know that the relation between these two legislative functions has been fraught with difficulty from the start. A series of battles across the latter half of the nineteenth century and the first half of the twentieth was intended to resolve, at least temporarily, the power balance between appropriations and authorizations (Fisher 1979; Shuman 1988: 63–64). Studies of the early postwar budget process emphasize the Appropriations Committees' role as guardian of the Treasury, a role grudgingly accepted by members on the authorizing committees because it was the one means Congress had to prevent the budget from spiraling out of control (Fenno 1962: 312; Ippolito 1981: 50–51; Schick 1983: 266; Gilmour 1990: 24–34; Shuman 1988: 200).[9] The de-

---

[9] One reflection of the growing dissatisfaction of authorizing committee members with their weak control over funding in the prereform budget system was the explosion of backdoor budgeting, entitlements, permanent authorizations, and indexing that markedly decreased the proportion of the federal budget that was channeled through the Appropriations

piction here is that the policy committees tend to authorize vastly more than Appropriations approves (Gilmour 1990: 30) and that partisanship was probably a larger factor across authorizations votes than across appropriations votes, both in committees and on the floor (Fenno 1966).

Especially since the onset of the new budget process, and even more so since the onset of reconciliation in 1980, budget scholars have been more likely to consider the authorizations-appropriations relationship. But expectations about party behavior are less than clear. Rational choice analysis suggests that the new institutional arrangements foster "an upward bias in spending, a special-interest bias in tax laws, unbalanced budgets and deficits, and a distributional attitude toward most policy decisions" (LeLoup 1983: 7). From this approach one would not, however, necessarily argue that there would be no conflict between the two parties, at least so long as the president's popularity is not overwhelming. Other institutionalist analyses suggest that partisanship was low on budget matters in the 1950s and high in the 1980s, with new features such as reconciliation and budget resolutions playing a large role in increasing partisanship (see also White and Wildavsky 1989), but they do not specify how partisanship is being measured in these periods (Gilmour 1990: 25, 115). The basic logic is that both budget resolutions and reconciliation bring into macro focus what the old budget system had fragmented. Fragmentation made the pieces easier for both parties to swallow; integration required basic choices about budget direction. To Fisher, "Increasing the size of a legislative vehicle—from an appropriations bill to a budget resolution—magnifies the scope of legislative conflict and encourages additional concessions to members" (cited in Ellwood 1983: 86).

Another possibility is that not so much the budget process but the need to limit spending as an antidote to deficits created a perverse environment where the declining quantity of annual spending directly controllable by Congress became ever more valuable as it became more scarce. The intensity of the debate thus intensified as the monies controlled by Congress diminished: Everyone wanted to preserve his or her share. On the surface, this need not lead to partisan conflict; regional conflict would be just as feasible. But with much of the debate framed in terms of guns versus butter, partisan positions took on heightened importance. The situation in the 1980s differed from the situation in the 1950s, another tight-budget era, because it was during the years between these two eras that the Dem-

---

Committees (Huitt 1990: ch. 15; Weaver 1988). Schick (1983) sees a distinction between Appropriations Committees that preferred to fund *agencies* and authorizations committees that sought to fund *programs*. This duality led outsiders such as interest groups to be more involved in pushing for funds in authorizations committees than in Appropriations. Eventually, Schick argues, Congress decentralized in order to facilitate this urge to distribute.

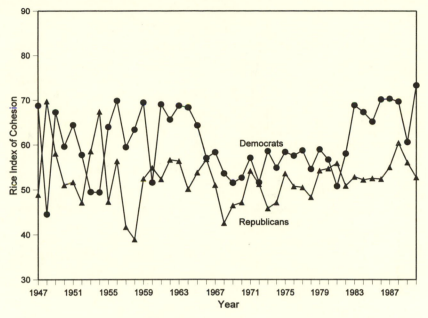

4.7 House Democratic and Republican Cohesion on Authorizations Votes

ocratic party moved toward a position that allowed greater accommodation for the expansion of the welfare state.

On the whole, there is a general disposition in the literature on the new budget process that there will be more party conflict in this process. It is not always clear whether this increased conflict is expected in both authorizations and appropriations. But to the extent studies argue that the appropriations process has taken on some of the aspects of authorizations and the authorizations process has tried to shortcut appropriations, and that both processes are guided by the strictures of the new budget process, a reasonable conjecture is that party cohesion and conflict should behave similarly across the two types of votes.

Trends in Appropriations and Authorizations

Figures 4.7 to 4.11 provide a graphical overview of the party cohesion trends in authorizations and appropriations. Comparing Democratic and Republican cohesion in figures 4.7 and 4.8 displays some striking contrasts. Democratic authorizations cohesion topped Republican cohesion in thirty-nine years, while Republican cohesion exceeded the Democratic level in five years. In four of those five years, the Republicans controlled

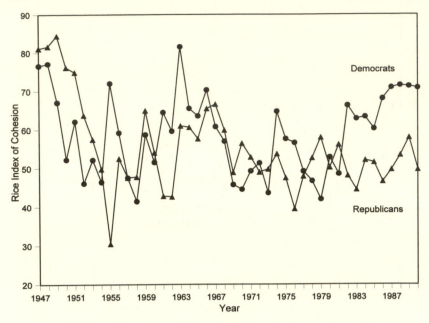

4.8 House Democratic and Republican Cohesion on Appropriations Votes

at least one house of Congress. The power to shape the contours of new or revised state activity is thus clearly a power that unites majority parties. For most of the fiscal state period, that means the Democrats. In appropriations, the parties are more nearly balanced: Democratic cohesion tops the Republican level in twenty-three of forty-four years. This pattern perhaps represents the incentives a minority party faces to acquire its share of federal largesse, even if it disapproved of a spending program's introduction. After 1974, the Democrats show more appropriations cohesiveness than Republicans in fourteen of the seventeen years. This pattern is consistent with Kiewiet and McCubbin's (1991) interpretation that the 1970s reforms were an effort by Democrats to enforce Democratic policy positions on the floor.

Looking across figures 4.7 and 4.8 shows that for thirty-one of forty-four years Democrats were more cohesive in authorizations than in appropriations. Republicans were about evenly split, with appropriations cohesion exceeding authorizations twenty-three times. From 1975 through 1990—marking the period of budget reform, congressional reform, and the dissolution of Keynesianism—the Democratic pattern does not change greatly as authorizations cohesion exceeds appropriations in twelve of sixteen years. For the Republicans, however, the 1975 to 1990 period marks a sharp departure from earlier party practice, with authorizations cohesion exceeding appropriations twelve years out of sixteen. One possible explanation of this switched pattern is that the authorizations process became comparably "easier" grounds for cohesion than appropriations because with deficit cutting the watchword, no major new programs were contemplated. With congressional budgetary control via appropriations shrinking because of entitlements, backdoor spending, and the like, the parties may have had a more difficult time holding their membership together for appropriations votes; members were now fighting over the few remaining scraps in the "controllable" budget. But the authorizations committees *also* were expected to cut programs in their jurisdictions and that certainly had the potential to disrupt party cohesion. Most generally, however, this change likely reflects the kind of battles that emerge as one kind of state gradually erodes and a new, as yet undefined, replacement takes its place—fights erupt over the creation of new programs, the elimination of old ones, and the resizing and reshaping of those that will continue. The Republicans apparently found it relatively easy to agree on a new public philosophy to replace the fiscal state philosophy; this was largely a matter of authorizations. They found unity more difficult on the implementation of these new ideas in the appropriations process.

Should one expect to find a gap between a party's cohesion level in authorizations and appropriations? The budget literature does not directly address this question, but reasonable inferences can be drawn. Studies in the new budget politics literature stress the reduced role of incrementalism in budgeting after the mid-1970s, suggesting that any cohesion gap present in the old budget system should begin to narrow as the "guardian of the treasury" role of the Appropriations Committees dissolves into a more accommodating stance toward authorizations. Kiewiet and McCubbins (1991), on the other hand, imply that appropriations and authorizations cohesion should show about the same level of (minor) disparity across time. That is, because the parties were policy motivated both in authorizations and appropriations, and because the reforms of the 1970s did not represent a major break with the logic underlying earlier budget politics, no great shift in the gap between a party's authorization and appropriation cohesion should be expected. Figure 4.9 graphs the cohesion gaps.[10] The pattern is mixed. Democratic gaps fluctuate within stable parameters over the period. The Republicans do show a slight tendency toward decreased disparities, that is, a tendency toward similar levels of cohesiveness in their authorizations and appropriations

---

[10] A gap is simply the absolute value of the difference between authorizations and appropriations cohesion for an individual party. For party conflict, the gap is the absolute value of the difference between authorizations and appropriations conflict as measured by either party votes or party dissimilarity.

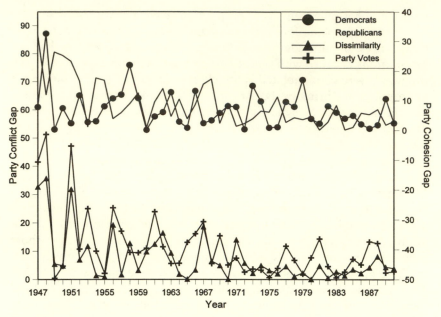

4.9 Cohesion Gaps and Conflict Gaps, House Authorizations and Appropriations Votes
Note: Democrats and Republicans on right axis, party votes and dissimilarity on left axis.

voting.[11] The weakness of the Republican trend, however, combined with the lack of change on the Democratic side suggests that Kiewiet and Mc-Cubbins's expectations are largely borne out. But in the party conflict gaps (fig. 4.9), where there is a more discernible downward trend (especially for party dissimilarity), the Kiewiet and McCubbins explanation seems less satisfying. Something clearly happens in the 1970s that changes budget politics and party voting behavior so that the party conflict levels in authorizations and appropriations became increasingly alike. That "something" is the collapse of the macroeconomic order of the fiscal state and not simply the introduction of changes in the buget process.

Figures 4.10 and 4.11 show that appropriations and authorizations conflict increased after the sharp decline of the late 1960s, particularly after 1979 for authorizations. (Omitting the unusually low figures for 1974 suggests that party conflict in authorizations held steady from 1970 through 1978.) Appropriations conflict began increasing after 1969, but the

[11] Regression analysis of the party gaps on a trend variable and a dummy variable for the 1975 to 1990 period indicate that neither the trend nor the dummy is significant for Democrats. For Republicans, the trend coefficient is significant while the dummy is insignificant at $p = .11$. Running the analysis just for the 1975 to 1990 period shows no significant trend for either party.

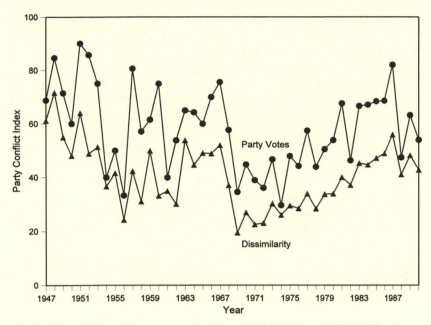

4.10 Party Conflict on Appropriations Votes in the House, 1947–1990

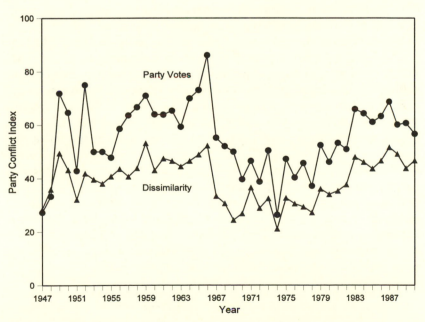

4.11 Party Conflict on Authorizations Votes in the House, 1947–1990

improvement is modest through 1979.[12] The broad range of congressional reform in 1974 and 1975 would seem to be less tightly connected to the resurgence of conflict than are specific budget reforms, especially reconciliation, first used in the stagflationist mire of the economic environment. Table 4.4 presents t-test comparisons of five-year sets of party cohesion and conflict data (1949–1953 versus 1954–1958; 1950–1954 versus 1955–1959; and so on). A t-value of 3.68 represents the .01 level of probability, which is advisable because of the small time periods being compared. A positive t-value indicates that the second set of years has a higher mean than the first set. The table shows that the introduction of reforms in 1974–1975 does not stand out as a key transformational year in party voting behavior; a better case can be made for the period from 1979 to 1982 and the impact of failed Keynesian macroeconomic management and the related introduction of reconciliation procedures.

The Economic-Political Model and Party Conflict on Authorizations and Appropriations

Neither authorizations nor appropriations would seem to be exclusively the domain of the economic or political environment. For example, one might expect to find party conflict on appropriations votes to be more likely to fluctuate as government responds to the business cycle. If authorizations bills more closely represent the pet projects of interest groups, one might expect voting on these bills to be especially connected to the political environment and less dependent on the economic environment. However, neither of these expectations is by any means obvious. One could plausibly argue that the authorizations process should respond to economic pressures with a push toward new programs during economic stress. The logrolling of the appropriations process on the other hand, might be seen as relatively immune to the economic environment and more closely tied to changes in the political environment. Thus, there is good reason to believe that both appropriations and authorizations could be influenced by economic and political conditions. Generally, I expect both economics and politics to matter. But because authorizations are directly about recasting the scope of the state and because the fiscal state features several "automatic" responses to economic troubles that do not require new appropriations, I expect the economic-political model to explain authorizations more effectively than appropriations.

[12] The general patterns of decline and resurgence vary somewhat for the two types of votes. Other than the different starting dates for conflict resurgence, the major mismatch is in the early years, where authorizations conflict is increasing or holding steady while appropriations conflict is declining. Correlations between the index of party dissimilarity for the two series are −.48 (1947–1956), .48 (1957–1969), −.05 (1970–1978), and .80 (1979–1990).

Table 4.4
Changes in Cohesion and Conflict in Appropriations and Authorizations, 1949–1986

	Democratic Cohesion		Republican Cohesion		Party Dissimilarity	
Year	Authorizations	Appropriations	Authorizations	Appropriations	Authorizations	Appropriations
1954	0.33	−0.39	−0.52	−4.17	0.04	−4.08
1955	2.57	0.66	−1.62	−2.11	1.81	−1.89
1956	1.21	−0.68	−1.06	−0.24	2.32	−1.89
1957	0.86	−0.38	−1.46	0.09	2.06	−0.37
1958	1.04	−0.05	−0.59	0.46	3.14	−0.59
1959	0.76	1.32	0.79	1.24	2.72	0.89
1960	−0.15	1.22	1.94	0.52	0.50	0.24
1961	1.27	3.00	1.32	−0.08	0.85	1.01
1962	0.57	2.77	1.93	1.10	0.83	1.31
1963	−0.11	2.43	0.75	2.63	−0.46	3.50
1964	−1.06	0.04	−1.44	1.84	−0.98	1.09
1965	−1.93	−0.80	−1.39	1.45	−1.41	0.26
1966	−7.78	−1.84	−1.87	1.23	−2.66	−0.74
1967	−4.09	−3.37	−2.72	−0.11	−6.79	−1.91
1968	−3.79	−4.39	−2.18	−3.27	−4.11	−6.93

(continued)

Table 4.4 (Continued)

Year	Democratic Cohesion		Republican Cohesion		Party Dissimilarity	
	Authorizations	*Appropriations*	*Authorizations*	*Appropriations*	*Authorizations*	*Appropriations*
1969	−1.99	***−6.17***	−0.65	***−4.77***	−2.59	***−6.84***
1970	−0.77	−1.58	−0.34	−2.13	−1.46	−2.51
1971	0.81	−0.39	0.55	−2.59	−0.56	−1.65
1972	0.89	0.70	0.58	−2.37	−0.40	−0.68
1973	3.55	1.12	0.50	−1.82	−0.07	1.16
1974	1.52	2.28	0.55	−1.08	−0.56	2.11
1975	1.82	−0.06	1.24	−0.97	0.67	2.68
1976	0.85	−0.88	0.62	−0.28	0.36	2.60
1977	−0.17	−1.76	1.53	1.70	1.20	2.88
1978	−1.18	−0.56	1.67	1.81	1.74	2.14
1979	0.57	−0.08	2.63	0.88	3.15	3.49
1980	0.74	1.85	1.31	0.30	2.80	3.76
1981	1.32	2.72	0.87	0.23	***3.68***	***4.91***
1982	***3.77***	***7.26***	−0.33	−1.88	***4.76***	3.89

Notes: Entries are t-values comparing the means of consecutive five-year series. The values across the 1954 line, for example, are the t-values for the mean comparisons of 1949–1953 versus 1954–1958. A positive value indicates that the second series has a higher mean than the first series. Entries in bold italic are significant at the .01 level.

Authorizations votes redefine or potentially redefine the scope of the state. Depression conditions in the 1930s produced a particularly profound example of this redefinition. Recessions provide, in smaller scale, some of the same opportunities for redefinition. When economic problems are considered amenable to Keynesian techniques, partisan voting on authorizations should converge. Those problems not conducive to Keynesian solutions create an opening for new ideas and party divergence. Table 4.5 indicates that this is precisely what happens during the fiscal state era. Authorizations conflict between the parties is especially well explained by the model in both its unadjusted and adjusted form. For unemployment, inflation, the interaction term, and reconciliation, the expected relationships prevail. All but one of the twelve economic coefficients reach significance. Reconciliation is significant for each estimation.

The pattern for the political variables differs somewhat across the forms of the model and across dissimilarity and party votes. Freshmen members have the expected impact on party votes (though not significantly) but not on dissimilarity. In each estimation, the size of the dominant Democratic faction is incorrectly signed. Vietnam and the post-midterm year are incorrectly signed in the party votes estimation but not near significance (two-tailed). Divided government displays mixed results. Other political variables produce the expected effects on authorizations conflict. This is a mixed bag of results for the political variables. It is the economic variables, however, that particularly capture expectations of party behavior derived from the constraints of the fiscal state. As noted above, these variables strongly support the predicted relationships.

Table 4.6 allows comparison with party behavior on appropriations votes. It is immediately apparent that the model does a far less effective job explaining party conflict in appropriations. Reconciliation has the expected significant effect in all four estimations, but with greater variance than for authorizations (the probability value is higher). Because reconciliation is primarily, though not exclusively, designed to force concessions from authorizing committees, this discrepancy is not surprising. With the exception of the adjusted form version of party votes, however, at least one economic variable is incorrectly signed in each estimation. Unemployment is correctly signed in each instance and significant in two of the four estimations. The political variables perform better. The size of the majority party and the Democratic dominant faction have inconsistent effects on appropriations conflict, but Vietnam, southern conservatism, new members, congressional elections, and the post-midterm year all have the expected effects, often significantly.[13] For the most part, the coefficients

[13] The finding on new members suggests that because freshmen have traditionally had less input in the appropriations process than the authorizations process, they are more inclined to follow the party lead on appropriations votes.

Table 4.5
House Party Conflict on Authorizations Votes, 1947–1990

	Party Dissimilarity		Party Votes	
Independent Variables	*Unadjusted Economic Variables*	*Adjusted Economic Variables*	*Unadjusted Economic Variables*	*Adjusted Economic Variables*
Constant	2.7571***	2.2239***	3.0088***	2.5592***
Economic:				
Unemployment	−.0428*	−.0221	−.0534**	−.0334*
Inflation	−.0740***	−.0366***	−.0696**	−.0314***
Unemployment*Inflation	.0074**	.0103*	.0079*	.0114**
Political:				
New members	−.0006	−.0006	.0000	.0001
R president, D Congress	.0055	−.0092	.0135	−.0033
R president, R Congress	−.0498	−.0138	−.1785	−.1584
R president, D House	.0017	−.0213	.0736	.0431
D president, R Congress	.5416	.7439	.2570	.3164
Vietnam	−.0106*	−.0134**	.0057	.0032
Majority size	.0148**	.0160**	.0179**	.0191**
Election	−.0027	−.0041	−.0664	−.0692
After midterm	.0730*	.0802*	−.0384	−.0347
Southern conservatism	−.0082*	−.0059	−.0112*	−.0090*
Dominant faction	−.0073	−.0114	−.0117	−.0161
Structural:				
Reconciliation	.2538***	.2452***	.2225***	.2268***
Party conflict$_{t-1}$	.2738**	.2918**	.3008**	.2880**
Standard error of regression	.1140†	.1191†	.1391†	.1398†
Corrected R^2	.744	.720	.633	.629
F-statistic	8.005***	7.211***	5.153***	5.093***

Note: Entries are unstandardized regression coefficients. For ease of presentation, standard errors have been omitted.

*$p \leq .10$; ** $p \leq .05$; *** $p \leq .01$, one-tailed test except for "R president, R Congress."

†This model was reestimated as generalized least squares, Prais-Winsten method, due to high values of the Breusch-Godfrey test for serial correlation with a lagged dependent variable.

on the political variables are of comparable size in the authorizations and appropriations estimations, with congressional elections providing one interesting (though nonsignificant) exception.

While these results accord with the anticipated results—authorizations conflict is better predicted than is appropriations conflict—the inconsistency in the economic variables is greater than expected in the appropri-

Table 4.6
House Party Conflict on Appropriations Votes, 1947–1990

Independent Variables	Party Dissimilarity		Party Votes	
	Unadjusted Economic Variables	Adjusted Economic Variables	Unadjusted Economic Variables	Adjusted Economic Variables
Constant	3.3498***	3.0973***	2.6381**	2.2078*
Economic:				
Unemployment	−.0286	−.0455*	−.0733	−.0876**
Inflation	.0209	−.0131	.0104	−.0010
Unemployment*Inflation	−.0047	−.0007	.0003	.0090
Political:				
New members	.0031*	.0030*	.0005	.0005
R president, D Congress	−.0564	−.0735	−.0020	−.0239
R president, R Congress	.0503	−.0037	−.0542	−.1441
R president, D House	.0394	.0090	.2820	.2474
D president, R Congress	.1210	.2123	.3803	.4153
Vietnam	−.0138*	−.0152*	−.0009	−.0045
Majority size	.0000	−.0002	.0250*	.0228*
Election	−.1612	−.1633	−.1313	−.1343
After midterm	.1138*	.1153*	.0941	.0996
Southern conservatism	−.0194***	−.0172**	−.0139*	−.0104
Dominant faction	.0050	.0021	−.0181	−.0197
Structural:				
Reconciliation	.2587*	.2578*	.2325*	.2237*
Party conflict$_{t-1}$	.4252**	.4267**	.3333	.3342
Standard error of regression	.1627†	.1630†	.2167†	.2174†
Corrected R^2	.677	.675	.373	.369
F-statistic	6.049***	6.019***	2.435**	2.411**

Note: Entries are unstandardized regression coefficients. For ease of presentation, standard errors have been omitted.

*$p \leq .10$; ** $p \leq .05$; ***$p \leq .01$, one-tailed test except for "R president, R Congress."

†This model was reestimated as generalized least squares, Prais-Winsten method, due to high values of the Breusch-Godfrey test for serial correlation with a lagged dependent variable.

ations estimation. One possibility is that the appropriations results are obscured by a rules change in 1970 that spurred appropriations amendments to be subject to formal roll-call votes. What this means is that before this date appropriations votes tended to be a smaller percentage of the votes than was true after the rules change. For some years, then, the party conflict indexes for appropriations are computed on relatively small numbers of votes, raising at least the possibility that the indexes for these years are less reliable than the indexes for later years. To test this possibility, I regressed the dependent variables in table 4.6 on the same set of independent variables plus a variable indicating the percentage of all votes that were appropriations votes. Once the percentage of appropriations votes is controlled for, unemployment, inflation, and the interaction term behave as expected in *all four* appropriations estimations. They are not as likely to reach significance as in the authorizations estimations, but that result was not unexpected. With this revision, the appropriations estimations resemble those for authorizations but at a lesser degree of strength. The results support the suggestion that, while economic and political conditions affect authorizations and appropriations conflict, authorizations are more likely to reflect state building and the "external" environment while appropriations relate more strongly to internal and political matters.

Conclusion

The fiscal state affects parties North and South and in both appropriations and authorizations. Looking at these two dichotomies refines and reinforces the interpretation of the fiscal state relationship between the economy and the parties presented in chapter 3. Democratic intraparty conflict is well explained by the economic-political model. As existing literature suggests, there are differences between North and South, authorizations and appropriations, in interparty behavior. The former partner in each of these dichotomies is more firmly linked with the patterns expected in the fiscal state; the interparty behavior typical in the fiscal state is more strongly the domain of northern Democrats and Republicans and authorizations votes. But the latter partners also behave in rough accordance with these patterns. And, as southern Democrats and appropriations became more like their counterparts, they conform more closely to the fiscal state pattern.

Separating votes and parties into these dichotomies provides additional refinement of the fiscal state's impact on party voting behavior, but it does not suggest that considering these votes or parties together in aggregate analysis is unwarranted.[14] In the end, the constraints of the fiscal state left the parties looking less relevant. With deference to the president, comparatively little to say on monetary policy, the acceptance of "automatic" policy, and consensus over the response to economic problems, the parties failed to convince a growing portion of the public that they deserved

[14] Of course, the aggregate set does not consist of authorizations or appropriations alone but also budget resolutions and votes on taxes and debt limits.

attention or support (Dennis 1975; Wattenberg 1990; Dennis and Owen 1994). The pattern of party voting, especially the urge to converge during economic stress, was not necessarily good for democratic choice or political parties.[15] The erosion of fiscal state constraints, beginning with the weakening Keynesian consensus, provided an opening for party contestation over new ideas. If these new ideas are linked with an institutional structure that favors parties, in a policy area the public cares about and believes government can affect, party-voter linkages will renew. Following a closer look at parties during recessions, I consider this possibility in chapter 6.

[15] I should note that while I remain agnostic on some of the major claims of the investment theory of political parties, many of my findings about party behavior are consistent with that approach (see Ferguson 1994).

5

Responding to Recession: Party Reactions and Policy Making during Economic Downturns

RECESSIONS PROVIDE a bright spotlight for parties to display their relevance. Recessions are periodic, feature high public attention to politics, deal with the underlying issue of the postwar party system, are linked to subsequent electoral outcomes, and offer the means, motive, and opportunity to reshape and restructure the fiscal state. And for parties rhetorically claiming economic managment to be their most impressive advantage over their adversary, a recession provides an exceptional opportunity to distinguish their programs from those of their opponent. Examining congressional roll-call votes provides a good sense of the macro response of the parties to changes in economic and political conditions. Roll-call analysis shows that if inflation remains low, partisan conflict diminishes as unemployment rises. But what about the party response during the course of a single recession? To understand how the fiscal state limits parties and how parties sometimes overcome those limits it is necessary to look closely at selected cases rather than focus on the broad scope of congressional voting over time. Looking at cases raises new questions about the interaction of the parties with changes in the economy and the messages sent to voters in these periods. In this chapter, I explore the following questions through qualitative analysis of archival and other primary data: What does the pattern of response look like in recessions? How do the party responses differ? What policy debates go on within the administration? How does the White House deal with the congressional parties in formulating economic policy during recessions? How do the parties attempt to present a common front to voters? Do presidential-congressional and House-Senate maneuvering make party positions more difficult to discern? What does this examination of recession politics suggest about the five constraints on parties in the fiscal state? At bottom, do the parties appear meaningful, distinctive, and significant to voters during recessions? By looking at how parties interact with the president, the nature and scope of fiscal state restructuring, the initiatives of party leaders, and how the parties build a policy response to economic issues, I explore the way parties overcame or remained limited by the structural and policy features of the fiscal state.

I examine party responses to the recessions of 1957–1958, 1974–1975,

Table 5.1
Selected Characteristics of Three Recessions

Characteristic	August 1957– April 1958	November 1973– March 1975	January 1980– July 1980
Months	9	17	7
Change in real output	−3.9%	−4.9	−2.3
Change in payroll employment	−4.3%	−2.9	−1.4
Change in unemployment rate	3.8 points	4.4	2.2
High unemployment rate	7.5%	9.0	7.8
Recovery in real output[a]	9.3%	8.0	3.4
Recovery in payroll employment[a]	4.8%	4.5	2.0
Recovery in unemployment rate[a]	−1.7 points	−1.0	−0.6
Party Delegations			
House	233D–200R	291D–144R[b]	276D–157R
Senate	49D–47R	60D–37R	58D–41R
President	Eisenhower (R)	Ford (R)	Carter (D)

Source: *Economic Report of the President* (Washington, D.C., Government Printing Office, 1993: 58–59).

[a] Economic improvement in first eighteen months after recession trough.

[b] The figures before January 1975 were 239D–192R (House) and 56D–42R (Senate).

and 1980. By providing variable conditions, these cases reflect many of the tendencies of postwar recession politics. Two of the recessions, 1957–1958 and 1974–1975, occurred under Republican presidents and divided government, while the 1980 recession took place during a unified Democratic term. The recessions vary in length—1980 is short, 1957–1958 is moderate, and 1974–1975 is long—although each recession was in some respects considered the sharpest economic decline since World War II. Two of the recessions, 1974–1975 and 1980, featured presidents running for or likely to run for reelection. The recessions of 1957–1958 and 1980 peaked in election years, unlike the recession of 1974–1975. In all three cases, the presidential party was electorally repudiated. Keynesianism as received wisdom was becoming more prominent around 1958, while by 1975 questions had set in, and by 1980 widespread skepticism was the rule. All three downturns share a Democratic majority in Congress. Table 5.1 and figures 5.1 and 5.2 present some

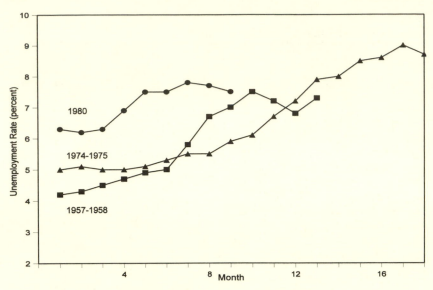

5.1 Monthly Unemployment Rates

Notes: Data points are the unemployment rates for the months during the recession. The first entry for each series marks the first month of the recession, with one exception: The first entry for the 1974–1975 recession is January 1974; the recession formally began in November 1973. The last three data points for each series represent the three months following the formal end of the recession.

basic characteristics of the three recessions. After reviewing these recessions, I discuss the tendencies in these cases and consider what these cases say about the five fiscal state constraints on parties presented in chapter 2.

The Recession of 1957–1958

Talk of inflation dominated economic policy preceding the recession of 1957–1958. President Dwight D. Eisenhower's proposed fiscal 1958 budget allowed for a small surplus—proper Keynesian strategy to defuse inflation—and a rejection of tax cuts.[1] 1957 was a grueling year. Head-

---

[1] Budget authority refers to an amount granted to an agency (or agencies). If an agency has budget authority of $100 million, it may spend any amount up to that figure; it need not spend all of the allotted authority. The amount that the agency spends is referred to as outlays. When Congress is debating the budget, it is most centrally debating the amount of budget authority to allow agencies. Outlays can consist of monies authorized currently or money to be spent per a previous year's appropriations (for example, a construction project may extend more than one year). Congress does not determine, through its appropriations process, the amount that will be spent in a given year. Some appropriations do come up an-

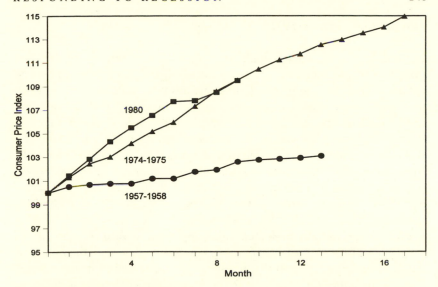

5.2 Monthly Consumer Price Index

Notes: Data points are the consumer price index values for the months during the recession. The CPI of 100 for the "0" month is the month before the recession formally begins, with one exception: The "0" month for the 1974–1975 recession is January 1974; the recession formally began in November 1973. The last three data points for each series represent the three months following the formal end of the recession.

ing into the recession, the legacy of the immediate past was a Republican party split between those elements willing to follow Eisenhower's accommodating stance to the New Deal and those elements favoring greater fiscal orthodoxy, loud Democratic complaints about administration economic policy, an administration focus on inflation, and a consensus between leaders of both parties and the administration that they warn each other about any proposed major deviations in economic policy.

---

nually. Others are given longer terms of authority. And still others are given effectively permanent appropriations. Most significant among this latter group are entitlements—programs in which the amount spent depends on the number of people meeting a legislatively mandated formula. These definitional wrinkles point to three features of budget and fiscal politics: (1) cutting or increasing appropriations often has its most significant impact in later years, not the present year; (2) much ongoing spending is "uncontrollable" because it is an entitlement or because it is being spent in fulfillment of prior commitments; and (3) a small percentage of fiscal-year outlays actually result from that years' appropriations process. White and Wildavsky note that "only 27.3 percent of the outlays in the government's 1980 fiscal year resulted from that year's appropriations process" (1989: 4).

Turning to Recession: 1958

Coming into 1958, the key budgetary question was how much domestic programs would need to be cut to allow increased military spending in response to Sputnik. From the administration's view, inflation remained the primary economic issue of the day, and the proposed budget contained level spending and another small surplus. But the recession that had begun in August 1957 was on the political agenda at the start of the year and soon would move to the top of that agenda (Morgan 1990: 99–100). By October 1957, Eisenhower acknowledged publicly that the economy was in a "breather," the future was "mixed," and that the government had to be "ready to move in when [it] possibly can" (*New York Times* [hereafter *NYT*], October 31, 1957, p. 1).

Both parties initially took a cautious approach toward recession cures. The Federal Reserve Board took the first action to deal with the recession, announcing a reduction in the discount rate it charged to member banks in mid-November. On December 23, as Democrats criticized the delay, the administration announced that it had "unfrozen" $177 million in housing program funds that Congress had appropriated despite presidential disapproval. J. William Fulbright (D-Arkansas), chair of the Senate Banking Committee, announced that he saw no need for anti-recession or anti-inflation legislation until it was clearer which was coming (*NYT*, January 5, 1958, p. 58). On January 10, Eisenhower's State of the Union address again stated his willingness to act to promote economic recovery if necessary.[2] Meanwhile, the Federal Reserve continued to take gradual steps to promote recovery. Within the administration, the chairman of the Council of Economic Advisers, Raymond J. Saulnier, argued that the spending in the budget was insufficient to speed recovery (Pach and Richardson 1991: 176).[3]

Democrats began in late January a two-pronged, loosely coordinated attack on Republican policies. First, Democrats, including Wilbur Mills (D-Arkansas), chair of the House Ways and Means Committee, and Sen-

---

[2] Stein (1969: 323) notes that neither the Budget Message nor the Economic Report of the President issued early in 1958 discussed any relationship between the budget and the recession.

[3] Other staffers warned, however, that Eisenhower might need to stay aloof because a presidential speech would only serve to link the president to economic conditions (Memo to the Assistant to the President, Sherman Adams, from Special Assistant Arthur Larson, January 28, 1958, in Branyan and Larsen 1971: 890). Eisenhower's chief economic advisers were Saulnier, Treasury Secretary Robert Anderson, Federal Reserve Board chair William McChesney Martin, and Gabriel Hauge, the administrative assistant to the president for economic affairs. These four met regularly as the Little Four. Similar structures were created in the Ford and Carter administrations.

ators John J. Sparkman (D-Alabama), Mike Mansfield (D-Montana), and Hubert H. Humphrey (D-Minnesota), suggested that Congress and the president might need to consider a tax cut to boost the economy (*NYT,* January 20, 1958, p. 1; February 1, 1958, p. 1). This was not an endorsement of a tax cut as such, but an endorsement of the idea of thinking about a tax cut.[4]

Second, Democrats introduced in early February individual pieces of legislation for economic recovery. These bills included assistance for public works and public improvements, increasing unemployment compensation and widening the range of covered workers, providing drought assistance to the Midwest and South, an omnibus housing bill to spur residential construction and slum clearance, and accelerating various kinds of federal spending (for example, hospital and highway construction) in high unemployment areas. On January 31, these items and others were packaged together by Senate Majority Leader Lyndon B. Johnson (D-Texas) as the Democratic ten-step response to the recession. There is scant evidence that anyone, including Democrats, made much of this "package" solution to the recession, but the package did reflect Johnson's ongoing strategy to hold the party together and was similar in form and content to his thirteen-point Democratic agenda announced in November 1955.[5] At the very least, Johnson's announcement and demands from organized interests forced an administration response (Morgan 1990: 103).

The administration's immediate response was that nothing much needed to be done to the economy. On February 10, Saulnier informed Eisenhower that monetary actions, acceleration of spending, and perhaps a tax cut were necessary to pull out of the recession. Eisenhower readily agreed to the first two items on the list while deferring on the third (Morgan 1990: 101). Treasury Secretary Anderson—the strongest pessimist within the administration on the advisability of tax cuts—publicly down-

---

[4] Indeed, Mills was a member of a Joint Economic Committee subcommittee that declared unanimously that tax cuts were not an obvious cure for the recession and that the best strategy was to wait and assess the results of increased defense spending and Federal Reserve monetary actions.

[5] See R. Oliver, "Congressional Program," October 26, 1955, Box 117, LBJA Subject File, Senate, United States, Leadership-Lyndon B. Johnson 1 of 2, Lyndon Baines Johnson Presidential Library (hereafter LBJL), for the first iteration of the program. The attraction of the budding program was that it could obtain broad Democratic support while requiring minimum Republican cooperation for passage. See also, file memos by George E. Reedy for chronologies of the Democratic response (Pre-Presidential Memo File, Box 6, Pre-Presidential Memo Files, Miscellaneous [Reedy, 1958], memos dated March 1958 and August 13, 1958, LBJL; and Reedy's oral history recollection of the 1955 "Program with a Heart" (interviewer Michael L. Gillette, August 16, 1983, interview 8, pp. 61–69). The November 1955 "Speech before Fund Raising Dinner, Democratic Advisory Committee of Texas," Whitney, Texas, is in Statements File, Box 18, LBJL.

played the utility of cutting taxes, while Eisenhower erroneously declared on February 12 that the slump had bottomed out and that jobs would pick up in March (Morgan 1990: 102). Administration officials declared that acceleration of spending in defense, postal affairs, highways, and housing programs amounted to a de facto anti-recession program (*NYT*, February 15, 1958, p. 10). Amid word that leading Democrats, including Rayburn, had indicated the possibility of investigating tax cuts, the White House announced that it, too, was considering such cuts.

On February 18, confident of an impending upturn, the Republican congressional leadership and the Eisenhower administration rejected the notion of tax cuts or other emergency measures to stimulate the economy. Republicans argued that monetary changes, stockpiled public works projects, and the acceleration of spending made other measures unnecessary. The Joint Economic Committee agreed, concluding with only one dissent that tax cuts were not necessary. Acceleration of spending, expansion of public assistance payments to the states, and the liberalization and extension of unemployment compensation were sufficient anti-recession remedies.[6] By the beginning of March, one reporter noted, "except for a new housing bill in the Senate, very little actual anti-recession legislation [was] under active consideration" (*NYT*, March 2, 1958, sec. IV, p. 3).

That assessment was not entirely fair. At the time, proposals for additional public works spending and unemployment compensation reforms were working their way through Congress as part of the Democratic package. By the second week in March, Eisenhower informed Republican leaders William Knowland in the Senate and Joseph Martin in the House that he was introducing new proposals to stanch a rush to pump-priming schemes. The president proposed new spending of $1 to 2 billion over the next two years, consisting of about one-third new outlays and two-thirds adjustments and accelerations of already appropriated funds. He also proposed extending unemployment compensation benefits for thirteen weeks for workers who had exhausted their benefits. Johnson labeled the new elements "a prompt, partial reaction to the new call for action issued in the Congress this past week" (*NYT*, March 9, 1958, p. 54). The administration had developed no contingency plans should the recession deepen (Morgan 1990: 101).[7]

---

[6] Memo from Roderick H. Riley, executive director, to Wright Patman, chairman, Joint Economic Committee, June 4, 1958, in Pre-presidential, Senate Files, Box 536, Committees Joint Economic, John F. Kennedy Presidential Library (hereafter JFKL).

[7] Vice President Richard M. Nixon indicated publicly that he strongly favored a tax cut. Saulnier also believed that a tax cut was justified (Morgan 1990: 121; Stein 1969: 331). The pro–tax cut argument was that tax cuts prevented a deeper economic decline, preempted "the spenders," were a basic administration goal, and lessened the likelihood of severe Republican losses in 1958. The Treasury considered twenty alternative tax cuts, and then reported only the revenue costs of the options to Eisenhower (Sloan 1991: 149).

If the administration assumed that Eisenhower's statement and subsequent activist posture (including well-publicized meetings with organized interests and members of Congress) would reassert White House control of the economic debate, it assumed wrong.[8] Some Republicans supported the call for tax cuts. Amid signs that the slump was deepening, Rep. Richard M. Simpson (R-Pennsylvania), the ranking Republican on Ways and Means and the chair of the National Republican Congressional Committee, called for an immediate income tax cut of about 10 percent (among other tax cuts totaling $6 billion) on the same day that the president issued his statement of new proposals (*NYT,* March 9, 1958, p. 56). Sen. Paul Douglas (D-Illinois), the leading Democratic proponent for tax cuts, announced he would introduce his own $5 billion tax cut. Eight Republican supporters of Eisenhower, including Sen. Jacob Javits (R-New York), called for $4 to 5 billion in anti-recession public works spending. In the immediate aftermath of Eisenhower's statement, both Democrats and Republicans were calling for more public works spending, more federal aid to depressed communities, and expanded unemployment compensation. But while concerned with the dollar totals, on balance the administration could not see much in the alternative proposals that would be seriously distasteful.

Columnist Edwin Dale aptly summed up the environment in Washington by noting that "At the end of the week, the degree of harmony and sweet reasonableness seemed dazzling" (*NYT,* March 16, 1958, sec. IV, p. 3; see also Stein 1969: 345). Both the Democrats and the Republicans agreed that a tax cut would be the next step. Republicans in the House and Senate voted with near unanimity for a $1.85 billion Democratic emergency housing bill (some Republican demands had been met through amendments) and for speeding up public works spending. Both parties wanted to extend unemployment compensation. Both agreed on accelerating spending in most areas, including $5.5 billion over two years for highways.

The party positions were not identical. Some Democrats were interested in establishing national standards for unemployment compensation and eliminating state-by-state variations, but most Democrats and nearly all Republicans rejected the notion. On March 19, when Eisenhower issued orders to speed up spending on $2.25 billion of publicly aided projects, Democrats complained that only $75 million of new spending would result when $2 billion might be more appropriate. The administration had preferred a longer-term focus to the housing bill that would raise the interest rate ceiling on government-guaranteed loans (thus encouraging

---

[8] Reichard (1975: 218–29) and Pach and Richardson (1991: 50) discuss the role of congressional liaison in the Eisenhower White House. Eisenhower was the first president to establish a permanent office of legislative liaison.

more lenders to participate); the Democratic countercyclical plan called for a special assistance program that would buy federally guaranteed loans at face value to open up the market for new loans. The plan that passed was closer to the Democratic model. Democrats wanted to commit roughly two and one-half times more funds to accelerated highway spending than the president, and they were willing to dip into general revenues rather than rely on the struggling highway trust fund. After substantial concessions by the Democrats, the bill was passed in a form that predominantly reflected the president's thinking. While these differences were important, agreement on the major tools available and their relative desirability was striking.

Among Democratic party leaders, the appearance of reasonableness was key: The worst thing for the party to do in an emergency was to obstruct the response of the administration.[9] To Johnson and Rayburn, the Democratic party's centrist supporters would credit the party if it helped Eisenhower extricate the country from its economic troubles. These supporters were not concerned about creating a "pure" Democratic anti-recession program. In the leadership's view, the best plan was to determine where events were leading and beat the administration to the punch with a proposal rather than worry whether the content of the proposal was markedly different from the administration's. Rayburn and Johnson indicated that they were waiting for leadership from the president: "Congress is not the action arm of the government" (Johnson, cited in Sundquist 1968: 24; see also Conkin 1986: 134–37).

With acceleration of spending accomplished or already proposed and new programs not likely to have any immediate economic impact, the move to tax cuts was viewed on all sides as the next logical step (Stein 1969: 328). But in the most striking display of the similarity of approach taken by the two parties in responding to the recession, Speaker Rayburn and Treasury Secretary Anderson reached a "gentleman's agreement" on March 12 that they would consult each other before initiating any tax cut legislation.[10] Neither party wanted to be undercut by the tax issue. Over

[9] The logic of this approach is spelled out in George E. Reedy, files memo, February 19, 1958, Pre-Presidential Memo File, Box 6, Pre-Presidential Memo File, Economy [Reedy, 1958], LBJL. Reedy's strategy counseled caution, specifics, mild criticism of the administration, and awareness of how criticism could backfire against the Democrats.

[10] Johnson, Rayburn, and Anderson, who forged the agreement to discuss any tax cut proposals, all hailed from Texas and had been longtime friends. Rayburn had the blessing of Ways and Means Democrats (Sundquist 1968: 27). It appears that Johnson informed the Democratic Policy Committee of his cooperation after the fact, although the committee voiced no loud opposition to the strategy (Minutes of Meeting, Democratic Policy Committee, March 19, 1958, Senate Files, Box 364, Senate Democratic Policy Committee, Minutes of March 8, 1955–June 24, 1960, LBJL). The AFL-CIO indicated it supported a tax cut as its preferred plan; the Chamber of Commerce placed a tax cut fourth on its list (State-

the next two days, the Senate overwhelmingly voted down tax cut proposals (including Douglas's by a 71 to 14 margin). At his April 9 news
conference, Eisenhower refused to support a tax cut in the near term. He
argued instead that the federal government had done its share and that
industry and consumers needed to do their part also. Party leaders on
both sides deflected a powerful array of tax cut proponents: the Advisory Council of the Democratic National Committee, the Committee for
Economic Development, the Rockefeller Brothers Fund Report, the U.S.
Chamber of Commerce, General Motors, J. P. Morgan and Company, the
AFL-CIO, and former CEA chair Arthur Burns (Sundquist 1968: 25).

Ending the Politics of Recession

To Eisenhower, inflation always threatened to become structural while unemployment was more truly cyclical (Sloan 1991: 145–48). A temporary
tax cut would probably be ineffective this late in the recession, but a permanent cut might well lead to future inflation; Democratic leaders and the
Treasury Department concurred (Stein 1969: 334). If the business cycle
must be interfered with, it should be done in a way that minimized the ex-
acerbation of any future inflation threat (Pach and Richardson 1991: 38,
176; Stein 1969: 319–20). Eisenhower's more aggressive posture became
concrete over the next several weeks as positive economic news arrived.
Over this period, the president vetoed a $1.7 billion Democratic rivers and
harbors bill,[11] announced his opposition to a bill approved 60 to 26 in
the Senate calling for community works projects,[12] and indicated his opposition to a Democratic plan approved by the House Ways and Means
Committee that would extend unemployment benefits by sixteen weeks.
That bill would also extend coverage to 1.8 million more workers and
would not require states to pay back the additional federal contribution
(Eisenhower had submitted his own more modest proposal that retained
all the features of the existing program while providing a federal loan to
allow states to increase by one-half the number of weeks a person could
receive benefits). He also signed the highway and housing bills mentioned
above but with a public statement of his displeasure and reluctance. By

---

ment of the AFL-CIO General Board on the Economy, April 28, 1958, in Senate Files Box
428, Reedy: Labor 2 of 2, LBJL; Letter to LBJ from the president of the U.S. Chamber of
Commerce, April 12, 1958, LBJA Subject File, Economy, National, Box 65, LBJL).

[11] When $350 million in new projects were removed from the July version of the bill,
Eisenhower signed.

[12] He also vetoed several bills that were not explicitly considered anti-recession proposals but which would have certainly increased federal spending, including, for example, aid
for airport construction and depressed areas redevelopment.

his news conference on April 23, Eisenhower was labeling the recession a "minor emergency" (especially in comparison with the communist threat) and urging that people not get "hysterical."

By the end of May, additional anti-recession action was concluded. In his news conference on May 28, Eisenhower declared that the recession had "largely spent its force" and that there would be no general tax cut. His statement ratified what all the major Democratic and Republican leaders had suggested the day before: There would be no tax cut in 1958. With economic statistics improving, other measures just starting to have an effect, and skepticism about whether a tax cut would help the situation or simply exacerbate future inflation, both sides could claim economic support for their view. Polls indicated that voters were uncertain about the usefulness of tax cuts. After appeals from Treasury Secretary Anderson and Director of the Budget Maurice H. Stans, the House Ways and Means Committee approved (21–2) the president's request to maintain current tax levels on a variety of excise taxes. The Senate voted 80 to 0 to approve Eisenhower's unemployment benefits proposal and sent it to the White House for the president's signature. Although the recession would emerge as a major campaign issue, for now the politics of the 1958 recession were over.

The Recession of 1974–1975

Like 1957–1958, the recession of 1974–1975 was the deepest to date of the postwar period. During 1974, inflation was, as President Gerald R. Ford put it, "public enemy number one." In a speech before Congress on October 8, 1974, Ford presented his plan to cut inflation, reduce energy consumption, and increase employment. Anti-inflation proposals included a 5 percent income tax surcharge on upper income earners and corporations; commitment to a $300 billion spending ceiling; and voluntary actions to hold down costs, prices, and wages. Anti-recession proposals included an increase in the investment tax credit, an increase in unemployment benefits, and the creation of public service jobs in depressed areas.[13]

The grace period for the October Plan was short. With the economy slowing down, Democrats in Congress arguing that slow economic growth now exceeded inflation as a problem, and Ford's own inclination to sign legislation boosting housing construction and public service employment, the administration reassessed its position. On November 18, following huge Democratic victories in the midterm elections, the Eco-

[13] For strategy, see Memo for William E. Timmons from Vern Loen through Max L. Friedensdorf, October 1, 1974, "President's Economic Speech," Economy (1), Loen and Leppert, Box 7, Gerald R. Ford Presidential Library (hereafter GRFL).

nomic Policy Board's (EPB) Executive Committee concluded that contingency plans were needed for dealing with the recession.[14] Accordingly, by the end of November, the administration had pushed its budget limit up to $302.2 billion amid new warnings by Alan Greenspan (chair of the Council of Economic Advisers) of an unexpectedly "marked contraction in production, employment, and incomes." With economists outside the administration pushing for tax cuts, Greenspan hinted in early December that a tax cut might be necessary to stimulate the economy.[15] Meetings with his economic advisers, the bipartisanship leadership of Congress, the Labor-Management [Advisory] Committee, and nongovernmental economists convinced Ford that the sentiment for a tax cut, in particular, was overwhelming. On December 20, the EPB agreed on the need for a temporary tax cut. The following day, Ford supported the idea, but not new spending programs (Porter 1980: 109–13).[16]

Tax Cuts

The major thrust of Gerald Ford's revised plan to stem the recession consisted of tax cuts. Announced first in a televised speech on January 13 and then elaborated in the State of the Union address two nights later, his

[14] "EPB Meeting Minutes, Oct. 10–22, 1974"; also October 23–31; minutes for meetings on October 16, 18, 24, 25, 31; in Seidman, Box 20, GRFL; "E.P.B. Meeting Minutes, Nov. 18–30, 1974," meeting of November 18, Seidman, Box 20, GRFL. Ford had suggested on September 12 that his advisers were to commence work on these contingency plans quickly. The Economic Policy Board brought together for daily discussions the top level of the administration officials dealing with economic policy. The EPB would delegate assignments to the departments and sought to provide the president with a consensus view on economic strategy or, minimally, identify key economic issues and lay out options for the president. The executive committee of the EPB, which was the most significant policy-making unit, consisted initially of the secretary of the treasury, chairman of the Council of Economic Advisers, director of the Office of Management and Budget, assistant to the president for economic affairs, and the executive director of the Council on International Economic Policy. Later, the secretaries of state, commerce, and labor were added. Other officials and staffers attended frequently.

[15] Treasury Secretary William Simon still favored a surtax (Hargrove and Morley 1984: 411). But L. William Seidman (executive director of the EPB) argued that it was time for the administration to listen to outside economists. The EPB agreed, however, that spending as an anti-recession tool outside the automatic stabilizers "is generally blunt, delayed, and out of phase" ("E.P.B. Meeting Minutes, Nov. 18–30, 1974," meeting of November 27, Seidman, Box 20, GRFL). See also Memo from Alan Greenspan to the President, November 26, 1974, "Current State of the Economy," Economy: Legislative Review, November 1974, Seidman, Box 63, GRFL; Ford (1979: 202, 227).

[16] The EPB had some difficulty reaching consensus on most of the particulars of the proposed tax bill ("Tax Proposals and Options," December 26, 1974, Taxes 11/74–12/74; "Tax Proposals and Options," January 4, 1975, Taxes 1/75–2/75; both Seidman, Box 166, GRFL).

anti-recession plan called for individual tax cuts (rebates of 1974 taxes) of $12 billion and business cuts (via an investment tax credit) of $4 billion. A more permanent income tax cut would be put into place if the revenues from energy taxes were adopted. His anti-inflation plan declared that there would be no new spending programs outside energy, that all cost-of-living adjustments in spending programs would be limited to 5 percent, and that budget cuts would slow the increase in federal spending.[17]

Ford's tax cut proposals went first to the House Ways and Means Committee. The committee approved $19.8 billion in cuts—$16.2 billion for individuals and $3.2 billion for businesses. Part of the cut would be a rebate on 1974 taxes while part would consist of reductions in withholding in 1975. Ways and Means also added $2.2 billion in tax increases. Compared to the president's plan, the bill provided more relief for lower income individuals and less for the middle and upper income groups, but Ford was prepared to accept such a distribution.[18] Republicans were mixed in their response, with six in support and five opposed. As a group, they supported cuts that were smaller, less lengthy, and more targeted to the middle class (*Congressional Quarterly Almanac* [hereafter *CQA*] 1975: 101). On February 27, the House passed the bill (H.R. 2166) 317 to 97; Democrats supported the bill 238 to 37, while Republicans voted 79 to 60 in favor.

The House bill was fairly close to the president's proposal. The Senate Finance Committee, however, made several changes. The committee deepened the cuts and shifted them more toward the middle class. It approved permanent rate reductions in the first four tax brackets and a bonus payment of $100 for each Social Security recipient. Some additional tax credits were added, including a 5 percent credit for the purchase of a newly constructed house (up to $2,000). The bill contained $23.3 billion in cuts for individuals, $7.4 billion for businesses, $3.7 billion in tax increases, $3.4 billion in new Social Security spending, and $0.2 billion in emergency unemployment benefits. The Senate passed the bill 60 to 29, with Republicans and southern Democrats voting against the bill by margins of 4 to 19 and 7 to 9, respectively. Republican objections concerned nearly all facets of the bill: the increased size of the cuts, the additional federal spending, and the permanence of some of the provisions.

---

[17] His energy program called for import fees, excise taxes, price decontrol of oil and gas, an acceleration of research and development, a synthetic fuels program, and increases in automobile gasoline mileage.

[18] Memo to the President from L. W. Seidman via Donald H. Rumsfeld, January 16, 1975, George Meany, Seidman, Box 195, GRFL; Memorandum of the meeting with the President and George Meany and L. William Seidman, January 17, 1975, George Meany, Seidman, Box 195, GRFL.

The conference committee report issued March 26 targeted individual cuts at $18.1 billion, business cuts at $4.8 billion, tax increases at $2.0 billion, Social Security spending at $1.7 billion, and emergency unemployment benefits at $0.2 billion. On the tax cuts, the bill that emerged was closer to the House and Ford plans, but Republicans in the conference were dissatisfied with provisions for a Social Security benefit, a home purchase credit, and tax reductions extending through 1975. Only one Republican agreed to sign the report; five refused. Rep. Barber Conable (R-New York) declared that the president should not feel compelled to support the bill despite its genesis in the White House (*CQA* 1975: 111).

On the floor, Republicans were more mixed in their view. The House passed the bill on March 26 by a vote of 287 to 125; Republicans voted 55 to 82.[19] This vote indicated that Ford could sustain a veto. On the same day, the Senate voted 45 to 16 to pass the bill, with Republicans slightly opposed (11–14). The bill then went to the president. For the next two days, the administration struggled to decide whether the president should sign the bill.

Most Republican members of Congress and Ford's legislative liaison staff assured the president that a veto could be sustained. Moderate Republicans were the most problematic regarding a veto, with Senators Robert Dole (R-Kansas), Robert Packwood (R-Oregon), Charles Percy (R-Illinois), and Howard Baker (R-Tennessee) all indicating to the administration that they were highly likely to support an override.[20] Democrats were more skeptical. Rep. Joe Waggonner (D-Louisiana) warned that a second bill might well be worse from the administration's point of view. Moreover, by vetoing the bill, the president risked the adverse future reactions of Finance Committee chair Russell B. Long (D-Louisiana) and new Ways and Means chair Al Ullman (D-Oregon). He might also weaken public confidence in his leadership. Rep. Dan Rostenkowski (D-Illinois) told liaison officials that "the President would make a terrible mistake by vetoing the bill."[21]

[19] Opposition in the House to some of the bill's new and revised provisions led to a vote to send the bill back to the conference committee. The vote to send the bill back was shy of a majority by a vote of 197 to 214.

[20] Memo to Jack Marsh from William T. Kendall and Patrick E. O Donnell, March 28, 1975, "Tax Reduction Act of 1975," Economy, February 1975–March 1976, Friedersdorf, Box 11, GRFL; Memo to the President from Vernon C. Loen through John Marsh, Don Rumsfeld, and Max Friedersdorf, March 28, 1975, "Tax Reduction Act Conference Report (H.R. 2166)," Economy, February 1975–March 1976, Friedersdorf, Box 11, GRFL. The liaison staff still recommended that the president sign the measure while making it clear that he expected reciprocal action in the future.

[21] Memo to the President from Max L. Friedersdorf, "Tax Reduction Bill," March 27, 1975, Economy, February 1975–March 1976, Friedersdorf, Box 11, GRFL. The liaison official noted that "Dan thinks the world of the President and wants to help him. . . . He is

In the White House, Seidman and Greenspan argued that the positive portions of the bill outweighed the negative; it would have positive economic effects and would bolster public confidence.[22] Treasury Secretary William Simon urged a veto. With a recently completed economic review indicating that unemployment would be worse than earlier anticipated while inflation would fare better, Ford signed the tax cut into law on March 30.

Public Sector Jobs and Public Works

As with the tax cuts, Democrats and Republicans quickly converged on the idea that some kind of public jobs provision was a necessary element of anti-recession strategy. Ford demonstrated his willingness to move down this policy path early in his presidency when, after meeting with labor leaders in September 1974, he released additional funding for a public service jobs program operating under the auspices of the Comprehensive Employment and Training Act of 1973 (CETA).[23] In effect, this action was an acceleration of CETA spending totaling $415 million and 85,000 jobs.

By the time Ford made his major inflation address in October, several jobs proposals were under consideration in Congress. The programs varied somewhat in their size, targeted populations, and triggers, but the proposals, from both parties, indicated commitment to substantial outlays for public jobs. Two Republican plans called for $4 to 4.5 billion and about 500,000 jobs (S. 2993, H.R. 16926); three Democratic plans ranged widely in proposed spending ($500 to $2 billion in S. 4079; $1 to 4 billion in H.R. 16596; $6.3 billion in H.R. 16150), with the largest of the three anticipating 900,000 jobs. When Ford recommended the creation of a Community Improvement Corps targeted toward small-scale and short-term beautification projects in his October 8 address, his proposal came in at the low end of the spending and jobs figures and attracted little interest.

---

very sincere in his support of the President." For other Democrats, see Memo to Jack Marsh from Russ Rourke, March 29, 1975, Taxes—Tax Reduction Act (3), Marsh, Box 32, GRFL.

[22] For the tax cut debate in the White House, see Memo to the President, "Tax Cut Bill," [March 27, 1975], Economic Affairs, Taxes—Tax Cuts 1975 (1), Seidman, Box 105, GRFL; Memo to the President from William Simon, "Tax Matters," ca. March 15, 1975, Taxes—Tax Cuts, 1975 (1), Seidman, Box 105; Memo to the President from L. William Seidman, "Tax Bill," March 28, 1975, President—Memos to 10/74–3/75, Seidman, Box 145, GRFL; Memo for the President from Robert K. Wolthius, March 28, 1975, "Tax Bill," Taxes—Tax Reduction Act (2), Marsh, Box 32, GRFL; Letter from Barry Goldwater to the President, March 31, 1975, Taxes—Tax Reduction Act (3), Marsh, Box 32, GRFL; Memo to the President from L. William Seidman, March 28, 1975, "Tax Cut Bill," Roger Porter Chronological File March 18–31, 1975, Seidman, Box 279, GRFL; Memo to the President from Jack Marsh, March 28, 1975, "Tax Bill," Taxes—Tax Reduction Act (3), Marsh, Box 32, GRFL.

[23] CETA was ordinarily considered a program to reduce structural rather than cyclical unemployment.

Not until December did both Democrats and Republicans feel pressed to move on the jobs legislation. Rejecting the administration's proposal, Congress passed a two-part jobs program. First, in an Emergency Public Jobs Program targeted to high unemployment areas, the bill provided $2.5 billion in fiscal year 1975 through Title VI of CETA for state and local governments to hire unemployed workers to perform community service jobs in health, education, sanitation, day care, recreation, and so on. About 300,000 jobs were anticipated. Second, through the Job Opportunities Program, the bill accelerated federal spending for labor-intensive public works projects. Despite misgivings about the programs' cost, the speed-up of public works, and that the jobs would be available to workers who had not exhausted their unemployment insurance, Ford signed the legislation. Party divisions during congressional deliberations were restrained; whether workers had to exhaust their benefits before claiming a public job caused much of the disagreement. Support for the individual bills in the House and Senate and the conference compromise was overwhelming with strong bipartisan support.

In the spring of 1975, public jobs were again tangled with public works. In the $5.3 billion Emergency Employment Appropriations Act, Democrats allocated $1.6 billion for new public service employment (partially through the CETA Title VI program); about $410 million for summer employment for youth; and the remainder for acceleration of public works projects, funding new maintenance and construction projects suggested by government agencies, and providing loans to small business. Republicans and Ford fully accepted the first two provisions. The real debate concerned the remaining $3.3 billion in the bill, which Republican leaders argued was costly and inflationary. Rank-and-file opinion was shakier: House Republicans voted against the bill 55 to 88 (original) and 49 to 91 (conference) and Senate Republicans split on the original vote 12 to 11 (the vote on the conference version was a voice vote). Not surprisingly, Republicans in areas hard hit by the recession found it difficult to vote against the bill, particularly since they anticipated a presidential veto.

Ford vetoed the bill on May 28, and Democrats immediately set out on an override effort. House Majority Leader Thomas P. O'Neill (D-Massachusetts) asserted that "We will not be facing a more important issue this session than this veto" (*CQA* 1975: 799). "If the majority cannot win this one, it cannot win any of them," challenged the House Minority Leader Robert Michel (R-Illinois). After heavy administration lobbying, the Democrats did not win (Reichley 1981: 328–29). Ford considered the vote to be perhaps the most important vote for the administration since he became president.[24] Just over one week later Congress

<hr />

[24] "Notes of the Cabinet Meeting, June 4th, 1975," 1975/06/04 Cabinet Meeting, Connor, Box 4, GRFL.

approved and the president signed legislation providing for the public jobs and summer jobs arrangements of the vetoed bill.

Public works spending was ensnared in another battle in 1976. In May 1975, the House passed with little debate a $5 billion local public works program for fiscal years 1976–1977 that was intended to produce 250,000 jobs (about two-thirds of the funds represented accelerated spending; the rest was new). Democratic support was near unanimous, while Republicans split 62 to 71. The Senate passed its version of the bill in late July and adopted the conference report by voice in December. United Democrats and a split Republican party passed the conference bill in the House the following January. Ford vetoed the now $6.1 billion bill because of its provision of $1.5 billion for countercyclical assistance to local and state governments to eliminate the need for them to cut programs or raise taxes.

Following a failure to override, congressional Democrats, with substantial Republican support, immediately went to work on a cheaper version of the bill. As passed, the new bill authorized $3.95 billion through fiscal 1977, with $2 billion for state and local public works projects, $1.25 billion for countercyclical aid, and $700 million for wastewater treatment plants. Ford again vetoed, but this time Republican defections were sufficient to override the veto. Ford signed the appropriations for the programs into law on October 1.

The administration's performance on job creation programs rankled many congressional Republicans. The party's conservative wing had the most difficulty with the administration's lack of a positive program and occasional compromises with Democrats (Rae 1989: 112–13, ch. 5). A legislative liaison staffer reported that House Republican leaders felt that "we do not have a recognizable program to combat measures such as the Humphrey-Hawkins Bill."[25] Moreover, the liaison staff found "great concern that we do not have a publicly visible program that emphasizes job creation in the private sector. Our approach has been passive and neg-

[25] The Humphrey-Hawkins bill, first introduced in 1974 and then again in 1975, sought to put enforcement power into the Employment Act of 1946. Its legislative history paralleled that of the earlier bill: The bill was continually weakened over time in order to widen support. For example, a call to reduce unemployment to 3 percent in eighteen months was increased to four years, the right to sue for a job was eliminated, attention to inflation targets were added, and so on. The idea of the bill was to have the president—not Congress—set economic goals and plans to reach them. Once approved, this overarching plan was to guide Congress. If the goals were not reached, countercyclical aid, jobs programs, and so on were to kick in automatically. The irony of this program was that, in a radical veneer, it managed to endorse most of the existing features of the fiscal state, including presidential leadership, automatic policy solutions, the bifurcation of monetary and fiscal policy, and the encouragement of plebiscites on macroeconomic targets. Failing to reach the floor in 1976, the bill finally passed in weak form in 1978 as a largely rhetorical statement that the president should seek low unemployment and low inflation.

ative. . . the public does not have a recognition that we propose anything other than letting the economy heal itself." Rep. Jack Kemp (R-New York) complained about lack of coordination between executive and legislative branch Republicans on job creation. Noting that "the Republican Party is in disarray and often without candidates *because* of this confusion on the Party's position, not vice versa," Kemp declared that "if the President will choose to align himself on economic and social issues with the traditional position of conservatives he will find a natural constituency coalescing around him in the Congress." To Kemp, "[I]n aggregate, [the electorate] sees little advantage to electing one party over another."[26]

This deterioration of congressional-executive Republican relations was striking given the administration's avowed strategy to consider the House Republicans its base. But it should have been no surprise. In the first Cabinet meeting of 1975, the president's political advisers stated that the administration's strategy was to be based on the president's concept of "floating coalitions"—support would be built on an issue-by-issue basis. The advisers warned that "we must be willing to move to the Democratic side of the aisle to get support; in fact we must be willing to move to the center and even perhaps slightly left of center to draw the Democratic votes necessary."[27] Like Eisenhower, Ford chose not to penalize party members for failure to adhere to the administration's fiscal agenda. Given the allure of Keynesian solutions in the fiscal state, this final piece of strategy was a virtual invitation for Republicans to defect in a recessionary environment.

Other Remedies to Recession

UNEMPLOYMENT INSURANCE

Extending unemployment insurance coverage is perhaps the most consistent response to recession in the postwar period. This is not surprising. Individuals who need help are clearly identifiable, areas with espe-

[26] Memo to the Economic Policy Board from William F. Gorog, "Administration Job Creation Initiatives," [n.d., ca. January 1976], Unemployment—Esch-Kemp Bill, Seidman, Box 109, GRFL. Kemp's remarks are as paraphrased by Gorog. Sen. William Brock voiced similar complaints about eroding the party's "philosophical consistency" in early 1975 (Memo to Jack March from William T. Kendall through Max L. Friedersdorf, "Senator Brock's Speech . . ." February 14, 1975, Congressional Relations, Memoranda, 1–2/75, Kendall, Box 12, GRFL).

[27] Moderate Republicans in the House supported this approach as early as December 1974 (Memo to the President from Ken Cole, "Report on Meeting with Republican House Members . . ." December 19, 1974, Cole, Kenneth (3), Seidman, Box 175, GRFL). See also Reichley (1981: 325–27, 332–36). Overall, Ford's relationship with Congress is assessed positively by both participants and scholars.

cially high unemployment are easily targeted, the additional aid is temporary in nature, and refusing to extend aid would register with many voters as a lack of empathy that would be difficult to explain. Ford first proposed extending unemployment insurance in his October 1974 speech, but Congress did not act until December, when it approved a two-part program. First, in the regular, permanent program—the program for all workers who qualified for unemployment coverage—Congress added another thirteen weeks of coverage, as Ford had suggested.[28] Second, a special, temporary program was established to provide up to twenty-six weeks of federally funded assistance for twelve million workers who fell outside the unemployment insurance system, especially farm and domestic workers and state and local employees. With some revisions, both programs were extended into 1977 with overwhelming bipartisan and presidential support.

HOUSING

By the time of Gerald Ford's October 8, 1974, inflation address, Congress had already acted with the assistance of the Nixon administration to increase the availability of home mortgages. Ford's October proposal to aid the housing industry called for an emergency one-year program that allowed the federal government to purchase conventional mortgages and government-insured mortgages from banks. With $3 billion available for such purposes, the intent was to free private funds for more mortgage loans. Dispute over the measure was negligible; it sailed through Congress in one week. In 1975, after Ford vetoed a Democratic bill that provided mortgage interest rate subsidies for new home purchases, Congress passed a second bill that extended the 1974 mortgage purchase program through mid-1976 (as Republicans favored) and provided some help for the unemployed facing foreclosures (H.R. 5398). On July 2, the president signed the bill, but the administration sat on the appropriated funds until January.

TAX CUT EXTENSION

Toward the end of 1975, congressional Republicans had become frustrated with the administration's approach to the recession. First, they complained that the Republican strategy was too executive-driven. Second, they feared that the Republican program appeared to voters as a string of negatives, of presidential vetoes, rather than a positive statement. These sentiments reemerged regarding the question about whether and how to

---

[28] Congress later added additional weeks.

extend the tax cuts enacted earlier in 1975 that were due to expire at the end of the year. Ford's staff handled the first problem by ensuring that congressional Republicans were kept informed.[29] The second problem was handled with a simple but politically attractive plan: The president would not extend tax cuts unless Congress agreed to a cap on spending.[30]

Although Democrats had been working out the details of a tax cut extension, Ford recognized that his action shifted the initiative to the administration.[31] On October 6, Ford proposed $27.7 billion in permanent tax cuts with $20.7 billion going to low- and middle-income individuals and the remainder to business. Ford also pledged to veto the cuts unless they were accompanied by a commitment to keep spending for the upcoming fiscal year below $395 billion (which was $28 billion below current budget projections). Democrats complained that Ford was disrupting the newly revised congressional budget procedure inaugurated by the Congressional Budget and Impoundment Control Act of 1974. Republicans on Capitol Hill were pleased. Barber Conable declared it "a bold grasp for presidential initiative where there hasn't been any" (CQA 1975: 135).

In mid-December, Democrats in both chambers, with some Republican support, passed a six-month tax cut extension by voice vote. Democrats argued that commitments to cut spending could be part of the new budget process in the first half of 1976. But Ford vetoed the bill the same day it was passed because of the omission of a commitment to keep spending below $395 billion in fiscal 1977. After failing to override, Democratic leaders in the House and Senate came up with a compromise package that cut taxes $8.4 billion ($7.4 billion to individuals) over six months and pledged to restrain fiscal year 1977 spending if the tax cuts were extended beyond June. Both chambers overwhelmingly passed the bill on December 19, and the president signed the tax cut extension four days later. Ford had to accede to the lack of a firm ceiling; congressional Democrats had to abandon the idea that they could extend the tax cuts past June without some kind of offset.[32]

[29] Memo to the President from Jack Marsh, October 6, 1975, Taxes—Tax Cuts/Spending Limitation Proposal 10/75–12/75, Marsh, Box 32, GRFL.

[30] Treasury Secretary Simon first suggested this kind of link in mid-1975 when he argued that the administration should cut a deal that had the administration accept the Democratic projections for the deficit for fiscal year 1976 if the Budget Committees would guarantee that spending be kept below their own $367 billion figure (Minutes of the Economic Policy Board Executive Committee Meeting, May 23, 1975, E.P.B. Meeting Minutes, May 21–31, 1975, Seidman, Box 21, GRFL).

[31] In a Cabinet meeting on October 8, Ford and his major economic advisers stressed the significance of not wavering on the proposed plan and of staying on the offensive rather than being reactive to Congress ("Cabinet Meeting, October 8th, 1975," 1975/10/08 Cabinet Meeting, James E. Connor, Box 5, GRFL).

[32] Ford was prepared to continue withholding at its current (1975) levels for sixty days without an agreement (W. F. Gorog, "Senate Tax Cut / Spending Limit Strategy," December 12, 1975, Taxes—Tax Cuts, 1975 (2), Seidman, Box 105, GRFL).

FEDERAL RESERVE RESTRUCTURING

One proposed structural reform of the fiscal state framework was designed to bring the Federal Reserve System under tighter congressional control. Proposed by House Banking Committee chair Henry S. Reuss (D-Wisconsin), H.R. 3160 stipulated that Congress would direct Fed policies on interest rates, the money supply, and credit allocation. Seven Democrats joined thirteen Republicans to defeat the measure in committee, 19 to 20. The administration strongly opposed the measure and there was no apparent support from Democratic leaders. A nonbinding resolution passed with overwhelming support by both parties. This resolution suggested the Fed pursue lower interest rates and looser monetary control and required the Fed chairman to attend two hearings per year on the Fed's upcoming plans. The Economic Policy Board saw this as a "near-optimum resolution of what started out as a very dangerous threat."[33]

The Recession of 1980

The 1980 recession was widely anticipated—in 1979. Instead, 1979 was a year dominated by inflation, especially following the second oil price shock administered by the Organization of Petroleum Exporting Countries. But the widely held view that recession was just around the corner created a historically unique situation where recession cures were part of the popular political dialogue well before the actual onset of recession. Slower growth than in 1978—though not yet contraction—confirmed the worst expectations of many observers. Despite the decline in growth, consumer price inflation accelerated to an 11.3 percent annualized rate. In this context, traditional Keynesian nostrums were less useful than in the past. Slowing down growth to cool inflation had not worked in 1979. Unless one was willing to abandon fine tuning for economic shock therapy through a deep, lasting recession, some other solution was necessary (Woolcock 1984).

Congressional Republicans attempted to fashion some alternative approach to economic management, some way to deal with simultaneous inflation and unemployment. They focused particularly on restoring economic incentives, encouraging investment and capital formation, and boosting a weak rate of productivity improvement.[34] Big government,

[33] Meeting Minutes of the Economic Policy Board Executive Committee, April 2, 1975, E.P.B. Meeting Minutes, April 1–8, 1975, Seidman, Box 21, GRFL.

[34] "This commitment [to new ideas for creating jobs and growth] is not based on one specific bill, but on the entire concept of restoring incentives in areas where they have all but been destroyed" (Rep. Jack Kemp, in "Governing Team Day," Republican National Committee Library, files).

they believed, had thwarted each of these keys to low-inflation growth. Old ideas were put to new uses. Tax cuts, for example, would stimulate growth *and* dampen inflation. Productivity and capital formation were always important, but now they were central to macroeconomic analysis.

Jimmy Carter found it difficult to look beyond the standard solutions (Hargrove 1988: 70–71). Responding to the Republican pressure and discontent among Democrats, Carter's economic advisers told him in late 1979 that he had two options for budget and economic policy in 1980.[35] The first option was to maintain the current policy posture, offering no major new initiatives except perhaps a youth employment program. A fiscal year 1981 budget deficit of $14 to 16 billion was forecast. The second option was to keep the current policy and add a "modest package" that would deal with long-term productivity improvement and control of inflation. Suggestions here included liberalization of depreciation for tax purposes, possible incentives for savings, and a youth employment and education program, among others. Under this scenario, the projected deficit was $21 to 23 billion. If Carter chose the second path, he could form a long-term program for productivity improvement and inflation control by packaging research and development and productivity-related spending already in the base budget with the new initiatives.[36]

Carter's advisers recommended the second option. There was no reason to wait until the necessity of a stimulus package became clear, they argued, because these were not stimulus ideas in the traditional Keynesian manner. The budget would still be tight despite anticipated increases in

[35] The Economic Policy Group (EPG) was the Carter version of Ford's EPB. Unlike EPB, however, it was never clear whether EPG was intended to be an analytical center or a coordinator of economic policy. The group started out very large but eventually a more manageable Steering Committee was developed. Carter asked Stuart Eizenstat, the head of his Domestic Affairs and Policy Staff (DPS), to monitor the EPG, but the connections between the EPG and the president remained ambiguous: "No one seemed to be in charge and people were going in different directions. Everyone felt powerless. When Alfred Kahn, head of the Council on Wage and Price Stability, tried to resign in the Summer of 1979 and was dissuaded by the president, he told [Charles] Schultze [chair of the Council of Economic Advisers] that he considered himself a fifth wheel; Schultze responded, No, I am. And Eizenstat amazed Kahn by saying that he did not feel in on final economic policy decisions either" (Hargrove 1988: 75–76).

[36] Memo to the President from Bill Miller, Stuart Eizenstat, Fred Kahn, and Charlie Schultze, "Final Options on the Budget and Economic Policy," December 20, 1979, White House Central Files (hereafter WHCF), Subject FG-104, FG12 7/1/79–12/31/79, Jimmy Carter Presidential Library (hereafter JCL). Alfred Kahn, chairman of the Council on Wage and Price Stability, was suggesting as far back as April 1979 that the administration had to consider the possibility that fiscal measures to control inflation were severely limited and that new solutions needed to be pursued—especially a focus on productivity. He expressed concern that recommendations to the president were "excessively sanitized" (Memo to the Vice President, W. Michael Blumenthal, Charles L. Schultze, James T. McIntyre, and Stuart Eizenstat from Alfred Kahn, "Attached Memo on Inflation Strategy," May 17, 1979, WHCF, BE-16, BE4–2 8/18/78–1/20/81, JCL).

unemployment. If he did not act, Congress would, and he would have to defend a "do-nothing" posture during the primaries and general election. Republicans, they reported, had taken the initiative away from the Democrats and were forging a bipartisan congressional consensus on the importance of incentives and productivity. But doing something traditionally considered inflationary as a means to *decrease* inflation and increase growth, in an environment of already high inflation, was a risk Carter was not prepared to take. With no official recession underway, it made sense in his view to administer the established medicine for curbing inflation. Last-minute appeals from Charles Schultze and Stuart Eizenstat were unsuccessful.[37]

Budgetary Restraint to Fight Inflation

Things were bad in 1979. They got worse in early 1980. By the end of February, both Carter and Federal Reserve chairman Paul Volcker were speaking of economic crisis. Political talk in Washington centered around the symbolic importance of a balanced budget and the—it was hoped—favorable impact such a move would have on public and financial market expectations (White and Wildavsky 1989: 29–30). With the economy slowing, the administration discouraged Democrats in Congress from pushing strong fiscal policy. Treasury Secretary Miller warned the Joint Economic Committee that "If we should at this point introduce a more stimulative fiscal policy, and we are wrong about the recession and the resilience of the economy is demonstrated once again, what we will have done is add to inflationary forces and we will see them showing up again in the economy and we will have many years where we will be set back a long way in our effort to starve out inflation. On the other hand, if we are more restrained and it turns out the economy deteriorates, we can move quickly to respond, and we would be prepared to move quickly to respond in some counteraction" (United States Congress, Joint Economic Committee 1980: 57).

[37] For Eizenstat, see Memo to the Economic Policy Group Executive Committee from Stuart Eizenstat, "Tax Proposals: Accelerated Depreciation," December 13, 1979, WHCF, FG-95, FG6–18, 1/20/77–1/20/81; Memo to the President from Stuart Eizenstat, December 22, 1979, WHCF, FI-11, FI4 12/1/79–12/31/79; and Memo to the President from Stu Eizenstat, December 26, 1979 (Lane Kirkland letter to President attached), WHCF, FI-11, FI4 1/1/80–1/31/80, JCL. As the head of the Domestic Policy Staff, Eizenstat played a key role in the transfer of information to the president. Along with Vice President Walter Mondale, Eizenstat was the most attentive of Carter's advisers to the major interest group supporters of the Democratic party and was a focal point for those in the administration frustrated with administration policy (Hargrove 1988: 43, 81; Campbell 1986: chs. 5–6; Thompson 1991). For Schultze, see Memo to the President from Charlie Schultze, "Final Budget Decision," December 22, 1979, WHCF, FI-11, FI4 12/1/79–12/31/79.

Congress did not receive this message—wait now and ask questions later—enthusiastically.[38] Members of the Joint Economic Committee told the administration's senior economic advisers that current economic policy did not promote productivity, growth, or business investment. Administration officials consistently brought the issue back to restrained budgets as a sign of seriousness on inflation. Schultze insisted that some steps were being taken on the supply side; the focus was not only demand restraint. And from Fed chairman Paul Volcker, the committee heard that doing almost anything now about depreciation, capital formation, and the like would encourage deficits and inflation. To Sen. Lloyd Bentsen (D-Texas), however, this view meant that "we are playing the thing like they did in 1974. That obviously wasn't successful" (United States Congress, Joint Economic Committee 1980: 103).

Unemployment for the first three months of 1980 was about half a point higher than in the second half of 1979, but it was stable. Inflation, by contrast, was increasing at about 1.3 percent per month. Despite the economic recession, the administration's attention remained largely on inflation. Budget restraint was not moderating inflation. Carter's advisers and staff urged him to be on the offensive promoting his policies, a public education role for which Carter evinced little enthusiasm. As some members of Congress grappled to find an alternative model to understand the economic problems, Carter held that the cure for unsuccessful Keynesianism was more Keynesianism. If budget restraint was not defusing inflation, more restraint was in order. Over the latter part of February and the early part of March, the administration refashioned its economic policy to produce a balanced budget via spending cuts. To lessen internecine interest group fighting among Democratic constituents, Eizenstat unsuccessfully recommended an across-the-board budget cut of 3 to 4 percent.[39]

In putting together the March version of the anti-inflation plan, Carter's staff had what was probably its most extensive and productive contact with rank-and-file and leadership Democrats, particularly the latter (Carter 1982: 527, 529; White and Wildavsky 1989: 31–34; Jones 1988: 195; Sinclair 1983: 181; Hargrove and Morley 1984: 493; Ferguson and Rogers 1981: 34–37). The program announced on March 14 consisted of

[38] Carter's difficulties with Congress are well known. Scholars give high grades to Ford and his congressional liaison but grant the Carter effort at best a low pass (Davis 1983: 64–66; Jones 1983: 117–21; cf. Ranney 1983, and McCleskey and McCleskey 1984; Jones 1988: chs. 4–5). Jones (1988) argues that Carter's interaction with Congress improved during his term; unfortunately, the policy problems became continually more difficult. Despite the generally negative assessments (from within the White House also), Yarbrough (1984: 165) and Jones (1988: 206) note that Carter's legislative success rate was in fact as good as or better than Lyndon Johnson's, a president often praised for his legislative skills.

[39] Memo to the President from Stuart Eizenstat, "Anti-Inflation Program," March 6, 1980, WHCF, BE-20, BE4-2 3/1/80–3/31/80, JCL.

a balanced budget; restraints on consumer credit, money market funds, and the liabilities of banks outside the Federal Reserve system through the provisions of the Credit Control Act of 1969; enhancement of the voluntary wage-price guidelines; energy conservation to reduce the impact of oil price shocks (largely through an oil import fee); and "structural" reforms to promote productivity, savings, and research and development.[40] The chief budgetary actions were reductions or cancellations of most of the new spending proposed in the earlier January budget and rescissions and deferrals of spending in a wide range of existing programs. Revised revenue and spending figures put the budget at anywhere from balanced to about $12 billion in surplus. "Structural" changes consisted of a call for deregulation of selected industries and an announced intention to seek productivity-enhancing tax cuts some time in the future.

The House Budget Committee passed a budget resolution that looked essentially like Carter's revised budget except for an explicit $10 billion business tax cut to enhance productivity (Sinclair 1983: 182–90). The Senate version of the budget resolution increased defense spending, cut domestic spending, and kept the same revenue as the House plan. When the Senate refused to change its position on defense spending, Democrats in the House, with the support of Carter and Speaker Thomas P. O'Neill— but not other Democratic leaders—rejected the conference compromise and sent the bill back to conference. Republicans voted against the compromise as well. After a second conference in which domestic spending was increased by less than $1 billion, both the Senate and the House approved the compromise on June 12. Democrats in both houses supported the measure; Republicans in the House voted overwhelmingly against the package, Republican senators split about evenly.

The approval of a purportedly balanced budget was no small achievement, and the administration was especially pleased that congressional Democrats proved willing to use the reconciliation procedures in the 1974 budget act to implement the plan. Under the reconciliation procedures, the Budget Committee directed the authorizations committees to compile about $8 billion in cuts and Ways and Means to come up with extra revenue. The whole set of proposals was voted on in a single no-amendment package (Sundquist 1981: 229–30). In other words, this procedure "reconciled" the spending approved by the authorizing committees with the spending limits approved by the Budget Committee. Carter was the key

[40] Memo to the President from G. William Miller, "Intensified Anti-Inflation Program," March 12, 1980, Counsel's Office, Cutler, 80, Inflation 3.12–31/80, JCL. Carter rejected balancing the budget by revising the automatic cost-of-living adjustments in entitlement programs or instituting a 1 percent across-the-board cut in these programs. He also rejected any kind of overall spending limitation or freeze. Finally, he declined to raise revenues through increasing tobacco and alcohol taxes, placing a surtax on upper income earners or corporations, or increasing the collections staff at the Internal Revenue Service.

here; had he not consulted extensively with members of Congress before his March address and kept firm on budget restraint through the spring, there would probably have been less commitment in Congress to using the new and controversial procedures.

Defusing the Recession

I am tempted to report of the 1980 anti-recession effort what historian Forrest McDonald wrote of early New Hampshire political history: "Not much happened" (1965: 117). "Not much got accomplished" might be a better summary. The sequence of response was unique: As I mentioned above, anti-recession talk was in the air in 1979; all that was missing was a recession. Members of Congress attached some ideas—such as anti-recession public works—to legislation in 1979. Nonetheless, although the recession arrived in January, it did not become the center of political attention until May or June. On May 28, Carter for the first time used the recession as a significant tool in his dealing with Congress. Urging defeat of the conference committee report on the first budget resolution because of its tilt toward defense spending and away from domestic spending, Carter noted that the country could not afford to let the recession get out of hand by further cutting programs that aid people in economic downturns (*CQA* 1980: 118). By that time, the decline in growth and employment was dramatic. The economy experienced its sharpest one-quarter GNP drop since the Great Depression. Leading indicators in April showed the greatest drop in their thirty-two-year Commerce Department history (White and Wildavsky 1989: 50–51). Yet, inflation was always of equal concern. In 1974–1975, politicians of both parties focused their attentions predominantly on recession despite high inflation. 1980 was different. The standard anti-recession devices kindled little enthusiasm. For politicians in 1980, recession politics as normally understood provided precious little political capital.[41]

TAXES

In this context, attention turned to tax cuts, particularly tax cuts that could be packaged as both anti-recession and anti-inflation. Some discussion of tax cuts had emerged during the debates over the budget resolutions. The question in these debates was whether to allow room in the budget plan for a tax cut in fiscal 1981. Although there was no need to

[41] My discussion is limited to new initiatives that are reasonably clearly designed to combat recession. For example, CETA public service jobs were reauthorized in 1980 at the same level as 1979, but these jobs would have existed regardless of the recession. Therefore, while voting on this reauthorization was undoubtedly affected by the recession, it is relatively difficult to talk about such a reauthorization as a new anti-recession response.

be specific about the actual shape of the tax cuts in the budget resolution, discussion centered mostly around business tax cuts that would allegedly increase productivity, decrease inflation, and decrease unemployment through increased business purchases of capital and other equipment. Senator Bentsen and Rep. James Jones (D-Oklahoma), a member of the Budget Committee and the Ways and Means Committee, were the most prominent Democrats calling for tax cuts. Many voices were heard on the Republican side. These included Barber Conable's introduction (along with Jones) of the 10–5–3 accelerated depreciation plan and the Kemp-Roth individual tax cut, which called for a 30 percent reduction in individual tax rates over a three-year period. In late February, Bentsen (as the chair) convinced the Joint Economic Committee to endorse his idea of a $25 billion business tax cut to improve long-term productivity. Most of the proposals in early 1980 had been circulating since tax politics took a more conservative turn in 1978 (Witte 1985: ch. 10). However, they took on a new urgency in the economic conditions of 1980, and their claims to boost growth became more attractive as unemployment rose.

A striking difference between the tax proposals of 1980 and those of the other recessions is that no one was talking about immediate tax cuts to boost the economy in 1980. With the underlying concern about inflation and with the existing deficit for fiscal 1980 expected to be about $60 billion, members of both parties saw little room for tax cuts, and Carter had been adamant that the deficit had to be controlled.

Because tight money was not likely to abate soon, Miller suggested to Carter on June 16 that he might want to begin thinking about tax cuts for fiscal year 1981.[42] Republican presidential nominee Ronald Reagan, warning against what "could well become the worst recession in half a century" (*CQA* 1980: 296), announced on June 25 his support of a 10 percent personal income tax rate cut for 1981 and the first phase of an accelerated depreciation plan for business. Most Republicans in the House and Senate enthusiastically supported the $22.3 billion cut. Moderate and liberal Republicans who feared the deficit implications of the three-year Kemp-Roth plan found the one-year Reagan plan palatable. The following day, Senate Democrats directed the Senate Finance Committee to report a tax cut bill by September 3 and formed a Senate Democratic Task Force on the Economy to develop a "comprehensive" economic policy. One staffer summed up the situation this way: "Right now, the economy-tax cut scene is chaotic, Democrats are going in all directions, and the President is behind the curve."[43]

[42] Memo to the President from G. William Miller, "Budget Review Session," June 16, 1980, SE 192, Economic Program [FCF, O/A 727] [1], JCL.

[43] Memo to Anne Wexler from Al From, "A Democratic Economic Strategy," July 10, 1980, SE 286, Tax Cut Proposal [CF, O/A 731], JCL.

The Finance Committee announced its plan on August 21. Gaining the support of committee Democrats and Republicans and candidate Reagan, the plan called for tax cuts of $39.4 billion in fiscal year 1981: $22 billion for individuals, $15 billion for business, and $2.4 billion for small business. The committee expected that the individual cuts would offset increases in Social Security taxes and inflation. The business cuts called for accelerated depreciation, tax rate reductions, research and development credits, and restructuring of the tax brackets.

Tax cuts got no further in 1980. Forced to respond by the Finance Committee action and the wide-ranging tax cut hearings in Ways and Means, and seeking the blessing of supporters of Sen. Edward M. Kennedy (D-Massachusetts), Carter reluctantly indicated on August 28 that in 1981 he would propose a tax cut of $27.6 billion. But Carter thought that cutting taxes was the wrong thing to do economically and his staff warned him that changing direction on taxes could create severe political difficulties with important allies like labor.[44] Party leaders and the rank-and-file in the House supported Carter's view that inflation and spending should be brought under control before tax cuts were enacted.[45] O'Neill announced as early as June 27—two days after the Reagan announcement—that he saw no way to complete action on a tax bill in 1980. Following the election, which transferred the presidency and the Senate to the Republicans and weakened the Democratic position in the House, the interest in enacting tax legislation waned in both parties. O'Neill made the obvious official when he announced that Carter promised him he would veto any postelection tax cut (*CQA* 1980: 298).

[44] Memo to the President from Stuart Eizenstat, [n.d.], Economic Policy, SE 192, Economic Program [CF, O/A 727] [1], JCL. See also, Memo to the President from the Economic Policy Group Steering Committee, "Economic Program for the 1980s," August 21, 1980, Counsel's Offices, Cutler 72, Economy, 11/79–8/80, JCL; Memo to the President from Stuart Eizenstat, "Economic Program," August 23, 1980, SE 192, Economic Program [CF, O/A 727] [1], JCL; Memo to G. William Miller from Al McDonald, "Plan/Timetable for Preparing Economic Positions," July 9, 1980, WHCF, FG-104, FG12 1/1/80–8/31/80; and Memo to Stuart Eizenstat from Anne Wexler and Al From, "Congressional Support for the President's Economic Program," August 19, 1980, SE 192, Economic Program [CF, O/A 727] [1], JCL. Schultze and the other major economic advisers thought Carter should act quickly, if only to have something positive to run on. As in 1979, they were overruled (Hargrove and Morley 1984: 495).

[45] One member of the legislative liaison staff reported that Ways and Means Democrats generally favored the cautious Carter approach, "But they are not firm. If a stampede develops, most will join it rather than be run over by it" (Memo to Frank Moore from Jeff Peterson, "Tax Cut Sentiment," July 24, 1980, SE 286, Tax Cut Proposal [CF, O/A 731], JCL). On testimony before Ways and Means, see Memo to Gene Godley et al. from Jeff Peterson, "House Members Testimony on Tax Cut," July 24, 1980, SE 286, Tax Cut Proposal [CF, O/A 731], JCL.

UNEMPLOYMENT COMPENSATION

Perhaps no other policy area better indicates the unusual nature of the anti-recession politics of 1980 than unemployment compensation. Given markedly different economic conditions and an officially much shorter recession than in 1957–1958 and 1974–1975, Congress failed to push through President Carter's request for additional unemployment insurance. In an economic revitalization address on August 28, Carter called for federally funded supplemental unemployment benefits for the long-term unemployed. On September 30, the House passed the president's request by a 336 to 71 vote (100–50 Republican, 236–21 Democratic), providing ten additional weeks for those who had exhausted their thirty-nine weeks of eligibility. In the Senate, the proposal got tangled up with reforms of the regular unemployment compensation and extended benefits programs. The Senate also added restrictions at the behest of Republicans that prevented supplemental benefits from going to workers who refused to accept new work, who were fired, or who quit their positions. Democrats added a lower trigger to allow the program to kick in earlier. The Senate approved the bill by voice vote, but with the two bills so far apart, a conference meeting was never held.

COUNTERCYCLICAL AID

Introduced during the 1974–1975 recession, countercyclical aid reemerged in 1980. This time, the proposal consisted of two parts: countercyclical aid to assist states and localities facing serious revenue shortages because of the recession, and targeted fiscal assistance to aid local communities that were in some measure still suffering the effects of the 1974–1975 recession. The White House argued that these twin programs were better than other anti-recession ideas, that the president could resist other costly anti-recession measures if he had these programs, and that the president would be in grave trouble in urban areas without the package because, as things stood, targeted fiscal assistance would be the only additional money spent during the primary season.[46] Although the House authorized $1 billion for a joint aid and assistance program, the ongoing state-federal revenue sharing program eventually sidetracked countercyclical aid. Revenue sharing had some political advantages over countercyclical assistance; it spread resources to more state governments and it did not have triggers to shut the aid off if the economy sufficiently improved.

[46] Memo to Stu Eizenstat and Jim McIntyre from Ralph Schlosstein, "Meeting with Congressman Jack Brooks on Counter-Cyclical Aid," November 13, 1979, SE 177, Counter-Cyclical [CF, O/A 727], JCL.

HOUSING

Stimulation of housing construction or housing purchases was a feature of all three recession periods discussed in this chapter. In 1980, this standard response was part of the reauthorization of housing programs. Under the rubric of the Section 235 Homeownership Assistance Program, Congress allowed more-affluent families to qualify for 75 percent of the $165 million in funds already appropriated for subsidized loans to low-income families. Proponents argued that including middle-class families in the program would accelerate the expenditure of already appropriated funds. The bill also authorized activation of a temporary program of payments to assist possible defaulters. Although other facets of the bill caused some conflict, debate on these provisions was essentially nonexistent. Carter signed the bill on October 8.

PUBLIC WORKS

The major public works proposal to deal with the recession came in a bill to fund the Economic Development Administration (EDA). In 1979, Carter had asked Congress to expand significantly the lending power of the EDA (to fund public works, business loans, educational assistance, and so on, in areas facing continuing economic distress). Both the House and Senate approved Carter's proposal late in 1979, but the House version of the bill contained a $2 billion anti-recession public works provision that would become effective if the unemployment rate exceeded 6.5 percent. The White House agreed with Republicans that the program cost too much and would not promote quick growth. With unemployment growing, Carter agreed in the summer of 1980 to a trimmed-down public works plan in order to move the bill, but Senate Democrats rejected Carter's concession. Just before the election, the major public works advocate in the House relented and the public works plan was scratched from the EDA bill.

Tendencies in Responding to Recession

Policies

Examination of these three recessions shows that there are no policies that are distinctively Democratic or Republican. Democrats are not alone when arguing for public sector jobs; Republicans and Democrats both call for tax cuts. Both parties demonstrated a willingness to choose from and support the entire array of anti-recession proposals at various times. To voters, this convergence over generalities is likely more notable than divergence over specifics. Add the intraparty conflict evidenced by Senate-House and presidential-congressional maneuvering, and distinctive "party" positions become even more difficult for voters to ascertain.

There are, however, different partisan proclivities. Democrats generally were willing to run larger deficits to stimulate the economy, although this bias nearly evaporates in 1980.[47] One way this difference is reflected is in the ongoing battle over triggers and targets. Indeed, these battles over scope—When does a program activate and whom does it benefit?—are a constant in anti-recession politics. As a rule, Democrats preferred lower triggers and widely targeted audiences while Republicans took the opposite tack. Democrats proved marginally more interested in public jobs and public works, although only in 1974–1975 was much accomplished in this direction. Republicans placed a much stronger emphasis on the automatic healing effects of the unemployment compensation system. There are, especially, differences over detail even when both parties agree on the need for a particular policy response. One would be hard-pressed to argue there is no party conflict: I have noted that party differences do not disappear entirely during economic stress, however it would be difficult in most instances to see the differences over detail as fundamentally different economic tools.

What are the policy responses? Across the three recessions, the policies that are considered are fairly consistent. There is little discussion of welfare or other transfer payments; most of these, of course, are working automatically. There is not much serious discussion of sector-specific solutions, even as the decline is generally acknowledged to be more severe in some industries than others, reflecting the arm's-length bias of fiscal state economic management.[48] There is little said of structural changes in the fiscal, monetary, or budgetary policy processes.[49] Instead, acceleration of spending, unemployment insurance extension, housing assistance, tax cuts, public works, and public jobs constitute the bulk of the proposals.

[47] This is consistent with work that suggests that partisan control of government leads to different economic outcomes (*if* we can assume that different policies produce these different results). The seminal statement here is Hibbs (1977). Although this research tends to rely heavily on the party of the president, research on congressional parties also indicates that appropriations decisions are influenced by economic conditions and party majority (Cox and McCubbins 1993).

[48] In both 1975 and 1980 there was discussion, and some action, encouraging the government to speed up its purchases of automobiles manufactured in the United States, but there was no pretense that these were stimulus programs on the order of magnitude of the housing assistance programs.

[49] The 1974 Budget Act certainly grew out of frustrations related to economic conditions—inflation provided President Nixon a pretext for widespread impoundment of congressionally appropriated funds—but it did not emerge as a result of the recession.

(Monetary policy is discussed below.) The most contentious debate occurs in the latter three areas.

Deeper economic decline makes adoption of these policies more likely. Comparing the response of the Eisenhower and Ford administrations demonstrates this point. Ideologically, these two Republican presidents were centrists or moderates in their own party. Given that the center of gravity in the Republican party had shifted slightly leftward in the years before the mid-1970s (Rae 1989; Reichley 1981), a Ford stance more accommodative to stimulation is not improbable. But in their rhetoric and economic commitments these presidents were more alike than different. Once they began acknowledging the recession, each made it clear that he would support stimulation of the economy parallel in scope to the depth and length of that decline. Eisenhower, in a relatively short recession, could adopt modest steps. Ford, in a more protracted decline, could adopt bolder steps. Ford also appeared interested in using public jobs as a tool to defuse opposition to his early focus on inflation.[50]

In each period, parties assemble policy "programs" to deal with recession. As a rule, no matter what the party or branch of government, these programs consist of a wide variety of stitched-together pieces of legislation consisting of both the new and the old that are a "program" only ex post facto. 1980 provides the closest instance to an exception to this rule: The Republican "program" was indeed stitched together of old elements, but these elements were narrowly focused on taxation. Carter's broad March and August programs were more in the traditional vein. For voters, these various programs were notable because they signaled which actors appeared to be responding actively to economic conditions.

Molehills into Mountains

Another notable tendency in the response to recession is the lag between the onset of the recession and any action designed to ameliorate the recession's effects. Even in 1980, when a recession had been widely anticipated through much of 1979, there was no extended discussion of the problems of the recession itself (as opposed to inflation) until midyear. The response was delayed in the other two cases as well. The lateness of the response provides credence for the argument that actions taken are likely to be procyclical rather than countercyclical in impact, thus accentuating rather than offsetting the problems in the business cycle. This argument assumes that the government will do a markedly better job pre-

[50] Table 5.1 indicates that when Ford first accepted public jobs proposals, in October 1974, the Democratic margin in Congress was not strikingly different from that faced by Eisenhower.

dicting the end of a recession than it did predicting its beginning. Based on these three cases, such an assumption seems reasonable; each administration's internal projection, specifically the projection of the Council of Economic Advisers, was accurate in predicting the business cycle trough. But the lingering effect of many of a recession's features, notably unemployment, can justify some relatively "late" action.

Part of the reason for the response delay is the imprecise nature of economic forecasting and economic knowledge. In all three of these recessions, officials were surprised by the extent or rapidity of the decline, whether measured by employment, growth, or production. The presidents were cautious also because each feared the consequence of jittery public confidence. Eisenhower, in particular, was inclined to understate the seriousness of the situation. As he learned, however, such caution can also lead to shaky public confidence about the president's understanding of the problem when economic figures do not show the improvement the president insists is just around the corner. Finally, this delay results from the strong influence official unemployment rates played in conceptions of when recession "really" starts. In each case, politicians tolerated decline for months—until the official unemployment rate began to show significant increases. Keynesianism's conservative formulation in the United States created this overemphasis on unemployment figures compared to other indicators of decline.[51]

Institutional Relations

One effect of this delay is that the nonpresidential party in Congress, whether minority (1980) or majority (1957–1958, 1974–1975), initiated the response to recession.[52] The reluctance of the president to act precipitously and the reluctance of the presidential party in Congress to rebuke its president leads to an initially passive approach by the presidential party. Once anti-recession activity is underway, the source of initiatives is more balanced. This balance results from an effort by the president and the presidential party to control the situation and minimize the political damage, and by the desire of the opposition party in Congress to put the

[51] Official unemployment statistics, as is well known, mask as well as reveal important economic trends. The masking is possible because the official rate excludes those who have given up trying to find employment and excludes those who are underemployed. It also does not measure the number of jobs lost during a recession or the likelihood of these jobs returning after the recession, although these figures may have more significant consequences for the economy.

[52] See Jones (1970) for a discussion of the options open to the minority legislative party. The strategic choices to be made are equally appropriate for a "majority" party facing a president of another party.

burden of leadership on the president. From the opponent's point of view, this sequence allows for criticism of the president's slow reaction and then, once he has been allowed to dominate the scene and respond, criticism that he proposes too little. To reverse the aphorism, too late and too little.

These changes in passivity and activity affect the relationship between the president and his party in Congress. Each recession goes through three broad phases where the congressional party embraces the president's view, then distances itself, then embraces the president's view again. This second embrace results from either improved economics (1957–1958, 1974–1975, partially 1980) or a sense that the other party will so fully appropriate the political gains from a given issue that it is best to fight to keep that issue off the agenda (partially 1957–1958 and 1974–1975, 1980).

Roll-call analysis shows that a classic Keynesian recession dampens, but does not eliminate, party distinctions across the aggregate of budget-related votes. What do the case studies, which focus on the major policy responses, suggest about this general finding?

While each case demonstrates some differences between the parties, the debate between the president and the nonpresidential party in Congress presents sharper party conflict than does the congressional party debate. Even on the major votes reviewed here, there are significant defections in the presidential party, particularly on votes of final passage. On occasion—most notably on taxes in 1958—the parties agree not to disagree on an important issue. And, as noted above, much of the debate that does go on within Congress revolves around triggers and targets rather than opposing policy prescriptions. This latter point is less true in 1980, where congressional Democrats tried at points to revive Keynesian-style policy prescriptions (usually with the tacit although unenthusiastic acceptance of the Carter administration). Republicans generally did not join in this effort, largely because they found it untenable to view 1980 as a classic recession amenable to Keynesian methods.

It is possible that the public may perceive more debate than the party conflict indexes would suggest because of the salience of the president's opinion on key issues. But even this statement presumes that the public is attentive to differences of fiscal policy detail and vote accordingly. More importantly, this public perception that there are party differences mostly reinforces the image of the president as centrally responsible for economic policy. Voters believed that Ronald Reagan would be preferable in combatting both unemployment and inflation chiefly because he was not Jimmy Carter (Burnham 1981a). In voting for "something different," voters are not casting specific policy choices nor saying that one party always excels in defusing either inflation or unemployment. If unemployment increases dramatically during a Democratic administration, voters do not retain that administration under the notion that Democrats are a "better" party for dampening unemployment. The same holds true for Republicans and inflation. That the party of the president does over time correlate to economic conditions in predictable ways says more about the demands of specific, highly organized interests in each party rather than policy decisions made by the aggregate electorate. Voters are not policy loyalists. They hold the president accountable whether he has a majority following in Congress or not. Party is weakened in the process.

The case studies also indicate the importance of House-Senate differences in policy solutions. To voters, "the party" encompasses both bodies. During the 1980 recession, the Democratic attempt to inject some Keynesian anti-recession thinking into the policy mix foundered frequently because of House-Senate conflict. This tendency makes it that much more difficult for voters to discern contrasting congressional party positions.

Case Studies and the Fiscal State

What do these cases say about the components of the fiscal state? I take each component in turn.

LOCATION OF FISCAL POLICY IN THE EXECUTIVE BRANCH

I noted above that the out-party leads in combatting the recession. After this initial period, the president and his party become more active in defining the agenda, though they do not exclusively control that agenda. What is remarkable in all three of these cases, however, is the extent to which the views of the president set boundaries for subsequent policy outcomes. Presidents may complain about bills at the margins, but it is rare (at least in these three cases) for a policy to succeed that has strong presidential opposition. It remains the president, then, who will largely determine the nature, pace, and scope of policy response to the recession. Even Jimmy Carter, perceived by both scholars and public alike as one of the most besieged and unsuccessful presidents in recent history, controlled the response to the recession of 1980. Particularly after his first budget failed to defuse inflation, Carter led an extraordinary effort to push through a balanced (or surplus, with the oil import fee) budget. Later, Carter argued that the conference report on the budget resolution should be defeated because its defense funding was too generous. After the defeat, a new compromise was not significantly less accommodating to defense spending, but the Carter balanced-budget focus remained. Most significantly, Carter, like Eisenhower, successfully averted a tax cut—despite widespread views that such a cut was inevitable. Even if his view was not popular, Carter's unyielding posture on the tax cut issue convinced Congress to avoid bringing the issue to a vote. Initiatives to deal with the recession, such as countercyclical aid, unemployment compensation, and youth employment, were administration products. While the administration did not get what it wanted in these areas, in other areas it did not have to accept programs it opposed. That is, these cases suggest that an administration may not get everything it wants, but it generally can live with that which is done.

The Ford administration provides another example. Sundquist (1981: 218–22) argues that the Democrats in Congress used the new budget procedures to control and define the response to the recession. But this view results from too close a focus on the politics of the (then new) budget resolution process. It is undoubtedly true that the Democratic Congress approved a series of measures that provided more stimulus for the economy than Ford would have preferred. But Ford was equally able, through liaison and through use of the veto, to prevent policies that he deeply opposed and to refine those that he could accept. And it is worth remembering the conditions under which Ford was operating: an overwhelming Democratic majority in Congress, an unelected president who was unpopular for his pardoning of Richard Nixon, the most severe downturn since the Great Depression, and the aftermath of a major scandal. The real surprise is how little congressional Democrats controlled economic politics in 1975.

What these cases show is that presidential beliefs and ideas matter. Clearly, the cases show that the president does not have absolute control over policy initiation and development (Peterson 1990; Bond and Fleisher 1990). But each of these presidents had a fairly strong sense of what they wanted to focus on in economic policy. During the recessions, they maintained that focus and created the outer boundaries on acceptable solutions to the current economic problems. This argument again may seem most surprising for Carter, who has been widely (and justifiably) criticized for his policy lurches from stimulus to restraint and back again. But while the charge holds true for his term, during the recession of 1980, Carter's economic policy was consistently focused on restraint, and he defied both his advisers and Congress to pursue that course.

AUTOMATIC STABILIZERS TAKE AWAY POTENTIAL PARTY ISSUES

Automatic stabilizers in the form of transfer payments were not a major part of the policy discussion in any of these three recessions. Two automatic stabilizers were discussed frequently. Deliberations over unemployment compensation focused on extending the length of the benefits. Debates emerged over the specifics of targeting and triggering. Essentially, however, these were bipartisan policy changes. There is no evidence that either party tried to appropriate this issue as its alone during subsequent election campaigns. The other automatic stabilizer that received some discussion was revenue reduction. In 1958, the parties agreed not to disagree on discretionary tax cuts. In 1975, both parties agreed that additional tax action was in order, with the Democrats offering a larger cut that was somewhat more beneficial for the lower-income brackets than the Republican-initiated bill. In 1980, the parties had their most serious conflict over discretionary tax policy. Tax cuts were one area where automatic stabilizers, that is, automatic revenue reduction, did not eliminate the possibility of additional discretionary action. With the stabilizers safely in place, however, action toward short-term tax cuts trailed further behind rhetoric.

SPLIT CONTROL BETWEEN MONETARY AND FISCAL POLICY

The case studies do not dwell on monetary policy because most of what the parties are doing during these recessions does not dwell on monetary policy. In the 1957–1958 and 1974–1975 recessions, the Fed loosened monetary policy to spur recovery. In 1980, the Fed clamped down to discourage inflation. Although discussions between the president's economic advisers and the Fed chairman were common, evidence of specific bargaining or policy trade-offs is scarce (Hargrove and Morley 1984; Kettl 1986). None of the parties in these three recessions adopted any strong, consistent, public views on monetary policy that was a major part of their political arguments or that would be likely to resonate with the public. Complaints about the Fed were intermittent and scattershot.

With the exception of the Reuss bill in 1975, neither party contemplated or initiated serious structural changes of the Fed-Congress or Fed-president relationship in these three periods. The Reuss bill had minimal support among Democrats and no support from party leaders. Whether all this constitutes "fedbashing" or not—keeping the Fed independent so that both Congress and the president can use it as a scapegoat—is not material here. What is significant is that the parties control over monetary policy is comparatively less than that over fiscal policy, the public views things this way, and neither party seriously tried to change this split.

MACROECONOMIC GOALS ENCOURAGE PLEBISCITARY VOTING

All three of these recessions resulted in repudiation of the presidential party. In 1980, the repudiation was reflected in the defeat of Jimmy Carter. He had defeated Gerald Ford in 1976 by complaining about the sluggish growth of the Ford era. Eisenhower's vice president (Richard Nixon), of course, lost the 1960 presidential election. In Congress, the presidential party suffered losses of incumbent seats and open seats that were among the postwar highs in 1958, 1974, and 1980. Most scholarly research shows that these losses were largely performance-based and that macroeconomic conditions were a notable though not solitary contributor to the defeats. Members of Congress risk defeat if their president performs poorly. Voters will reach the president through Congress if necessary. Indeed, if voters were holding *Congress* accountable for economic conditions, it is rather odd that in the 1957–1958 and 1974–1975 recessions they punished not the *majority* party but rather the minority party of the president. The large Republican losses in the first two recessions and the Democratic losses in the last send one message: Do more, even if you do not control Congress. Given that both parties choose from the same portfolio of remedies with great regularity, the policy substance of this exhortation is not obvious.

KEYNESIANISM AS A CONSTRAINT

Recessions could be good for parties. Parties could emphasize their differences with their rivals not only in rhetoric but in action. They could lay out distinctive visions of state-society relations and some vision of the "good society." In the fiscal state, however, recessions do not help parties. Not only do the structural components just discussed create problems, so does Keynesianism itself. If the economy is working well, economic issues fall from public attention. If the economy is working poorly, the parties find themselves rushing to proffer rather similar solutions to the problems. The solutions to recession were chosen from a consistent range of alternatives that fit easily within a Keynesian understanding of economic problems.

As Keynesianism moved from accepted doctrine (1957–1958), to questioned doctrine (1974–1975), to contested doctrine (1980), the debate between the parties on the major policies appeared to heighten. Stated more conservatively, we see a distinction between the experiences of 1957–1958 and 1974–1975 on one hand and 1980 on the other. There is nothing surprising about the policies considered in 1957–1958 or 1974–1975. By 1980, politicians were having a difficult time describing the problem that faced them, let alone analyzing it and prescribing a cure. In 1980, most of the trusty standards of the past—even unemployment insurance—failed. Republicans began rushing off to greet supply-side economics and its pro-growth, anti-inflation, productivity-oriented tax cuts. Democrats were uncomfortably still holding hands with Keynes. Although he had little to tell them about their current dilemma, without his grip they were not quite sure where to go. If Keynesian understandings become less tenable, or if Keynesian problems are no longer the most pressing problems, parties have an opportunity to overcome a key constraint of the fiscal state. Both roll-call analysis and case studies suggest that this is precisely what began happening in the late 1970s.

Party revival in the 1980s would prove to be partial because the changes in the fiscal state were partial. The tendency toward convergence in fiscal policy was partially reversed as the declining utility of Keynesianism fostered intraparty cohesion and interparty conflict in Congress. Voters, however, were not yet sure that these ill-defined differences were relevant. The structural limits—president versus Congress, monetary versus fiscal policy, automatic stabilizers and uncontrollable spending, and plebiscitary voting—remained, as did the perceptions and behaviors these constraints encouraged among voters. In the short-run, voters dissatisfied with party performance faced the choice of exit, voice, or loyalty (Hirschman 1970). Many chose to exit from voting, from loyal partisanship, and from the belief that parties can matter. Party would become more salient to voters and nonvoters when they saw congressional parties controlling a policy area that was widely considered important and on which the parties had important differences.

6

Parties, Politics, and the Fiscal State

ERAS DEMARCATED by significant state-building episodes constitute party eras in American political development. The influence, appeal, and centrality of political parties depends heavily on the nature of the state and dominant policy concerns in a political era. State structures will by design or inadvertence affect the likelihood that in these party eras parties play a centrally important policy-making role and are perceived that way by voters and elites. Some policies are particularly well-suited to be the basis of strong parties, others encourage weak parties. For the postwar party era, the fiscal state defines the structural and political environment within which parties operated. A central force behind the decline of political parties, the fiscal state also provides insights needed to explain the partial resurgence of American parties. In this book, I follow the thread of the fiscal state through postwar American party politics, not to argue that nothing else influences that politics but to suggest that the nature of the state and its policy have a vital influence on the status of political parties.

The formation of the fiscal state in institutional and policy struggles from 1937 through 1946 had serious implications for the long-term position of the parties. Weaker parties were the result of conscious design, unexpected consequence, and an unfavorable policy issue. Keynesian beliefs made the House parties converge when unemployment or inflation was a solitary problem (Democrats became more cohesive, Republicans less), but the potential for party divergence increased when both inflation and unemployment occurred simultaneously. When the focus turns to regional party splits and differences between authorizations and appropriations, this finding still generally holds. Roll-call analysis shows that the relevant environment for understanding the fall and rise of parties in the House includes not just the political and institutional environments emphasized in other studies but also economics and the state. Those elements are also clear in the party response to three recessions. Looking at the development of Democratic and Republican anti-recession strategies and the sequence and nature of the response, I stress both the opportunities and limits that the recessions presented to the parties. Limits outweighed opportunities.

Throughout this book, the discussion has emphasized differences with other interpretations of American parties. The analysis is bolstered, however, by its consistency with other findings on American politics. As I indicate in chapter 1, scholars such as Fenno (1973), Lowi (1979) and McCormick (1986) explore the notion that some policies are more easily exploited by parties than others. Kelly (1994: 164) notes that retrospective voting models and other explanations of voter behavior rely implicitly on the notion that citizens' expectations of the state will change as the state changes, and these changed expectations produce changes in behavior. It would not make much sense for citizens to vote retrospectively in most versions of that model unless they assigned economic responsibility to the president. These points are true as well for Shafer's (1991b) notion that the United States is in an "electoral order" where citizens value Democrats and Congress for certain responsibilities and Republicans and the president for others. Ferguson's (1994) investment approach to parties argues, as does the fiscal state approach, that there are systematic reasons to expect weak links between masses and elites and that the competition between the parties remains dominated by basic economic conflicts. Realignment theory stresses the importance and long-term influence of issues raised in a realigning period for the following decades of policy and electoral politics (Burnham 1970; Carmines 1994). Kelly's (1994) discussion of divided government presents data indicating that problems with the New Deal party system began in the 1950s rather than later. I do not necessarily agree in each instance with the interpretations these authors offer. The key point is that a substantial body of research has produced findings that are consistent with the fiscal state approach, and I have used these findings as a point of departure.[1] The fiscal state approach provides better leverage to incorporate these and other findings, to understand both party decline *and* resurgence, and to suggest why resurgence might appear in some portions of the party system but not others.

In this chapter, I turn to alternative explanations of recent American party politics, suggest an "interregnum" understanding of the past two decades of American political history, discuss some social and economic developments that might serve as the basis for full party revitalization, and consider the 1992 and 1994 elections in the context of the fiscal state.

Beyond the Tripartite Party

The study of American political parties is compartmentalized. With the rise of the tripartite model of parties—party as organization, party in the electorate, party in Congress[2]—political scientists began to develop so-

[1] For instance, Kelly (1994) sees sharp "punctuated change" in the 1950s where I see gradual change; Carmines (1994) places a heavier emphasis on generational change and population replacement than would I.

[2] The specific components of the triad might be stated slightly differently in other accounts.

phisticated theories of each of these compartments. The connections between these different components received less consideration. The task of
party theory should now be to link these components and reintegrate the
study of political parties.[3]

An integrated approach forces students to be more cautious about
overstating the impact of the revival of party in one single arena such as
organization or Congress. Realignment of party elites while growing
numbers of voters distance themselves from both the parties and politics weakens the claim that parties are resurgent. If voters are sending
ever more pure parties to Washington as a statistical artifact—for
example, because attrition and flight from the electorate leaves a smaller pool of participants, and these citizens tend to hold stronger party
views than nonactive individuals—claims of revitalization are questionable.

The fiscal state had important implications for several levels of party.
Parties in the system became less important as more of the important policy-making became executive policy. Parties in Congress saw their cohesion and conflict affected by both political and economic variables that
were driven by widespread Keynesian understandings of the political
economy; Keynesian logic led to party convergence during economic
downturns. Party among voters tended toward decline as voters perceived
the president to be responsible for economic policy; with this view, voters
were free to conduct presidential plebiscites and to stress the individual
candidates for Congress rather than the party. (The congressional inclination to converge during recessionary periods rather than offer significant alternatives reinforces these voting tendencies.) As members increasingly presented themselves in candidate-centered campaigns and
presidential candidates built personal organizations to run primary campaigns, the rise of a private market of campaign services threatened party
organizations (a case of the "institutional displacement" mentioned in
chapter 2). The party organizations recast their direction to be able to provide services to candidates, but these adaptations could not occur without funds. These funds were scarce until the first and second waves of the
interregnum order threw the party system into flux.[4] Ordinary middle-
class citizens who felt their identity and security threatened then poured
money into Republican headquarters. The Democrats followed. The parties can demand support from the public with all the high-tech equipment

---

[3] Baer and Bositis (1988) provide an excellent overview of the theories of American parties and argue that it is time to move away from the trinity model of parties and toward a
unified model.

[4] This point is not sufficiently recognized in arguments about revived party organizations.
It is true that new technologies greatly assisted fundraising efforts; it is also the case that increased funds were necessary before large-scale investments in technology were possible.

at their disposal, but the public response will be meager until the public has a reason to supply the funds: The erosion of the fiscal state provided an opening for party organizational resurgence.

Why did parties in the public stagnate while congressional parties revived? On the positive side, the decline of party among the citizenry in some respects leveled off in the 1980s (Dennis 1986; Wattenberg 1990) as the grip of the fiscal state loosened slightly. Voters were aware that the congressional parties had polarized, even if they were uncertain how this polarization dealt with major concerns. For example, for the 1972 through 1990 period the correlation between the election-year index of House party dissimilarity and the public's perception of party ideological differences was a moderate .56. When the public's focus on congressional parties was not obscured by presidential candidates—that is, in midterm election years—the correlation was .72. On the other hand, the public did wonder whether the arguments mattered. During the loud and long 1991–1992 partisan debate about tax cuts to spur economic recovery, for instance, 78 percent of the public believed that a tax cut would make "just some" or "very little" difference in improving the economy, while another 4 percent were unsure.[5]

Public awareness of polarization in Congress can be seen as a positive sign for the parties, but in turnout, attitudes toward parties, and voting behavior, party decline in the electorate continued. The basic reason is that the fiscal state constraints on parties were still powerful, even with the declining usefulness of Keynesian policy. The structural limits remained, as did the perceptions and behaviors these structural features encouraged. Some of these limits weakened: Congress engaged in macrobudgeting, and reconciliation procedures potentially intruded on automatic policy. But at the end of the day, American politics and political parties still operated under the constraints of the fiscal state. Until a new organizing framework supplanted Keynesianism for policy making, voters would continue to view congressional party performance as uneven and, to some extent, incomprehensible. They perceived their world changing rapidly while political elites slowly shifted positions in a confusing pattern. If the desultory and, to most observers, irrelevant debate over anti-recession tax cuts in early 1992 was the best the parties could offer to deal with new economic realities, the voters cannot be blamed for not responding more enthusiastically to the changes in the legislative parties. Until parties regain the policy control they have lost, voters and nonvoters will turn away.

[5] Sources: For index of party dissimilarity, chapter 3; for public perceptions, American National Election Studies Cumulative Data File, 1952–1990, v556; for tax cut opinions, NBC News/*Wall Street Journal* Poll, January 23, 1992.

The Three R' s: Alternative Historical Perspectives on Recent Party Politics

With the partial revival of parties has come a revival of scholarly interest in parties. I have cited or discussed several of these studies in other chapters. Here, I focus on three approaches to understanding recent American party politics—realignment, reform, and race.[6]

Realignment

Major debates have engulfed critical realignment analysis since the mid-1980s. The puzzle of the missing realignment was a major cause of this theoretical disarray. Extrapolating from past realignment cycles, analysts expected a realignment sometime around 1964 or 1968. No realignment occurred; that is, no realignment in the classic form identified for the 1850s, 1890s, or 1930s.[7] Among other things, these realignments significantly shifted party loyalty and mobilized new groups, occurred at several levels of the political system in the same "critical" period, inaugurated periods of long-term voting stability, initiated institutional changes, and produced major policy change. When no realignment of this type emerged in the late 1960s, scholars took one of two paths: They tried to make refinements to the model to account for the "missing" realignment (Burnham 1991, 1994), or they abandoned the idea of realignment altogether, suggesting that even the historical cases presented as critical realignments were not convincing (Shafer 1991a). For present purposes, I will travel

[6] These are not the only three that might be chosen. Students of European political parties have explored the possibility that affluence leads to the rise of postmaterialist values (lifestyles and quality of life) that disrupt traditional partisan alignments (Inglehart 1990; Dalton and Kuechler 1990; Dalton, Beck, and Flanagan 1984; Steel and Tsurutani 1986, among others; see also, Hays 1981). Scholars have paid some attention to this possibility in the United States, but extended treatments are rare and the emphasis has been largely on the splits between "economic liberals" and "social liberals" in the Democratic party. Layman and Carmines's (1992) analysis finds that party alignments remain dominated by class and economic concerns, but they note that ideological self-placement increasingly depends on one's position on postmaterialist issues. Carmines (1994) notes, as have others, that the Reagan coalition was particularly vulnerable to defection by fiscally conservative but socially liberal professionals.

[7] Observers scrutinized every presidential election after 1964 for signs of long-term realignment (Segal 1968; Phillips 1969; Burnham 1968, 1981a; Lawrence and Fleisher 1987; Hurley 1991). Some analysts have begun to suggest that we indeed have seen a realignment or a new party system, but of a rather different sort (Aldrich and Niemi 1990; Burnham 1994; Aldrich 1995). The consensus remains that a realignment in the classic sense has yet to occur (Wattenberg 1990; Buell 1987; Beck 1988).

down the first path and indicate how a consideration of the fiscal state might assist those operating in this tradition.

The theoretical point to be made is simple. Realignment analysts need to look at the defining issues of a critical realignment and see how these issues play themselves out in practice. In the 1930s, the defining issue was the state as an economic actor, embodied in one form in the budget. But this defining issue is inherently problematic because it defuses the issues that led to the new system. Indeed, the issues are particularly defused during periods of recession. In the fiscal state, the realignment sequence is distorted. Burnham (1970) has suggested that cycles of socioeconomic development, largely based on changes in the division of labor, create the underlying strain that leads to realignment.[8] If something should interfere with these cycles, and especially their outward manifestations as inflation or unemployment, the politics that are said to accompany these economic cycles might also be disrupted.

In short, critical realignment theorists left out the state. Once the state intervenes in the business cycle, any political cycle that depends on economic conditions will be potentially disrupted. Although they talked about great policy change after realignment, realignment theorists neglected to consider that this great policy change could work to thwart future critical realignments.

There was no reason to expect a classic critical realignment in 1964 or 1968 because the New Deal system had gone a long way toward undermining the expression of the sort of economic and social convulsions historically associated with critical realignment. Historically, critical realignments have been "surrogates for revolution" (Burnham 1982: 101) that reconnect the party system around socioeconomic reality. But in a period of reasonably successful managed economics the political system does not behave and react as it did in a period of nationally unregulated capitalism. The result of economic and social turmoil in 1964 and 1968 would be sometimes withdrawal from politics, sometimes newfound and temporary alliance, but not critical realignment. Past realignments needed a triggering event before the political explosion would take place; successful economic management defused the necessary triggering event.

Historically, critical realignment involved three interrelated but distinct realignments: legislative (party balance and voting), state (changes in policy and institutional powers), and voter (party identification and support).

---

[8] Sundquist (1973), conversely, argues that there is no underlying driving force to realignment; realignment depends on the fortuitous appearance on the agenda of extremely divisive and salient issues. Berry (1991) suggests that critical realignment can be accommodated to long-wave theories of economic growth and development. The "long swing" cycles identified for the labor process and labor markets also bears some resemblance to the realignment cycles (Gordon, Edwards, and Reich 1982).

Throughout American political history, these three realignments seemed to occur simultaneously; it was easy to consider them inextricably linked. But the present period is different; now they are not so obviously connected.[9] Part of the reason for the disconnection was mentioned above: The fiscal state successfully thwarted serious economic crises and obstructed those triggers that had in the past generated lasting change at all three levels of realignment. As the undergirding of the economy introduced in the 1930s and 1940s weakens and the problems this undergirding was designed to ameliorate are no longer the most important disturbances in the economy, the possibility for a triggering event and a critical realignment are enhanced.

Reform in Congress

The increased partisanship in Congress has resulted in a new surge of interest in political parties.[10] One set of arguments suggests that improved party strength emerged out of reforms in the 1970s that strengthened the position of the party caucus (Hammond 1991). Another set argues that reforms strengthening the position of party leaders led to more consistent parties (Sinclair 1983, 1989). A third line of argument contends that voters sent more ideologically consistent parties to Washington (Collie and Brady 1985; Brady 1990; Bensel 1984). A final approach stresses that both leaders and members were important—party leaders could more easily lead ideologically consistent party members. In this view, leadership is rounding up like-minded members (Aldrich 1995).[11] In an important work, Rohde (1991, 1992; see also Ornstein and Rohde 1978) connects several of these arguments: Voters who in the 1950s sent to Congress heterogeneous parties began in the early 1970s to send more ideologically consistent parties to Congress; members rejected the existing distinction of power with congressional reforms in the 1970s; and leaders then had both the means, motives, and

[9] Burnham (1991) discusses possible subcategories of realignments. Party-based realignments, he suggests, are only one type of realignment, albeit the historically most familiar. Policy realignment can occur without classic realigning voting behavior, although *some* change in voter behavior—even in a dealigning direction—is probably necessary. Ferguson (1982, 1994) has more broadly made the argument that scholars are mistaken to look for realignment in voter coalitions; rather, coalitions among industrial elites are key.

[10] I focus here on party in the legislature. Cotter et al. (1984), Bibby (1990), Herrnson (1990), and Gibson and Scarrow (1993) provide overviews of the changes in party organization in the United States. Panebianco (1989) provides a more general overview.

[11] This view is consistent with the notion that presidents are more likely to engage in facilitative leadership—pushing along a process or change that has substantial support—rather than directive leadership that points policy or the country in a starkly different direction with little public or political support (Edwards and Wayne 1990; cf. Peterson 1990; Bond and Fleisher 1990).

opportunities to exercise leadership. Underneath the party change, then, lie party coalitions that are increasingly similar from district to district.

Sorting out these related but competing lines of analysis is difficult. Were leaders dealing with more malleable members because of ideological consistency, for example, or were strong leaders molding the opinion of a fairly disparate group of party members? Roll-call votes themselves cannot answer the question because they help measure, or define, consistency. What roll-call analysis can do is determine whether aggregate voting patterns changed in ways that are comprehensible from the reform approach or any other approach. In chapter 3, I indicate that analysis of House votes provides some support for the basic ideas that reform and changes in the composition of the Democratic party enhance party cohesion and party conflict. Here, I suggest some problems that plague the consistency and reform-based approaches. Stating these objections does not demonstrate the correctness of the fiscal state approach; it does indicate that some skepticism is warranted before attributing the recent revival of congressional parties to reform or consistency changes alone.

Consider first consistency. Voter and congressional consistency are bounded. Undoubtedly, party coalitions witnessed secular change. But it was in the mid-to-late 1970s, after the reforms, that the Democrats were considered the "everyone" party, dominant in a "one-and-a-half" party system (Ladd 1977, 1978). The Democratic coalition was widening; nearly all major social groupings were predisposed to consider themselves Democrats. Coalitions that are a mile wide and an inch deep tend not to be terribly consistent. Instead, the demands coming from such a coalition are wide and varied. For several elections following 1974, the Democrats were winning suburban Republican seats and representing constituencies whose interests varied from those of traditional Democrats. This does not mean that party members in Congress were becoming less ideologically consistent (although one could logically make that argument [Edsall 1984]), but it does question how much of this consistency can be explained by referring to voters. Rohde (1991, 1992) argues that southern Democrats and northern Democrats were finding that their constituencies were increasingly similar, but except for comparisons of southern Democratic identifiers with northern Democratic identifiers, no evidence is presented that demonstrates that the southern Democratic congressional district resembles that of the North in constituency characteristics. Figures in chapter 3 of this book indicate that congressional voting cohesion was as high in the 1950s as in the 1980s, yet, according to the consistent-member argument, the 1950s parties were highly heterogeneous.[12]

---

[12] Rohde (1991, 1992) points out that different types of votes are differentially likely to be partisan. Final passage votes are much less likely to be partisan than are procedural votes or amendments. This of course makes the relatively high cohesion and conflict levels in the

Ticket splitting reaffirms the point. Voters are quite willing to cross party lines to vote for an incumbent. In 1988, just over half of all Democrats voted for a House Republican incumbent running for reelection, while the same proportion of Republicans voted for House Democratic incumbents (Abramson, Aldrich, and Rohde 1990: 270). Constituencies under such conditions are likely to be diverse and certainly include more than the party identifiers. Since the 1950s, indeed, since the turn of the century, an increasing proportion of voters has voted for a presidential candidate of one party and a congressional candidate of another party. Many voters indicate multiple party identifications, where party identification depends on the office being contested.[13] These developments simply suggest that scholars must look before they leap from consistent legislators to consistent voters.

Even independent of voter consistency, the argument about more internally consistent House party membership needs to be limited. The improvement in interparty differences has been much more striking than the improvement in intraparty cohesion, but this is a difficult distinction to make from within the consistent member framework. Similarly, proponents of the consistency idea stress important changes in the South while overlooking equally important changes in the North. It is true that northern and southern House Democrats have become more alike in their voting patterns. Notably, however, as southern Democrats were becoming more cohesive in the late 1960s and 1970s, northern Democrats were becoming *less* cohesive. At least part of the apparent homogeneity in the Democratic party, then, results ironically from a more confused and less consistent northern party.

The consistent-member approach also tends to overlook the position of the Republican party. Rohde (1991: 120–27) provides an exception. He notes that Republicans are generally less cohesive than Democrats, that their cohesion has not improved as rapidly as the Democrats, and that polarization between the northeastern and other wings of the party has grown (cf. Bailey 1988: 3–9, 65, 113–14). Rohde suggests that the difference lies in the fact that the reform process was centered in the Democratic party. This suggestion, though plausible, gives little analytical leverage on the period *before* the reforms when Democrats were already more cohesive than Republicans.[14] By contrast, the fiscal state approach

1950s all the more remarkable; not only did they occur when parties were heterogeneous, they also occurred when comparatively few votes were held on amendments.

[13] The winter 1992 (vol. 13) issue of the *Midsouth Political Science Journal* presents several analyses on segmented partisanship in the public.

[14] Both Cox and McCubbins (1993) and Kiewiet and McCubbins (1991) suggest that the majority position of the Democratic party is the key: The majority party members set rules and structure the process in the House in a way favorable to their interests, which allows for relatively higher levels of cohesion.

links the formation of that state more closely to the Democratic party and therefore expects on average higher levels of Democratic cohesion.

Now consider reform. When institutional change coincides with economic change, it is difficult to separate the two analytically. The reform explanation centers on responses to internal grievances in Congress or grievances with the president, but the fiscal state approach suggests that it is preferable to consider the possible connections between economic ("external") change and the generation of these "internal" demands. Rather than suggesting that the institution affects cohesion and conflict isolated from external events (or that one need not explicitly refer to these events to explain the levels of cohesion and conflict), it is more plausible to begin with the notion that parties will tend to be more distinctive when they have more to fight about. Indeed, it is hard to explain the changes in cohesion and conflict after 1950 by reference only to dichotomous structural variables that were not changing until the mid-to-late 1970s.

The consistency and reform literatures show that the definition of a "strong party" is not settled. Does a strong party require centralized leadership that can extract concessions or conduct exchanges with party members through the use of negative and positive sanctions? Or can a strong party be a party where voting is highly cohesive but leadership is relatively weak and dispersed? I suggest in chapter 1 that we think about party strength in terms of party control over policy domains and widespread acceptance of the notion that the parties are responsible for a given policy area.[15] The key ingredient is not the role of leaders but whether the parties are meaningful cue givers to voters, members of Congress, and other branches of government. In this view, the question of leadership recedes to the background; the more immediate question is whether parties have some meaning or relevance for citizens and participants. Parties can be strong without strong party leaders. The reality is likely to lie between the extremes. Leadership is important: At different times, the transaction costs of building cohesion can vary, but leadership will generally decrease the costs, even with a generally homogeneous group of party members. That can increase the likelihood of parties appearing meaningful to the public, *if* they have control of important and contentious policy areas.

Race

A third strand in the analysis of recent American party politics argues that race and racial issues have been at the center of a realigned party system (Carmines and Stimson 1989; Edsall and Edsall 1991; Weissberg 1991;

[15] Other ingredients were party differences on issues deemed significant by voters and elites. See Carmines, McIver, and Stimson (1987) for a compatible view, expressed as part of the conditions under which parties realign or fail to realign.

Carmines 1994; cf. Piven 1992). Racial issues polarized the parties after 1964 and led to significant shifts in public support for the two parties, including increased Republican support by white southerners and the northern working class. At the presidential level at least, a new conservative coalition ruled American politics after 1968.

In their analysis of the partisan politics of race, Carmines and Stimson (1989) reject both the dramatic change required in critical realignment analysis and the slow change dictated by secular realignment analysis. Instead, they adopt an "issue evolution" framework in which new issues alter the issue profiles of party coalitions but need not result in dramatic effects such as a new majority party at all voting levels. The authors present a "dynamic growth" model of polarization where conversion of existing voters and mobilization of new voters occur after the "critical moment." Generational replacement occurs in small incremental change after the critical moment. Gradual growth of polarization in the early years after the critical moment and partial decay in issue polarization years later are outcomes of normal population replacement.[16] "Dealignment," or an increase in self-identified partisan independence, results when three things occur: the existing alignment is no longer "vivid" (that is, it is old), the stability of the old issues on the agenda is disrupted, and parties take clear positions on the new issues. If any of these three variables is absent, the old alignment continues (Carmines, McIver, and Stimson 1987).

Carmines and Stimson argue that racial issues have presented the chief and most important issue evolution of recent American politics. In impressive detail, they show how positions on racial issues have changed among presidential candidates, members of Congress, party activists, and the mass public. They are undoubtedly correct to assert that an important change has occurred in the politics of race and that it is a change that intimately involves the political parties. Their argument is compelling and rigorous. The central problem with the issue evolution framework, though, is the nature of the new issue. Will this issue "drive" the party system, or is it just one important issue among many? Will a new consistency on an issue necessarily be associated with a reversal of party decline? If not, then this theory informs us more about changing coalitions than about the rise and decline of party. Nowhere do Carmines and Stimson show that racial issues are comparatively more important than others or consider whether these issues might be part of some larger cluster of issues. According to Abramowitz (1994), social welfare and national security issues were far more salient concerns to white Democratic defectors

[16] Using survey research that reconstructs data back to 1932, Carmines and Stimson (1989: 142–48) find that government provision of jobs (used as a proxy New Deal issue) became less a focus of partisan conflict, with most of the change coming from a slightly increased conservatism among the Democrats in the populace. Interestingly, most of the change took place from 1932 to 1948, not in more recent years.

than were racial issues. An election process increasingly dominated by incumbents also seems ill-suited for an issue evolution explanation. The rapid return of incumbents to office would suggest that parties would be less flexible over time, not more, but this theory presupposes such flexibility. Although the theory stresses heavily the increased party polarization in congressional voting on race, the most significant mass voting behavior changes have been at the presidential level. Within the issue evolution framework, such a discrepancy is puzzling.

Qualitative analysis of the recent politics of race (Edsall and Edsall 1991) reaches the same conclusions as the quantitative analysis in the issue evolution approach. Unfortunately, it suffers from the same problems. In their first chapter Edsall and Edsall (1991) show in convincing and elegant detail that the changes in the party system after the mid-1960s were related to a whole host of issues that might be summarized as social management. That is, the notion that government can perfect society is the main axis of dispute in the social policy and regulatory innovations of these decades. They are issues that many voters perceive as cultural attacks on their identity, attacks based as much on class and status as race (Rieder 1989; Phillips 1990). Edsall and Edsall seek to reduce this complexity to race and race alone, but ultimately they cannot do so. There is no solid evidence that important recent election results can be based primarily on racial issues. Many of the issues they identify—taxation, for example—result as much from economic conditions and the failures of economic management as they do from any explicit link to race.

My point here is not that race does not matter. Rather, I suggest that racial issues compete with many others, and their importance appears to be inversely related to economic conditions. The race argument points to Republican presidential victories as proof of the power of the new conservative ideology and coalition. It is equally true, however, that these Republican presidents won reelection when the economy was doing well. They lost reelection in 1976 and 1992 when the economy performed poorly. Other analyses of recent American politics suggest that the complex of issues that came to the forefront in the late 1960s are not easily summarized as "racial" but more accurately, as noted above, as "social management." Dionne (1991) emphasizes racial issues, but also family issues and foreign policy (see also Shafer 1991b). Ferguson and Rogers (1986) suggest that business coalitions changed for concrete reasons of economic conditions, not race, and question the depth of the rightward turn in American public opinion. Petrocik (1987) indicates that between 1952 and 1984 party identifiers polarized more on welfare issues than racial issues and that polarization grew on both issues (obviously these two issue areas are related). Burnham (1981a) suggests that crises in culture, empire, and economics were all responsible for the move toward

Republican presidencies. Green and Guth (1991) show that Reagan-era activists (big financial contributors) were aligned more on a traditional New Deal left-right spectrum than any other. Layman and Carmines (1992) find much the same among the mass public, while Shafer and Claggett (1994) concur that economic and welfare preferences are "much more strongly" tied to party identification than are cultural and national preferences.[17] Finally, it is difficult to reconcile the presumed importance of polarization on racial issues with the evidence of declining voter turnout, especially among those groups said to be most distressed by the Democrats racial liberalism. In an earlier work, Edsall (1984) indicated that working-class Democrats were not necessarily endorsing the Republicans racial conservatism; rather, they were exiting the electorate in large numbers (see also Burnham 1987; Piven and Cloward 1988; Piven 1992). Dionne's claim that these new nonvoters were not impressed with the issue stances and concerns of either party is probably correct. The security and identity dilemmas that the public experienced went beyond race and depended on changes such as the globalization of the economy that all countries had difficulties managing in the 1980s. The dramatic cuts in the welfare state, changes in the majority party, and rising political discontent in overwhelmingly homogeneous countries like Sweden suggest caution in relying too heavily on race. One cannot ignore the importance of race in American politics; one also cannot reduce recent American politics to race. Below, I suggest that this complex of issues about economics, social management, identity, and security is a key to understanding the recent evolution of the fiscal state party era and the possibilities for a new party era.

Thoughts on the Interregnum Order

Scholarly and popular ruminations about the "crisis" in American politics abounded in the 1970s and 1980s and remain prominent in the 1990s. The appropriateness of the crisis label is not significant here. Rather, I believe that the fiscal state approach might add to our understanding of the turmoil of the past twenty-five years. Admittedly, broad brush strokes are employed in painting this particular canvas. I organize these generous

[17] The Shafer and Claggett study highlights some interesting strategic dilemmas for the parties, especially the Democrats. They find that the Democrats should be very successful, *if* strong Democrats are allowed to set the party agenda. However, when independent Democrats set the stage for issue debate and candidate selection, the advantage shifts to the Republicans. They find that independent Democrats are alone on the left end regarding cultural matters, while all others, including strong Democrats, cluster around the conservative end of the spectrum.

extrapolations of the fiscal state approach under the rubric of the interregnum order, that is, the political order between the eras of the public philosophy defined by the fiscal state and that to be defined by some future state. It is a period when, as Antonio Gramsci intoned, "the crisis consists precisely in the fact that the old is dying and the new cannot be born; in this interregnum a great variety of morbid symptoms appears" (1971: 276).

One interesting feature of the cohesion and conflict data in chapter 3 is timing: Cohesion and conflict peak in the early 1960s and reach a very low ebb in 1969.[18] What might these switchpoints represent? I suggest that this data reflects an incipient and ultimately failed attempt to replace the Keynesian logic of American politics; this period was the first wave of the interregnum order.[19]

By 1964, the New Deal coalition seemed to have lost its cohesiveness and electoral strength.[20] In 1964, serious struggle began over the replacement of that 1930s system—a system that had transformed the nature of the American state. Through 1969, the Great Society was the visible result of the effort to build a new political order by forging a new political settlement regarding the role of the state.[21] This effort had its genesis in the growing domination of the Democratic party by northern liberals beginning in the late 1950s.[22] It was an attempt to design the successor to the fiscal state.

But in 1969, conservative and moderate Democrats and Republicans began an assault on the Great Society. Supportive of or willing to tolerate the state inaugurated by the New Deal, they opposed the idea of replacing the fiscal state organization of American politics with the Great Society. Budgets—the defining charter of the modern state—were the logical locus for the attack. Unlike the New Deal, the Great Society was

[18] This description is accurate generally; all the time series do not follow precisely this pattern.

[19] Burnham's (1985) discussion of an "interregnum state," as he notes, is based on my early draft of the ideas in this section.

[20] Indeed, Burnham (1968) notes that the results of the 1964 presidential election resembled the geographical voting distribution common from 1896 to 1928 rather than the pattern inaugurated during the 1930s. The difference between 1964 and 1896 is that in 1896 the Democrats were stronger in the western and southern "colonial periphery" while the Republicans won the northeastern and midwestern "metropole"; but in 1964, the Democrats were dominant in the metropole and the Republicans stronger in the periphery. There are many other available discussions of the early problems of the New Deal coalition. A good recent effort is Piven (1992).

[21] Drucker (1967) refers to the Great Society as an attempt to produce a "managed society" akin to the New Deal's "managed economy."

[22] This effort is consistent with Carmines's (1994) discussion of political losers introducing new dimensions to the issue agenda. Spatial models like Carmines's are foreshadowed in classic works by Sundquist (1983) and Schattschneider (1960).

not institutionalized to a great degree and depended on the continued dominance of the Democratic party in presidential and legislative elections. (There were exceptions to this broad statement, most notably the Medicare program.) The opponents of the Great Society did not immediately exhibit high levels of cohesion and unity. Many, particularly in the Republican party, worried about finding themselves on the wrong side of history again. Richard Nixon, for example, embraced Keynesianism but not the Great Society. Nonetheless, some of his reforms (not all enacted) in welfare, job training, and general revenue sharing were careful to indicate concern with Great Society issues without necessarily adopting the Great Society specifics.

The Great Society, then, represented the first wave of the interregnum order. The interregnum order was subject to such immediate attack because the Great Society was a policy realignment built in the absence of profound electoral realignment.[23] Electoral realignment was thwarted because the fiscal state muted economic crisis. In the absence of such crisis, politics ran on two tiers—Keynesian and Great Society—in this interim period. These two tiers are paralleled by the often-noted split within the Democratic party between the "old" economic liberals and the "new" social liberals.

Inflation and unemployment were relatively low in the 1960s, growth and investment high; the success of macroeconomic fine tuning took those issues more-or-less off the "front burner" and opened political space for the other defining issues of the 1960s. Parties based on New Deal issues had great difficulty incorporating the new political forces of the 1960s that squeezed into this widening political space (Baer and Bositis 1988, 1993). This failure encouraged the attempt by some party members to realign the policy concerns of the American state. But these would-be state builders incorrectly assumed that the voters would follow their clarion call. By the 1970s, the renewed importance of traditional, Keynesian economic politics made these "new" issues vulnerable to attack.

In this context, what is the meaning of the rise of Ronald Reagan in the late 1970s? Reagan achieved some success in attacking parts of all the New Deal tenets: regulation, domestic spending, economic management, social welfare, growing federal power, and international political economy. But he did not attempt to eradicate these bases of economic undergirding. Rather, Reagan's ostensible goal was a virtually full repeal of the Great Society via an aggressive budget strategy that dominated the politics of the early to middle 1980s and contributed to, though they did not

---

[23] The Democrats lost forty-eight seats in the 1966 House elections and four more in 1968, bringing them approximately back to their pre-1959 level. The 1966 and 1968 elections lowered the Democrats Senate advantage from thirty-six to fourteen seats.

solely cause, massive budget deficits.[24] As the president attempted to re-define state-economy relations, politics was fiscalized around the budget and the deficit and party conflict increased. Budget crises and the threat of government shutdown were staples of the news. Resentment of Reagan's strategy by Great Society defenders is reflected in Speaker Thomas P. O'Neill's (D-Massachusetts) lament that

> I have never seen anything like this in my life, to be perfectly truthful. What is the authority for this? Does this mean that anytime the President of the United States is interested in a piece of legislation, he merely sends it over? You do not have any regard for the process, for open hearings, discussion as to who it affects, of what it does to the economy? But because a man who does not understand or know our process sends it over, are we to take it in bulk? ... Do we have the right to legislate? Do we have the right to meet our target or can he in one package deregulate, delegislate, the things that have taken years to do? (LeLoup 1982: 321)

Ironically, like the Great Society before him, Reagan hoisted a policy realignment on fragile electoral reeds. Voter endorsement of the Reagan revolution was tentative, and the administration often found its biggest obstacles to be fellow Republicans (Stockman 1986). Congress remained stubbornly Democratic while Republicans continued to win presidential elections. But unless voters sensed that a stronger party system was in place—in the sense of party strength laid out earlier in chapter 1—they would continue to base their vote for the president and members of Congress on different calculations.

If the failed attempt to supersede the Keynesian consensus with the Great Society marked the first wave of the interregnum order, the failures of Keynesianism itself led to the second wave. By the mid-to-late 1970s the efficacy of the Keynesian analytical apparatus that supported the fiscal state was in serious dispute. Difficulties explaining the condition of the American economy in this period, the increasing integration of the world economy, and the lack of relevant policy prescriptions provided by the Keynesian framework raised a large theoretical battle within the economics profession (Chrystal, 1983; Thurow, 1983; Dow, 1985; Blinder, 1989) and created confusion among politicians and policy makers about what economic course to follow.

[24] White and Wildavsky (1989) note that other factors contributed importantly to the budget deficits, including an unusually bad economy in the 1970s and early 1980s, changing demographics, and escalating health care costs. Moreover, federal government revenue as a percentage of the gross national product spurted during the Carter years, and unless one was willing to argue that Americans were ready to endorse a jump-shift in the level of taxation, it was likely that taxes were going to be reduced. For all their gravity, the major impact of the tax changes during the Reagan years was to bring revenues as a percentage of gross national product more in line with the level preceding the late 1970s.

These problems with Keynesianism weakened one fiscal-state constraint on contemporary political parties. A positive development for the parties, the erosion of support for Keynesianism encouraged new contestation about the future of the American political economy. Past understandings about the empirical and normative relationship between state and economy were thrown in question. Party differences in Congress heightened as members of the two parties sought to define new positions in a rapidly changing environment. Party organizations, particularly at the national level, became more active and successful in using new technologies to tap into the growing anxiety resulting from the loss of economic stability and predictability. The Republicans were particularly successful in using these newfound resources to recruit candidates who would spread the message about restructuring the state. Despite these positive changes for the position of party in American politics, the other constraints of the fiscal state remained. Party in the electorate continued to stagnate.

If the failures of economic management marked the second wave of the interregnum order, the first wave (the Great Society) created at least some of these problems. Keynesianism was most weakened by its inability to explain convincingly the economic conditions of the 1970s. But budgetary changes emerging from the Great Society also weakened Keynesianism. In pursuit of the Great Society and then in pursuit of its elimination, the budget was transformed from an economic instrument to a more fully economic, social, military, and regulatory instrument.[25] The budget became the prize. Making the budget's goals so extensive, and parts of the budget so resistant to change, made it much more difficult to use as a prime fiscal policy tool. Ironically, then, the Great Society weakened Keynesianism not by restructuring the fiscal state but by sharply diminishing the government's ability to use the budget to fine-tune the economy. As if to highlight how little Keynesianism revealed about contemporary political economy, by the mid-1980s, discussions about increasing or decreasing the deficit had no obvious relationship to the condition of the economy.

This interregnum order is well reflected in the debates about the 1990–1991 recession. With purportedly massive ongoing deficit stimulus, additional stimulus—the standard Keynesian prescription—appeared untenable.[26] On the other hand, the standard monetary prescriptions were

---

[25] As noted in chapter 3 (note 5) this transformation is apparent in a comparison of Joint Economic Committee hearings on the *Economic Report of the President* at the outset and conclusion of the 1960s (see United States Congress, Joint Economic Committee 1963, 1969).

[26] Purportedly is the operative word. A full Keynesian analysis would stress that the nominal deficit is not as important as the deficit necessary to produce full employment, but politically that is a difficult distinction to make. Prescriptions about deficits as proportions of gross national product are equally difficult to coat in soothing political language.

slow to produce growth. In late 1991, discussion centered around minor stimulus via tax cuts, because other options were not self-evident. And even these cuts were to be offset by higher taxes elsewhere (Democrats) or spending cuts (Republicans) because of budget-process changes installed by the 1990 deficit-cutting agreement. By requiring a "pay-as-you-go" procedure for any new nonemergency spending increases or tax cuts, the budget agreement sharply curtailed the government's already feeble ability to engage in discretionary Keynesian fine-tuning.[27] In 1992, old standbys such as tax credits for housing purchases were added to the mix. In the end, the only results on the fiscal side were reducing the tax withholding taken from workers paychecks (even though the total taxes to be paid by April 15 did not change) and extending unemployment benefits. Although the Democrats accepted the major components of President Bush's stimulus plan, Bush backed off from his own plan when congressional Republicans complained. When the Democrats sought to put the president on the spot by adding a high-income tax increase, Bush's veto was assured. None of this had much to do with improving the economy, because there was little concrete sense of what would work.

New organizing frameworks for state-society and state-economy relations were only in their infancy. On the Republican side, there was renewed commitment to the basic principles of supply-side economic analysis and the notion of a conservative "opportunity society" to replace the welfare state. From Democrats, especially with Bill Clinton's election, one heard more about public investment and reinvestment and, although Democrats avoided the term, industrial policy. Each of these alternatives dealt with fundamental problems that were untouched by standard fiscal and monetary policy prescriptions. But these options were not well formulated and each side appeared willing to borrow from the other. Given this confusion, it is not surprising that in the 1990–1991 recession politicians rushed to assert the old-time religion and that the parties talked about using the same policy instruments, though in marginally different ways. It is also unsurprising that voters in 1992 expressed great frustration with and lack of trust in government. While polarization and cohesion revived among elites, the public was decreasingly attached to the party system. Congressional parties, distant from their electoral base, were dancing inside a jar. This, in essence, is the politics of the interregnum order.

[27] Because the recession was officially over by late 1991, extra spending could no longer be considered emergency spending under the budget agreement. The ability to fine-tune the economy was already feeble because of the ever increasing proportion of the budget dedicated to mandatory spending (primarily entitlements and net interest payments). Mandatory spending determined 36.3 percent of federal outlays in 1970; by 1990, this spending totaled 59.9 percent of all outlays (United States Office of Management and Budget 1994: table 8.3).

Beyond the Interregnum Order?

Even if Keynesianism still worked, the problems Keynesianism solves are no longer the central economic problems. In Offe's words: "The Keynesian welfare state . . . has operated on the basis of the false theory that the problems it is able to deal with are the only problems of the capitalist political economy, or at least the permanently dominating ones" (1983: 239). Keynesianism can be viewed as a system that once handled quite well the surface symptoms of more deeply rooted economic problems, without necessarily addressing those problems explicitly.

What are the alternatives? What might encourage voter participation? What policy areas might be conducive to strong parties? In other words, what policy areas might be the domain of congressional parties, be areas on which the parties offer distinctive differences, and be areas about which voters and elites care?

One possibility is that supporters of political parties should look more closely than they have previously at reform ideas such as a balanced budget amendment and congressional term limits. Scholars can produce lists of negative consequences arising from the adoption of either of these alternatives. A balanced budget amendment would be a charade dependent on scenarios, rosy and otherwise. It might not be good economic policy. Term limits will increase the power of staff, bureaucrats, and lobbyists, and is yet another way to limit the public's democratic choice. For either amendment, if something can go wrong, it will. And if no one ever thought about it going wrong, you can count on it happening.

I find several of these complaints compelling. Procedural devices do not ordinarily solve political problems and restricting democratic options is troubling. But opponents of these reforms often argue as if the existing way of doing things is somehow "natural" and that a balanced budget amendment or term limits would be an "artificial" burden on the democratic process. *Any* rules, including rules that allow budget deficits or rules that allow lifetime careers in Congress, are artificial. It is not difficult to interpret the existing rules as limiting democracy in certain ways. Therefore, decisions about which reforms are desirable depend on what values one wishes to promote in the political system and what are the best available means to those ends. It is not irrational for citizens to value rotation of elites in office, just as many academic departments require rotation of the position of department chair.[28]

My point here is not to argue for these reforms but to suggest that they cannot be as easily dismissed as many political scientists would like. For

[28] Granted, unlike politicians, many if not most academics do not cherish extended periods devoted to administrative duties.

the status of parties, each of these reforms offers something of value. If nothing else, a balanced budget amendment would force to the surface explicit considerations of the proper mode of state-society relations. The deficit is indeed a conflict over ends more than means (White and Wildavsky 1989), but a deficit in the hundreds of billions of dollars allows one to submerge this conflict rather than confront it. Forcing the issues to the surface could possibly introduce alternative arenas for party contestation beyond the relatively fruitless domain of fiscal policy. As for term limits, political scientists often work themselves into a box. Sometimes, for example, we argue that the problems in Washington are essentially caused by the public because the public is unwilling to accept sacrifice or to support the politicians who make "hard choices." At the same time, we argue that politicians cannot make such hard choices because their careers are on the line. If that is true, why not remove politicians from this uncomfortable position? Congressional history certainly suggests that politicians in the nineteenth century who did not see Congress as a long-term career were more likely to support party policy, not less. Perhaps the American people have it right: rather than change the voting habits of a hundred million citizens, why not change the career paths of a few hundred lawyers? As Congress protects itself from itself when it establishes commissions to handle politically sensitive issues or establishes a trade remedy process that favors bureaucratic and not legislative routes to protection, the American people may be crying "stop us before we reelect and spend again."

Rather than dwelling on reforms, perhaps more important for present purposes is to consider important developments in the economy and society that might support stronger parties. Worldwide changes in production and labor markets over the past two decades have had profound effects on the American economy and have raised a host of new issues to prominence.[29] Productivity, infrastructure investment, technological flexibility, human capital investment, competitiveness, and international competition are the most obvious. In the United States, changes in production intersect with a deteriorating position in the world economy and widespread concern about trade deficits, declining living standards, and stagnant incomes. Concerns about personal identity and family security appear to tie together many of these fears in much the same manner as trade policy did in the late nineteenth century.

[29] Suggestive accounts of these transformations are Block (1977), Harrison and Sum (1979), Epstein (1981), Bluestone and Harrison (1982), Gordon, Edwards, and Reich (1982), Noyelle (1982, 1983), Stanback and Noyelle (1982), Cohen and Rogers (1983), Bowles, Gordon, and Weisskopf (1984), Piore and Sabel (1984), Starr (1988), Blinder (1989), Block (1990), Burtless (1990), Kuttner (1991), Nau (1992), Reich (1992), Graham (1992), and Tyson (1993).

Can these issues, concerns, and fears become the basis of a new period of party strength? Prominent members of the two parties have broached the issues: In the 1988 Democratic primaries, Rep. Richard Gephardt (D-Missouri) attempted to make the case for trade protection. Democrats in the 1992 primaries pitched their message at "the middle class" (variously defined) and debated the merits of trade promotion, trade restriction, and strategic trade policy. Bill Clinton stressed the virtues of industrial policy in his successful campaign and sought to tie together a wide array of changes in social and economic policy under the rubric of security. In the Republican party, conservatives have stressed the notion of the "opportunity society." To date these forays into the thicket of issues above has been tentative, especially on the Democratic side where the politics of issues such as trade and the role of labor in the Democratic coalition have become complex. The resurgence of party conflict on trade issues discussed in chapter 1 was most prominent from 1983 to 1988 and diminished afterward. The intense debates over the North American Free Trade Agreement (NAFTA) in 1993 and the General Agreement on Tariffs and Trade in 1994 are signs of this complexity. Even with NAFTA, the more partisan of the two debates, party lines were blurred. It is not clear exactly where the axis of conflict over these issues might be located or whether Americans will see personal opportunity and personal security as opposite ends of a single dimension or separate dimensions altogether. Some kind of major socioeconomic crash might provide the impetus to cut through this complexity, but the fiscal state, even with considerable strains, has so far proved resilient in preventing such a crash from occurring. One can hardly encourage a crash to revive parties at the voter level, but the slow disintegration of trust in politics is equally foreboding.

The Election of 1992

One interpretation of the 1992 election is obvious: George Bush got a wake-up call in New Hampshire in February, but he never heard the bell. As the alarm kept ringing through the primary season and through the Republican convention, Bush continued to press the snooze button, content to wait just a little bit longer before confronting the depth of his political troubles. Had Bush dealt with domestic issues earlier, had he not given his convention over to the social and religious right in Houston and gotten lost in the mire of "family values," and had he run a better campaign, perhaps he would have won in 1992. But to a large extent these were problems throughout Bush's presidency, and voters are rightly skeptical about campaign conversions.

Rather than view the election of Bill Clinton as a result of Bush's cam-

paign errors (Maggiotto and Wekkin 1993), it is more instructive to view
this election as a reflection of two major historical forces. I briefly mention
the first and discuss the second more fully. The first major historical force
was the collapse of the old communist order and the subsequent loss of the
cold war as a key principle of American politics. Despite his talk of a new
world order, Bush provided few details on just what that term entailed.

The second key historical force reflected in the election was a crisis in
political economy. This crisis had two components, one empirical and one
theoretical. Empirically, Americans had endured declining living standards, declining incomes, and witnessed the diminished position of the
United States in the world economy. Analysts were puzzled in their attempts to understand the public angst during the 1990–1991 recession, a
recession that by recent historical measures was not particularly long and
not especially deep. Unemployment rates of 7.8 percent paled in comparison to the rates near 10 percent during the 1982 and 1974–1975 recessions. (The recovery from the 1990–1991 recession was, however, the
slowest of the postwar era.) But the angst was due to something adroitly
hit upon by Clinton during the campaign: The structure of the economy
had changed. Unlike in previous recessions, people feared that lost jobs
would never return; they were feeling the impact of years in which families did indeed have to "work more and more to make the same amount
or less"; they saw vast numbers of middle-income jobs, both blue and
white collar, disappear; they could not see much, if any, future improvement for their own, or their children's, job prospects. Competitive threats
from Europe and Asia were widespread, and Eastern Europe threatened
more erosion of lower paying jobs. More was going on in 1992 than just
the recession. By most measures, the economy under Bush was sporting
its worst performance since World War II. Had the unemployment rate
been 6.8 percent instead of 7.8 percent, it is unlikely that much would
have changed for George Bush. Bush did not cause this broader crisis in
the political economy, and perhaps neither did the Republican presidents
who were in office for sixteen of the previous twenty years. But, just as
clearly, neither Bush nor the former presidents did much to condition
these changes or alleviate the stresses inherent in such widespread transitions from one type of economy to another. The closest Bush came to understanding the situation was when he noted publicly that economies were
changing worldwide. To Bush, that was important only because on some
measures the American situation was not as grim as in other countries.
An observation of that kind explains next to nothing to citizens wonder-
ing what has been going on, what is likely to happen, and what the effect
will be on themselves and their families.

The second component of the crisis in political economy helps explain
why Bush failed to react to the massive social and economic changes go-

ing on and, indeed, expressed little understanding that such changes were surely underway: There was at the time no viable economic theory for macroeconomic management. Neither Keynesianism, the dominant technique for managing the economy from the end of World War II through the middle 1970s, nor supply-side economics, the putative heir to Keynesian theory, had much credibility by the early 1990s.[30] Neither Bush nor his advisers had much of a sense of what to do in the absence of a guiding theory of how to manage the economy in a transitional era. During most of the Reagan and Bush period, the heavy lifting in economic policy fell not to supply-side policy formulated in the White House but to monetary policy formulated by the Federal Reserve. It was a sign of the depth of the policy crisis that all the traditional tricks of monetary policy, including the lowest interest rates in decades, were deployed with little effect during the slow growth period of the early 1990s. With none of the three major macroeconomic theories working, where was one to turn? The public surely did not know whether Bill Clinton had the answer, but they just as surely knew that Bush, whose only well-known economic principle was his unwillingness to raise taxes, did not. By talking about "trickle down" and by committing himself to countering the harsh consequences of the market via job retraining, lifetime education, and the like, Clinton tapped into these concerns. Politicians around the world have eagerly sought to delink government from responsibility for economic outputs by asserting that the market has a will of its own; Clinton countered that there might be new and useful ways for government to modify the impact of the market.[31] A Republican who expressed some awareness of the magnitude of these changes would have had a better chance at retaining the presidency.

George Bush once scoffed when he was criticized for lacking "vision."

---

[30] Keynesianism collapsed because of its inability to dissect and cure stagflation—simultaneously high inflation and unemployment. Indeed, from within the logic of the theory, stagflation was a virtual impossibility. Nor could Keynesians explain why an economy would remain sluggish in the face of huge budget deficits. Supply-side economics claimed to have a solution to stagflation, but in the process created or acquiesced in the development of new problems: increasingly large budget deficits that consumed more and more of the federal budget, a tax system increasingly disadvantageous to the middle class (especially because of the burden of payroll taxes for Social Security and Medicare), and relatively meager improvements in private investment outside real estate.

[31] John Goldthorpe (1987) has suggested that the political logic of the Keynesian compromise may linger on long past its economic viability. Keynesianism was a historic compromise between contending ideologies and class interests that produced consensus on previously destabilizing and divisive issues. Labor got protection from the vagaries of the market via unemployment insurance, retraining, and the like. Economies remained essentially capitalist in most respects; Keynesianism posed no grave threats to the key institutions, power, or advantages of capitalist society. But, politically, Keynesianism did produce an unwillingness to accept the consequences of sharp social inequalities produced by the market.

In the end, "the vision thing" (as he called it) had the last laugh, as Bush's failure to speak meaningfully about the historic transitions in global economics, politics, and diplomacy sunk his presidency. In a transitional period, the prospect of electing an administration (Reagan–Bush) to its fourth term has limited appeal, particularly an administration perceived as unresponsive to the challenges at hand.

But all this hardly put the Democrats in a position of strength from which to conclude the interregnum order. If one believes that small business is the major catalyst in the economy, it will be politically difficult and dangerous to impose new government mandates on those businesses, as Clinton discovered in his failed universal health insurance initiative. Clinton had to tread carefully around the "middle middle" class (voters whose family income was $30,000 to $50,000 annually). This group gave strong support to Ross Perot (*New York Times,* November 8, 1992), was skeptical of Clinton's reliability and honesty, and was well represented in small business. Indeed, the Democrats were still stuck with the dilemma that became manifest in the 1970s and 1980s: The party sought to appeal to the working class, the middle class, and business. Leaning too heavily toward any of these groups risked alienating the others, as Jimmy Carter discovered. Because those groups demographically most predisposed to vote Democratic were also most predisposed to avoid voting, Clinton stressed universal social welfare initiatives (new programs that would be open to people of all income groups). However, middle class entitlement programs like Social Security and Medicare have proven to be tremendous drains on federal resources. Moreover, the election results indicated that in one concrete way the Reagan revolution lived on: The size of government probably could not get any larger (although budget priorities could change). New taxes would be a very difficult sell, as the passage of antitax proposals and tax limitation referendums around the country on election day showed. This made the control of medical costs imperative because of their budget-busting tendencies. At the same time, health care reform was the most complex and contentious change that Clinton proposed and one likely to burden small businesses. Finally, while Clinton's analysis of the economy was adroit, it was an analysis that set a high standard for governing. Under a more Keynesian politics, it would be sufficient for Clinton to reduce the unemployment rate a point or so, but in the early 1990s, that type of change would not move the public. Clinton told the public that the country was past Keynes, past focusing on unemployment rates, and into an era where competitiveness, education, job security, and middle-income job growth were the real concerns of government. It came to haunt Clinton that the public believed him. Despite his best efforts in 1994 to emphasize the improvements in employment and economic growth since he assumed office, voters were not impressed.

If the policy position of the party was precarious, its electoral position was equally tenuous. Clinton managed only 43.2 percent of the vote. Only Richard Nixon in 1968 (43.2 percent), Woodrow Wilson in 1912 (41.8 percent), and Abraham Lincoln in 1860 (39.8 percent), all in multicandidate races, have had this small a share of the national vote entering office. In only three states did Clinton garner more than 50 percent of the vote. Clinton was only the third Democrat in this century to win while losing seats in the House of Representatives, joining Wilson in 1912 and John F. Kennedy in 1960. He gained no seats in the Senate. Coattails were all but invisible. In twenty-one Senate races won by Democrats, the Senate candidate outpolled Clinton in raw votes in all twenty-one. In eight gubernatorial elections won by Democrats, Clinton was outpolled by the candidate for governor in all eight. And of course, Ross Perot captured about a fifth of the electorate, challenging Theodore Roosevelt for the best third-party showing in the twentieth century. The vote for Perot was an indicator of the level of public discontent and lack of confidence in the parties in 1992. Forty to 50 percent of the public believed that neither party represented their values. Only 29 percent expressed support for the current two-party system.[32] In short, the 1992 election did not represent an overwhelming Democratic victory from the top of the political system to the bottom, nor had a new axis of political competition clearly emerged to erase the remaining structural constraints of the fiscal state.

The Election of 1994

The Republican victory in the 1994 midterm election provided a punctuation point to the recent evolution of the fiscal state and the winding down of the interregnum order. Democratic attempts to achieve political, welfare, and health care reform after Clinton's election in 1992 had come to naught, and despite a modestly growing economy, the president had failed to erase the fears of insecurity, stagnant income, and declining living standards and opportunities that had been the bedrock of his victory two years earlier. The resulting Republican victory in 1994 extended from local and

---

[32] "Neither political party represents my views anymore": Strongly disagree 17.3 percent; Somewhat disagree 31.1; Somewhat agree 32.3; Strongly agree 19.1 (*USA Today*, August 27, 1990). "Which party comes closer to sharing your values?": Democrats 30.1 percent; Republicans 28.9; Neither 41.0 (*USA Today*, December 10, 1991). "Which one of the following would you prefer?": A continuation of the two-party system of Democrats and Republicans 29.1 percent; Elections in which candidates run as individuals without any party labels 37.1; The growth of one or more new parties that could effectively challenge the Democrats and Republicans 32.0 (Harris Survey 921105, question D4, July 1992). Source: University of North Carolina, Institute for Research in Social Science, Public Opinion Item Index, online.

state offices up through Congress and was expansive enough to allow Republicans to claim credibly that they were the country's new majority party or, at worst, on an equal footing with the Democrats. Following their capture of Congress, Republicans set to work to redefine the relationship of the American state to the economy and society. Organizational reforms in the House centralized power in party leaders hands. House Republicans proceeded in a disciplined fashion to implement the campaign promises contained in their Contract with America. In some ways, their actions were advantageous for parties. Policy initiative was clearly located in the congressional party arena, particularly with the new majority party. Substantive offerings emerged from party officials at lower levels, especially governors. Haley Barbour, the Republican National Committee chair, was regularly included in party legislative strategy discussions and began almost immediately a series of party-building "talks" with voters over talk radio outlets. Republicans did not announce President Clinton's budget "dead on arrival" in February 1995—an attempt to keep Clinton "in the loop" for blame as budget cuts took hold. But his framework of ever continuing deficits was rejected, even though the major difference in the Clinton and Republican budgets would apparently take place years in the future. In one telling symbolic gesture, a House committee recommended doing away with the president's Council of Economic Advisers, the body established in the Employment Act of 1946.

If there was any doubt that Keynesianism as a policy framework was defunct, the first few months of the Republican Congress erased the doubt. Discussions began regarding ways to replace the Keynesian-favored progressive income tax system with a flat-rate or consumption tax system designed to promote the supply side of saving and investment. Republican budget plans included granting control of many programs to the states through block grants that would not grow as economic conditions deteriorated. To accomplish this budgetary change, the concept of "entitlement" was stripped from the programs handed back to the states. If the Republicans proved successful, the automatic stabilizers that had defused economic troubles so often during the fiscal state period would be sharply scaled back. Indeed, if the Republican balanced budget goal was strictly enforced, spending reductions would be needed during recessions to meet reduced tax revenue, opening up substantial grounds for partisan debate. An attempt to pass a balanced budget amendment failed in 1995. Despite that defeat, both the House and the Senate passed a budget resolution that would balance the budget by 2002 if economic assumptions and projections proved accurate. Party cohesion was extraordinary. Initially, President Clinton joined with congressional Democrats in an ode to the fiscal state, arguing that the Republican plans for ending entitlements and requiring a balanced budget would destroy the economy's ability to heal itself during economic downturns. By midyear, however, it was not clear if the president was prepared to defend social program entitlements. He expressed his support for balancing the budget in ten years instead of seven, but later he agreed to the Republican timetable. Congressional Democrats, angered by Clinton's move toward the center, preferred a stark challenge to the Republican agenda.

With the abandonment of Keynesianism, the prominence of congressional parties, and the weakening of automatic stabilizers, the Republican agenda in 1995 addressed some of the key constraints on parties in the fiscal state. The other constraints were less clear. Certainly the Fed was at the center of business cycle management in 1995. But this matters only if the axis of competition between the parties is to lie primarily on macroeconomic management issues. With the ascendancy of Congress and the erosion of Keynesianism, would voters continue to conduct presidential plebiscites on macroeconomic performance? Certainly the futurist, transformational tone of the Republican leadership, particularly House Speaker Newt Gingrich (R-Georgia), did not suggest that voters should make their political decisions based on the latest blips in the inflation, unemployment, or growth rates.

But could the Republican attempts to restructure the state, which did not appear in any version to promise a smooth, gently changing business cycle, survive plebiscitary style voter behavior? This is where the impact of the 1994 election is less obvious. One part of the Republican party preferred to define party competition on social, religious, and moral policy grounds. Others preferred to emphasize reform of the political process. Another wing gave priority to reform of affirmative action, immigration, welfare, and criminal justice laws. Some touted radical devolution of power to state and local governments and a strong libertarian vision of private property and gun ownership rights, sentiments that reached their apogee in the militia, patriot, and county autonomy movements. Yet another contingent saw economic growth through supply-side incentives and fewer restrictions on business as the driving force. Republican party leaders preferred to define the competition as the scope of government involvement in individual lives. At the same time, when responding to charges that their budget priorities inflicted pain, the same leaders often emphasized that they still were allowing government to grow, but at a slower clip. It was indeed striking that Republicans often worked within Democratic policy legacies, proposing to reform and refine but not eliminate Medicare, food stamps, the school lunch program, student loans, welfare, environmental protection, the National Labor Relations Board, and an array of other programs. It was equally striking that the new "conservative opportunity society" agenda had relatively little to do with the kinds of economic stresses and anxieties that drove the 1992 election and that led many voters to try the Republicans in 1994. Despite assurances that removing regulatory, legal, and tax restrictions on business would lead to an entrepreneurial boom ultimately benefiting the average worker, and that welfare reforms would end dependency, there was little in the Republican plans that would clearly identify the Republicans as the party that would raise incomes and increase security. (It was ironic that, one year after the failure of President Clinton's health care reform plan, surveys showed that voters still identified health security as one of the country's very top needs but that neither party had a plan to offer.) Added to this mix was the confusion in the Democratic party about how to respond to the Republican ascendancy. Political actors groped for another organizing framework, but as the fiscal state continued to wither, the grounds for future party competition remained unclear. For voters to return to parties, they must be convinced that the parties are in control of a policy domain that is fundamentally important and on which significant differences exist.

Writing early in the Republican Congress, one can only be cautious about the actual implementation of these policy and structural changes. Like the blindfolded men touching the elephant, it is dangerous to project based only on the limited experience we have, ignorant of important events and episodes that can disrupt what appears to be a smooth trajectory of developments. Indeed, the fiscal state constructed from 1937 to 1946 ultimately looked substantially different from the industrial cartelization and limited short-term relief programs one might have projected in 1933, or the extensive social democracy one might have expected in 1935 with the National Labor Relations and Social Security Acts. More safely, I would suggest that the possibilities for party in American politics look better in the mid-1990s than they have since the establishment of the fiscal state. The two existing major parties may be reconstituted and remain dominant. Perhaps they will be joined or replaced by a new competitor. The key point is that, from social values to a redefinition of government's economic responsibility, the dimensions for party competition being discussed in 1995 appear to be more hospitable for strong parties than the settings provided by the fiscal state. Of course, the proof will be in the details. Both the structure of policy making and the content of policy are crucial, and the restructuring of both is only in its incipiency.

Conclusion

The 1880s and 1890s are often considered the founding period of modern American society. In that period, the United States became a large-scale manufacturing country and power shifted from planters to industrialists and financiers. Worldwide, countries scrambled for markets, and many in the United States saw the capture of foreign markets as a way to solve social and economic problems induced by industrialization. Divided government was normal, with different parties holding different branches. Citizens and journalists believed corruption was widespread, and political reforms built a merit-based bureaucracy, required voter registration, and weakened the grip of party around the country. Unions were weak, and workers feared a degradation of skills and pay because of new technology. To deal with overproduction and competition, employers cut wages. There were clear regional differences in economic development. The national state was in many respects distant; in particular, the rise of industrialism and its effects on the cities was essentially outside the realm of political debate. Government at the state level was the focus of most health, safety, and regulatory initiatives, education reforms, and the like. A conservative Supreme Court placed property rights at the peak of constitutional importance. After a period of fighting the very divisive Civil War, the country unified around a "splendid little war" in 1898.

Similarities between the past and the present are obvious, though not complete. The 1890s ended with the great electoral blowup of 1896. 1992 was not our 1896. 1996 or 2000 may be. Decisions will be made about policy direction that will shape state-economy relations and politics for the next few decades. The role of political institutions such as political parties, and indeed the health of democracy, needs to be an explicit part of the agenda. The discontent with politics, parties, and government ironically reinforces the need for strong parties to perform their linkage function. No inherent logic of history requires party collapse and no such law demands renewal or ensures that parties will follow the pattern or path that is best for democracy or the parties' long-term relevance. Revival is not easy, but parties can be relevant. State structure and policy can smother or enhance the relevance, role, and reputation of political parties. Politics will decide. States are shaped not only by forces but by politics and choices. As in the 1930s and the abortive attempt of the 1960s, the parties themselves can play a role in shaping this state and defining a new party era. In the case of political parties, the cure for the problems of politics is indeed more politics.

Appendix

Budget-Related Roll-Call Votes, 1947–1990

Table A.1
Major Budget-Related Categories

Year	N	Appropriation	Authorization	Debt Limit	Tax	Budget Resolution
			Percentage of Votes Considering:			
1947	38	42.1	29.0	0.0	21.1	7.9
1948	29	44.8	31.0	0.0	17.2	6.9
1949	41	17.1	78.1	0.0	4.9	0.0
1950	44	11.4	77.3	0.0	11.4	0.0
1951	48	62.5	29.2	0.0	8.3	0.0
1952	28	50.0	42.9	0.0	0.0	0.0
1953	28	57.1	28.6	7.1	7.1	0.0
1954	31	16.1	58.1	0.0	19.4	0.0
1955	30	13.3	76.7	3.3	6.7	0.0
1956	35	17.1	82.9	0.0	0.0	0.0
1957	56	55.4	39.3	0.0	0.0	0.0
1958	42	16.7	71.4	7.1	0.0	0.0
1959	48	27.1	64.6	4.2	4.2	0.0
1960	39	20.5	64.1	5.1	15.4	0.0
1961	54	27.8	66.7	1.9	3.7	0.0
1962	47	27.7	55.3	8.5	8.5	0.0
1963	64	31.3	50.0	12.5	6.3	0.0
1964	59	23.7	67.8	1.7	6.8	0.0
1965	71	21.1	73.2	2.8	2.8	0.0
1966	67	29.9	53.7	3.0	13.4	0.0
1967	89	46.1	42.7	7.9	3.4	0.0
1968	79	32.9	60.8	0.0	7.6	0.0
1969	62	41.9	45.2	0.0	12.9	0.0
1970	97	29.9	65.0	2.1	2.1	0.0
1971	103	39.8	56.3	1.9	1.9	0.0
1972	106	44.3	46.2	6.6	1.9	0.0
1973	199	31.2	53.8	5.0	4.0	0.0
1974	161	39.8	56.5	1.2	1.2	1.2
1975	251	29.9	44.6	4.4	16.7	4.8
1976	222	35.6	49.1	1.8	7.7	5.9
1977	255	31.4	46.3	2.0	10.2	11.8
1978	294	34.0	46.6	3.1	7.1	9.2

(continued)

Table A.1   *(Continued)*

		Percentage of Votes Considering:				
Year	*N*	*Appropriation*	*Authorization*	*Debt Limit*	*Tax*	*Budget Resolution*
1979	270	32.2	44.4	4.1	3.3	16.7
1980	248	41.1	37.5	3.2	5.7	13.3
1981	157	43.3	38.2	1.3	4.5	12.7
1982	217	31.8	46.1	0.0	5.5	16.1
1983	190	37.9	54.2	1.6	4.2	2.1
1984	200	36.5	52.0	3.0	2.0	6.5
1985	227	33.5	51.1	4.4	2.6	7.5
1986	212	40.6	47.6	1.9	1.4	8.0
1987	199	39.2	48.2	3.5	1.5	7.5
1988	158	37.3	52.5	0.0	3.2	2.5
1989	189	46.0	39.2	1.6	2.7	9.0
1990	247	40.5	47.8	4.1	4.1	5.7

Note: Entries omit consensus votes—votes with 90 percent or more of Democrats voting in the same direction as 90 percent or more of Republicans. Budget resolution votes include legislative budget votes in 1947 and 1948.

Table A.2
Selected Major Policy Areas

Year	N	Trade[a]	Defense	Agriculture	All Rules[b]	Rule for Immediate Passage
					Percentage of Votes Considering:	
1947	38	0.0	0.0	29.0	7.9	2.6
1948	29	0.0	0.0	10.3	6.9	3.4
1949	41	0.0	14.6	9.8	19.5	4.9
1950	44	4.6	0.0	2.3	6.8	0.0
1951	48	2.1	6.3	8.3	14.6	4.2
1952	28	0.0	17.9	3.6	21.4	10.7
1953	28	0.0	25.0	7.1	0.0	0.0
1954	31	0.0	12.9	3.2	16.1	3.2
1955	30	0.0	10.0	10.0	10.0	6.7
1956	35	0.0	14.3	20.0	17.1	5.7
1957	56	0.0	12.5	5.4	1.8	1.8
1958	42	0.0	14.3	11.9	31.0	11.9
1959	48	2.1	10.4	16.7	2.1	2.1
1960	39	2.6	2.6	7.7	15.4	5.1
1961	54	0.0	7.4	9.3	3.7	1.9
1962	47	0.0	0.0	10.6	8.5	2.1
1963	64	4.7	6.3	14.1	12.5	3.1
1964	59	3.4	0.0	8.5	8.5	5.1
1965	71	2.8	4.2	8.5	8.5	0.0
1966	67	1.5	0.0	1.5	6.0	0.0
1967	89	0.0	1.1	2.3	5.6	0.0
1968	79	3.8	5.1	8.9	5.1	1.3
1969	62	0.0	17.7	6.5	8.1	3.2
1970	97	0.0	9.3	3.1	7.2	1.0
1971	103	0.0	12.6	4.9	6.8	2.9
1972	106	0.0	12.3	0.9	12.3	3.8
1973	199	1.5	11.6	12.6	8.5	4.5
1974	161	2.5	16.2	2.5	15.5	10.6
1975	251	0.8	13.9	6.4	10.0	4.0
1976	222	0.9	16.7	2.3	11.7	4.1
1977	255	1.6	15.3	7.1	7.8	0.0
1978	294	4.4	12.9	5.4	5.1	0.0
1979	270	0.0	12.2	0.7	4.8	1.1
1980	248	1.6	6.9	2.8	13.3	4.4
1981	157	0.0	21.0	9.6	9.6	2.5
1982	217	0.5	15.2	4.2	9.7	3.2

(continued)

Table A.2   *(Continued)*

				Percentage of Votes Considering:		
Year	*N*	*Trade*[a]	*Defense*	*Agriculture*	*All Rules*[b]	*Rule for Immediate Passage*
1983	190	3.2	9.5	5.8	26.3	9.5
1984	200	0.0	14.5	4.0	9.5	5.0
1985	227	0.0	18.9	11.5	16.3	4.0
1986	212	2.8	17.5	3.8	14.6	2.4
1987	199	0.0	14.1	1.5	21.1	2.0
1988	158	1.9	20.3	6.3	19.0	5.1
1989	189	0.5	15.3	2.1	13.2	4.8
1990	247	0.8	10.9	11.7	18.2	6.5

Note: Entries omit consensus votes—votes with 90 percent or more of Democrats voting in the same direction as 90 percent or more of Republicans.

[a] The Trade column in table A.2 includes only those votes falling into one of the five categories in table A.1. Additional trade votes were used to calculate the indexes reported in chapter 1.

[b] The first Rules column includes all votes considering rules. The second column, a subset of the first, includes only those votes calling for a suspension of the rules and immediate passage of a bill with no amendments.

Bibliography

Aaron, Henry. 1990. Statement before the Committee on Rules, Subcommittee on the Legislative Process, United States Congress, House of Representatives, March 21. Manuscript.

Abramowitz, Alan I. 1994. "Issue Evolution Reconsidered: Racial Attitudes and Partisanship in the U.S. Electorate." *American Journal of Political Science* 38: 1–24.

Abramowitz, Alan I., Albert D. Cover, and Helmut Norpoth. 1986. "The President's Party in Midterm Elections: Going from Bad to Worse." *American Journal of Political Science* 30: 562–76.

Abramson, Paul R. 1976. "Generational Change and the Decline of Party Identification in America, 1952–1974." *American Political Science Review* 70: 469–78.

Abramson, Paul R., John H. Aldrich, and David W. Rohde. 1990. *Change and Continuity in the 1988 Elections*. Washington, D.C.: CQ Press.

Adamany, David. 1980. "The Supreme Court's Role in Critical Elections." In Richard J. Trilling and Bruce A. Campbell, eds., *Realignment in American Politics: Toward a Theory*. Austin: University of Texas Press.

Advisory Commission on Intergovernmental Relations. 1986. *The Transformation in American Politics: Implications for Federalism*. Washington, D.C.: Government Printing Office.

Aldrich, John. 1988. "Modeling the Party-in-the-Legislature." Paper prepared for the annual meeting of the American Political Science Association, Washington, D.C., September 1–4.

———. 1995. *Why Parties? The Origins and Transformation of Party Politics in America*. Chicago: University of Chicago Press.

Aldrich, John, and Richard G. Niemi. 1990. "The Sixth American Party System: The 1960s Realignment and the Candidate-Centered Parties." Working Paper 107, Duke University Program in Political Economy.

Alesina, Alberto. 1987. "Macroeconomic Policy in a Two-Party System as a Repeated Game." *Quarterly Journal of Economics* 102: 651–78.

———. 1988. "Macroeconomics and Politics." *National Bureau of Economic Research Macroeconomic Annual* 1988: 11–55.

Alesina, Alberto, John Londregan, and Howard Rosenthal. 1993. "A Model of the Political Economy of the United States." *American Political Science Review* 87: 12–33.

Alesina, Alberto, and Howard Rosenthal. 1989. "Partisan Cycles in Congressional Elections and the Macroeconomy." *American Political Science Review* 83: 373–98.

———. 1995. *Partisan Politics, Divided Government, and the Economy*. New York: Cambridge University Press.

Alesina, Alberto, and Jeffrey Sachs. 1988. "Political Parties and the Business

Cycle in the United States, 1948–1984." *Journal of Money, Credit, and Banking* 20: 63–82.

Alford, John R., and David W. Brady. 1989. "Personal and Partisan Advantage in U.S. Congressional Elections, 1846–1986." In Lawrence C. Dodd and Bruce I. Oppenheimer, eds., *Congress Reconsidered*. 4th ed. Washington, D.C.: CQ Press.

Alt, James E. 1984. "Dealignment and the Dynamics of Partisanship in Britain." In Russell J. Dalton, Scott C. Flanagan, and Paul Allen Beck, eds., *Electoral Change in Advanced Industrial Democracies: Realignment or Dealignment?* Princeton: Princeton University Press.

———. 1985. "Political Parties, World Demand, and Unemployment: Domestic and International Sources of Economic Activity." *American Political Science Review* 79: 1016–40.

Alvarez, R. Michael, Geoffrey Garrett, and Peter Lange. 1991. "Government Partisanship, Labor Organization, and Macroeconomic Performance." *American Political Science Review* 85: 539–56.

APSA Committee on Political Parties. 1950. "Toward a More Responsible Party System." *American Political Science Review* 44 (Supplement).

Arcelus, Francisco, and Allan H. Meltzer. 1975. "The Effect of Aggregate Economic Variables on Congressional Elections." *American Political Science Review* 69: 1232–39.

Argersinger, Peter H. 1992. *Structure, Process, and Party: Essays in American Political History*. Armonk, N.Y.: M. E. Sharpe.

Baer, Denise L., and David A. Bositis. 1988. *Elite Cadres and Party Coalitions: Representing the Public in Party Politics*. Westport, Conn.: Greenwood Press.

———. 1993. *Politics and Linkage in a Democratic Society*. Englewood Cliffs, N.J.: Prentice-Hall.

Bailey, Christopher J. 1988. *The Republican Party in the U.S. Senate, 1974–1984: Party Change and Institutional Development*. New York: St. Martin's Press.

Bailey, Stephen K. 1959. *The Condition of Our National Political Parties*. Washington, D.C.: Fund for the Republic.

Barrie, Robert W. 1987. *Congress and the Executive: The Making of the United States Foreign Trade Policy, 1789–1968*. New York: Garland.

Baldwin, Robert. 1986. *The Political Economy of U.S. Import Policy*. Cambridge: MIT Press.

Bauer, Raymond A., Ithiel de Sola Pool, and Lewis Anthony Dexter. 1963. *American Business and Public Policy: The Politics of Foreign Trade*. New York: Atherton Press.

Beck, Morris. 1980. "The Public Sector and Economic Stability." In United States Congress, Joint Economic Committee, *The Business Cycle and Public Policy, 1929–80*. Washington, D.C.: Government Printing Office.

Beck, Paul Allen. 1974. "A Socialization Theory of Partisan Realignment." In Richard G. Niemi and Associates, eds., *The Politics of Future Citizens: New Dimensions in the Political Socialization of Children*. San Francisco: Jossey-Bass.

———. 1984. "The Dealignment Era in America." In Russell J. Dalton, Scott C. Flanagan, and Paul Allen Beck, eds., *Electoral Change in Advanced Industrial*

Democracies: Realignment or Dealignment? Princeton: Princeton University Press.

———. 1988. "Incomplete Realignment: The Reagan Legacy for Parties and Elections." In Charles O. Jones, ed., *The Reagan Legacy: Promise and Performance*. Chatham, N.J.: Chatham House.

Bensel, Richard F. 1984. *Sectionalism and American Political Development*. Madison: University of Wisconsin Press.

———. 1990. *Yankee Leviathan: The Origins of Central State Authority in America, 1859–1877*. New York: Cambridge University Press.

Berger, Suzanne. 1979. "Politics and Antipolitics in Western Europe in the Seventies." *Daedalus* 108: 27–50.

———. 1981. "Introduction." In Suzanne Berger, ed., *Organizing Interests in Western Europe: Pluralism, Corporatism, and the Transformation of Politics*. New York: Cambridge University Press.

Berry, Brian J. L. 1991. *Long-Wave Rhythms in Economic Development and Political Behavior*. Baltimore: Johns Hopkins University Press.

Bibby, John F. 1990. "Party Organization at the State Level." In L. Sandy Maisel, ed., *The Parties Respond: Changes in the American Party System*. Boulder, Colo.: Westview Press.

Bibby, John F., James L. Gibson, Cornelius P. Cotter, and Robert J. Huckshorn. 1983. "Trends in Party Organizational Strength, 1960–1980." *International Political Science Review* 4: 21–27.

Blinder, Alan S. 1989. *Macroeconomics under Debate*. New York: Harvester Wheatsheaf.

Block, Fred L. 1977. *The Origins of International Economic Disorder: A Study of United States Monetary Policy from World War II to the Present*. Berkeley: University of California Press.

———. 1990. *Postindustrial Possibilities: A Critique of Economic Discourse*. Berkeley: University of California Press.

Bloom, Howard S., and H. Douglas Price. 1975. "Voter Response to Short-Run Economic Conditions: The Asymmetric Effect of Prosperity and Recession." *American Political Science Review* 69: 1240–54.

Bluestone, Barry, and Bennett Harrison. 1982. *The Deindustrialization of America: Plant Closings, Community Abandonment, and the Dismantling of Basic Industry*. New York: Basic Books.

Blumenthal, Sidney. 1982. *The Permanent Campaign*. 2d ed. New York: Simon and Schuster.

Boltho, Andrea, ed. 1982. *The European Economy: Growth and Crisis*. New York: Oxford University Press.

Bond, Jon R., and Richard Fleisher. 1990. *The President in the Legislative Arena*. Chicago: University of Chicago Press.

Born, Richard. 1990. "Surge and Decline, Negative Voting, and the Midterm Loss Phenomenon: A Simultaneous Choice Analysis." *American Journal of Political Science* 34: 615–45.

Bowles, Samuel, David M. Gordon, and Thomas E. Weisskopf. 1984. *Beyond the Waste Land: A Democratic Alternative to Economic Decline*. Garden City, N.Y.: Anchor Press.

Brady, David W. 1978. "Critical Elections, Congressional Parties, and Clusters of Policy Changes." *British Journal of Political Science* 8: 79–99.

———. 1980. "Elections, Congress, and Public Policy Changes, 1886–1960." In Richard J. Trilling and Bruce A. Campbell, eds., *Realignment in American Politics: Toward a Theory.* Austin: University of Texas Press.

———. 1988. *Critical Elections and Congressional Policy Making.* Stanford: Stanford University Press.

———. 1990. "Coalitions in the U.S. Congress." In L. Sandy Maisel, ed., *The Parties Respond: Changes in the American Party System.* Boulder, Colo.: Westview Press.

Brady, David W., Joseph Cooper, and Patricia A. Hurley. 1979. "The Decline of Party in the U.S. House of Representatives, 1887–1968." *Legislative Studies Quarterly* 4: 381–407.

Brady, David W., with Joseph Stewart Jr. 1982. "Congressional Party Realignment and Transformations of Public Policy in Three Realignment Eras." *American Journal of Political Science* 26: 333–60.

Brand, Donald R. 1993. "Political Parties and the New Deal." In Peter W. Schramm and Bradford P. Wilson, eds., *American Political Parties and Constitutional Politics.* Lanham, Md.: Rowman and Littlefield.

Branyan, Robert L., and Lawrence H. Larsen. 1971. *The Eisenhower Administration, 1953–1960: A Documentary History.* Vol. 2. New York: Random House.

Bridges, Amy. 1986. "Becoming American: The Working Classes in the United States before the Civil War." In Ira Katznelson and Aristide R. Zolberg, eds., *Working-Class Formation: Nineteenth-Century Patterns in Western Europe and the United States.* Princeton: Princeton University Press.

———. 1994. "Creating Cultures of Reform." *Studies in American Political Development* 8: 1–23.

Brinkley, Alan. 1989. "The New Deal and the Idea of the State." In Steve Fraser and Gary Gerstle, eds., *The Rise and Fall of the New Deal Order.* Princeton: Princeton University Press.

Brock, William A., and Stephen P. Magee. 1978. "The Economics of Special Interest Politics: The Case of the Tariff." *American Economic Review Papers and Proceedings* 68: 246–50.

Broder, David S. 1972. *The Party's Over: The Failure of Politics in America.* New York: Harper.

Budge, Ian, and Richard I. Hofferbert. 1990. "Mandates and Policy Outputs: U.S. Party Platforms and Federal Expenditures." *American Political Science Review* 84: 111–32.

Buell, Emmett H., Jr. 1987. "Review Essay: The 1984 Elections." *Journal of Politics* 49: 581–95.

Burk, Robert F. 1990. *The Corporate State and the Broker State: The DuPonts and American National Politics, 1925–1940.* Cambridge: Harvard University Press.

Burnham, Walter Dean. 1968. "American Voting Behavior and the 1964 Election." *Midwest Journal of Political Science* 12: 1–40.

———. 1970. *Critical Elections and the Mainsprings of American Politics.* New York: Norton.

———. 1975. "Insulation and Responsiveness in Congressional Elections." *Political Science Quarterly* 90: 411–35.

———. 1981a. "The 1980 Earthquake: Realignment, Reaction, or What?" In Thomas Ferguson and Joel Rogers, eds., *The Hidden Election: Politics and Economics in the 1980 Presidential Campaign.* New York: Pantheon.

———. 1981b. "The System of 1896: An Analysis." In Paul Kleppner, ed., *The Evolution of American Electoral Systems.* Westport, Conn.: Greenwood Press.

———. 1982. *The Current Crisis in American Politics.* New York: Oxford University Press.

———. 1984. "Parties and Political Modernization." In Richard L. McCormick, ed., *Political Parties and the Modern State.* New Brunswick, N.J.: Rutgers University Press.

———. 1985. "The 1984 Election and the Future of American Politics." In Ellis Sandoz and Cecil Crabb, eds., *Election '84: Landslide without a Mandate?* New York: New American Library.

———. 1987. "The Turnout Problem." In A. James Reichley, ed., *Elections American Style.* Washington, D.C.: Brookings Institution.

———. 1991. "Critical Realignment: Dead or Alive?" In Byron E. Shafer, ed., *The End of Realignment? Interpreting American Electoral Eras.* Madison: University of Wisconsin Press.

———. 1994. "Pattern Recognition and 'Doing' Political History: Art, Science, or Bootless Enterprise?" In Lawrence C. Dodd and Calvin Jillson, eds., *The Dynamics of American Politics: Approaches and Interpretations.* Boulder, Colo.: Westview Press.

Burtless, Gary, ed. 1990. *A Future of Lousy Jobs? The Changing Structure of U.S. Wages.* Washington, D.C.: Brookings Institution.

Cain, Bruce, John Ferejohn, and Morris Fiorina. 1987. *The Personal Vote: Constituency Service and Electoral Independence.* Cambridge: Harvard University Press.

Cameron, David R. 1984a. "The Politics and Economics of the Business Cycle." In Thomas Ferguson and Joel Rogers, eds., *The Political Economy: Readings in the Politics and Economics of American Public Policy.* Armonk, N.Y.: M. E. Sharpe.

———. 1984b. "Social Democracy, Corporatism, Labor Quiescence, and the Representation of Economic Interest in Advanced Capitalist Society." In John H. Goldthorpe, ed., *Order and Conflict in Contemporary Capitalism: Studies in the Political Economy of Western European Nations.* New York: Oxford University Press.

Campbell, Colin. 1986. *Managing the Presidency: Carter, Reagan, and the Search for Executive Harmony.* Pittsburgh: University of Pittsburgh Press.

Campbell, James E. 1991. "The Presidential Surge and Its Midterm Decline in Congressional Elections, 1868–1988." *Journal of Politics* 53: 477–87.

———. 1993. *The Presidential Pulse of Congressional Elections.* Lexington: University Press of Kentucky.

Carmines, Edward G. 1994. "Political Issues, Party Alignments, Spatial Models, and the Post–New Deal Party System." In Lawrence C. Dodd and Calvin Jillson, eds., *New Perspectives on American Politics.* Washington, D.C.: CQ Press.

Carmines, Edward G., John P. McIver, and James A. Stimson. 1987. "Unrealized Partisanship: A Theory of Dealignment." *Journal of Politics* 49: 377–400.

Carmines, Edward G., and James A. Stimson. 1981. "Issue Evolution, Population Replacement, and Normal Partisan Change." *American Political Science Review* 75: 107–18.

———. 1984. "The Dynamics of Issue Evolution: The United States." In Russell J. Dalton, Scott C. Flanagan, and Paul Allen Beck, eds. *Electoral Change in Advanced Industrial Democracies: Realignment or Dealignment?* Princeton: Princeton University Press.

———. 1986. "On the Structure and Sequence of Issue Evolution." *American Political Science Review* 80: 901–20.

———. 1989. *Issue Evolution: Race and the Transformation of American Politics.* Princeton: Princeton University Press.

Carter, Jimmy. 1982. *Keeping Faith: Memoirs of a President.* New York: Bantam Books.

Cavanagh, Thomas E., and James L. Sundquist. 1985. "The New Two-Party System." In John E. Chubb and Paul E. Peterson, eds., *The New Direction in American Politics.* Washington, D.C.: Brookings Institution.

Chamberlain, Lawrence H. 1940. *The President, Congress, and Legislation.* New York: Columbia University Press.

Chambers, William N. 1975. "Party Development and the American Mainstream." In William N. Chambers and Walter Dean Burnham, eds., *The American Party Systems: Stages of Political Development.* 2d ed. New York: Oxford University Press.

Chappell, Henry W., Jr., and William R. Keech. 1985. "A New View of Political Accountability for Economic Performance." *American Political Science Review* 79: 10–27.

Chase-Dunn, Christopher. 1980. "The Development of Core Capitalism in the Ante-Bellum United States." In A. Bergessen, ed., *Studies in the Modern World System.* New York: Academic Press.

Chrystal, K. A. 1983. *Controversies in Macroeconomics.* 2d ed. Oxford, England: Philip Alan.

Chubb, John E., and Paul E. Peterson. 1985. "Realignment and Institutionalization." In John E. Chubb and Paul E. Peterson, eds., *The New Direction in American Politics.* Washington, D.C.: Brookings Institution.

Clausen, Aage. 1973. *How Congressmen Decide: A Policy Focus.* New York: St. Martin's Press.

Clausen, Aage, and Rodney Anderson. 1994. "Partisan and Ideological Alignments in Congressional Voting during the Carter and Reagan Administrations." Paper prepared for the annual meeting of the American Political Science Association, New York, September 1–4.

Clubb, Jerome M., William H. Flanigan, and Nancy H. Zingale. 1980. *Partisan Realignment: Voters, Parties, and Government in American History.* Beverly Hills, Calif.: Sage.

———. 1989. "Partisan Realignment Revisited." Paper prepared for the annual meeting of the American Political Science Association, Atlanta, August 31–September 3.

Clubb, Jerome M., and Santa A. Traugott. 1977. "Partisan Cleavage and Cohesion in the House of Representatives, 1861–1974." *Journal of Interdisciplinary History* 7: 375–401.

Cohen, Joshua, and Joel Rogers. 1983. *On Democracy: Toward a Transformation of American Society.* New York: Penguin.

Coleman, John J. 1991. "Economic Conditions and Party Cohesion." Paper prepared for the annual meeting of the American Political Science Association, Washington, D.C., August 29–September 1.

———. 1992. "Economics, Recessions, and Party Decline: American Parties in the Fiscal State." Ph.D. diss., Massachusetts Institute of Technology.

———. 1994. "Party Organizational Strength and Partisanship in the Public." Paper prepared for the annual meeting of the American Political Science Association, New York, September 1–4.

Coleman, John J., and David B. Yoffie. 1990. "Institutional Incentives for Protection: The American Use of Voluntary Export Restraints." In Frank J. Macchiarola, ed., *International Trade: The Changing Role of the United States.* New York: Academy of Political Science.

Collie, Melissa P. 1984. "Voting Behavior in Legislatures." *Legislative Studies Quarterly* 9: 3–50.

———. 1988a. "The Rise of Coalition Politics: Voting in the U.S. House, 1933–1980." *Legislative Studies Quarterly* 13: 321–42.

———. 1988b. "Universalism and the Parties in the U.S. House of Representatives, 1921–1980." *American Journal of Political Science* 32: 865–83.

———. 1989. "Electoral Patterns and Voting Alignments in the U.S. House, 1886–1986." *Legislative Studies Quarterly* 14: 107–27.

Collie, Melissa P., and David W. Brady. 1985. "The Decline of Partisan Voting Coalitions in the House of Representatives." In Lawrence C. Dodd and Bruce I. Oppenheimer, eds., *Congress Reconsidered.* 3d ed. Washington, D.C.: CQ Press.

Collins, Robert M. 1981. *The Business Response to Keynes, 1929–1964.* New York: Columbia University Press.

Conkin, Paul K. 1975. *The New Deal.* 2d ed. Arlington Heights, Ill.: Harlan Davidson, Inc.

———. 1986. *Big Daddy from the Pedernales: Lyndon Baines Johnson.* Boston: Twayne.

Conybeare, John A. C. 1983. "Tariff Protection in Developed and Developing Countries: A Cross-Sectional and Longitudinal Analysis." *International Organization* 37: 441–67.

Cooper, Joseph, and Patricia Hurley. 1977. "The Electoral Basis of Party Voting: Patterns and Trends in the U.S. House of Representatives, 1887–1969." In Louis Maisel and Joseph Cooper, eds., *The Impact of the Electoral Process.* Beverly Hills, Calif.: Sage.

Cotter, Cornelius P., and John F. Bibby. 1980. "Institutional Development of Parties and the Thesis of Party Decline." *Political Science Quarterly* 95: 1–27.

Cotter, Cornelius P., James L. Gibson, John F. Bibby, and Robert J. Huckshorn. 1984. *Party Organizations in American Politics.* New York: Praeger.

Cotter, Patrick R. 1985. "The Decline in Partisanship: A Test of Four Explanations." *American Politics Quarterly* 13: 51–77.

Cover, Albert D., Neil Pinney, and George Serra. 1994. "Voting Behavior in the House and Senate: Regional Shifts and Contemporary Changes in Party Coalitions." Paper prepared for the annual meeting of the American Political Science Association, New York, September 1–4.

Cox, Gary W., and Mathew D. McCubbins. 1993. *Legislative Leviathan: Party Government in the House.* Berkeley: University of California Press.

Crewe, Ivor, B. Sarlvik, and James Alt. 1977. "Partisan Dealignment in Britain, 1964–1974." *British Journal of Political Science* 7: 129–90.

Crotty, William. 1984. *American Parties in Decline.* 2d ed. Boston: Little, Brown.

———. 1991. "Political Parties: Issues and Trends." In William Crotty, ed., *Political Science: Looking to the Future.* Vol. 4. Evanston, Ill.: Northwestern University Press.

Dalton, Russell J., Paul Allen Beck, and Scott C. Flanagan. 1984. "Electoral Change in Advanced Industrial Democracies." In Russell J. Dalton, Scott C. Flanagan, and Paul Allen Beck, eds., *Electoral Change in Advanced Industrial Democracies: Realignment or Dealignment?* Princeton: Princeton University Press.

Dalton, Russell J., Scott C. Flanagan, and Paul Allen Beck, eds. 1984. *Electoral Change in Advanced Industrial Democracies: Realignment or Dealignment?* Princeton: Princeton University Press.

Dalton, Russell F., and Manfred Kuechler, eds. 1990. *Challenging the Political Order: New Social and Political Movements in the Western Democracies.* New York: Oxford University Press.

Davidson, Roger H., ed. 1992. *The Postreform Congress.* New York: St. Martin' s.

Davis, Eric L. 1983. "Congressional Liaison: The People and the Institutions." In Anthony King, ed., *Both Ends of the Avenue: The Presidency, the Executive Branch, and Congress.* Washington, D.C.: American Enterprise Institute.

Deckard, Barbara Sinclair. 1976. "Political Upheaval and Congressional Voting: The Effects of the 1960s on Voting Patterns in the House of Representatives." *Journal of Politics* 38: 326–45.

Deckard, Barbara, and John Stanley. 1974. "Party Decomposition and Region: The House of Representatives, 1945–1970." *Western Political Quarterly* 27: 248–64.

Dennis, Jack. 1975. "Trends in Public Support for the American Party System." *British Journal of Political Science* 5: 187–230.

———. 1986. "Public Support for the Party System, 1964–1984." Paper prepared for the annual meeting of the American Political Science Association, Washington, D.C., August 28–31.

Dennis, Jack, and Diana Owen. 1994. "Anti-Partyism and Support for Perot, 1992–93." Paper prepared for the Workshop on Anti-Party Sentiment, ECPR Joint Sessions of Workshops, Madrid, Spain, April 17–22.

Destler, I. M. 1992. *American Trade Politics: System under Stress.* 2d. ed. Washington, D.C.: Institute for International Economics.

Dionne, E. J., Jr. 1991. *Why Americans Hate Politics.* New York: Simon and Schuster.

Dodd, Lawrence C., and Richard L. Schott. 1979. *Congress and the Administrative State.* New York: John Wiley and Sons.

Dow, Sheila C. 1985. *Macroeconomic Thought: A Methodological Approach.* New York: Basil Blackwell.

Downs, Anthony. 1957. *An Economic Theory of Democracy.* New York: Harper and Row.

Drucker, Peter F. 1967. "New Political Alignments in the Great Society." In Bertram M. Gross, ed., *A Great Society?* New York: Basic Books.

Dwyre, Diana. 1992. "Is Winning Everything? Party Strategies for the U.S. House of Representatives." Paper prepared for the annual meeting of the American Political Science Association, Chicago, September 3–6.

Eden, Robert. 1993. "The New Deal Revaluation of Partisanship." In Peter W. Schramm and Bradford P. Wilson, eds., *American Political Parties and Constitutional Politics.* Lanham, Md.: Rowman and Littlefield.

Edsall, Thomas Byrne. 1984. *The New Politics of Inequality.* New York: Norton.

Edsall, Thomas Byrne, and Mary D. Edsall. 1991. *Chain Reaction: The Impact of Race, Rights, and Taxes on American Politics.* New York: Norton.

Edwards, George C., III, and Stephen J. Wayne. 1990. *Presidential Leadership: Politics and Policy Making.* 2d ed. New York: St. Martin's Press.

Eisner, Robert, and Paul J. Pieper. 1984. "A New View of the Federal Debt and Budget Deficits." *American Economic Review* 74: 11–29.

Eldersveld, Samuel J. 1982. *Political Parties in American Society.* New York: Basic Books.

Ellwood, John W. 1983. "Budget Control in a Redistributive Environment." In Allen Schick, ed., *Making Economic Policy in Congress.* Washington, D.C.: American Enterprise Institute.

Epstein, Gerald. 1981. "Domestic Stagflation and Monetary Policy: The Federal Reserve and the Hidden Election." In Thomas Ferguson and Joel Rogers, eds., *The Hidden Election: Politics and Economics in the 1980 Presidential Campaign.* New York: Pantheon.

Erikson, Robert S. 1988. "The Puzzle of Midterm Loss." *Journal of Politics* 50: 1011–29.

———. 1990. "Economic Conditions and the Congressional Vote: A Review of the Macrolevel Evidence." *American Journal of Political Science* 34: 373–99.

Esping-Andersen, Gosta. 1990. *The Three Worlds of Welfare Capitalism.* Princeton: Princeton University Press.

Esty, Daniel C., and Richard E. Caves. 1983. "Market Structure and Political Influence: New Data on Political Expenditures, Activities, and Success." *Economic Inquiry* 21: 24–38.

Eubank, Robert B. 1985. "Incumbent Effects on Individual-Level Voting Behavior in Congressional Elections: A Decade of Exaggeration." *Journal of Politics* 47: 958–67.

Fenno, Richard F., Jr. 1962. "The House Appropriations Committee as a Political System: The Problem of Integration." *American Political Science Review* 56: 310–24.

———. 1966. *The Power of the Purse.* Boston: Little, Brown.

———. 1973. *Congressmen in Committees.* Boston: Little, Brown.

Ferguson, Thomas. 1982. "Party Realignment and American Industrial Structure:

The Investment Theory of Political Parties in Historical Perspective." *Research in Political Economy* 6: 1–82.

———. 1984. "From Normalcy to New Deal: Industrial Structure, Party Competition, and American Public Policy in the Great Depression." *International Organization* 38: 41–94.

———. 1994. "'Organized Capitalism,' Fiscal Policy, and the 1992 Democratic Campaign." In Lawrence C. Dodd and Calvin Jillson, eds., *New Perspectives on American Politics.* Washington, D.C.: CQ Press.

Ferguson, Thomas, and Joel Rogers. 1981. "The Reagan Victory: Corporate Coalitions in the 1980 Campaign." In Thomas Ferguson and Joel Rogers, eds., *The Hidden Election: Politics and Economics in the 1980 Presidential Campaign.* New York: Pantheon.

———. 1986. *Right Turn: The Decline of the Democrats and the Future of American Politics.* New York: Hill and Wang.

Finer, S. E. 1984. "The Decline of Party?" In Vernon Bogdanor, ed., *Parties and Democracy in Britain and America.* New York: Praeger.

Finger, J. Michael, H. Keith Hall, and Douglas R. Nelson. 1982. "The Political Economy of Administered Protection." *American Economic Review* 72: 452–66.

Fiorina, Morris P. 1977. *Congress: Keystone of the Washington Establishment.* New Haven: Yale University Press.

———. 1980. "The Decline of Collective Responsibility in American Politics." *Daedulus* 109: 25–45.

———. 1981. *Retrospective Voting in American National Elections.* New Haven: Yale University Press.

———. 1987. "Party Government in the United States: Diagnosis and Prognosis." In Richard S. Katz, ed., *Party Governments: European and American Experiences.* New York: Walter de Gruyter.

———. 1990. "The Electorate in the Voting Booth." In L. Sandy Maisel, ed., *The Parties Respond: Changes in the American Party System.* Boulder, Colo.: Westview Press.

Fisher, Louis. 1972. *President and Congress: Power and Policy.* New York: Free Press.

———. 1979. "The Authorization-Appropriation Process in Congress: Formal Rules and Informal Practices." *Catholic University Law Review* 29: 51–105.

———. 1990. Testimony before the Committee on Rules, Subcommittee on the Legislative Process, United States Congress, House of Representatives, March 21. Manuscript.

Flanigan, William H., and Nancy H. Zingale. 1985. "United States." In Ivor Crewe and David Denver, eds., *Electoral Change in Western Democracies: Patterns and Sources of Electoral Volatility.* London: Croon Helm.

Ford, Gerald R. 1979. *A Time to Heal: The Autobiography of Gerald R. Ford.* New York: Harper and Row.

Formisano, Ronald P. 1993. "The New Political History and the Election of 1840." *Journal of Interdisciplinary History* 23: 661–82.

———. 1994. "The Invention of the Ethnocultural Interpretation." *American Historical Review* 99: 453–77.

Frantzich, Stephen. 1989. *Political Parties in the Technological Age.* New York: Longman.

Freddi, Giorgio. 1986. "Bureaucratic Rationalities and the Prospect for Party Government." In Francis G. Castles and Rudolf Wildenmann, eds., *Visions and Realities of Party Government.* New York: Walter de Gruyter.

Freidel, Frank. 1990. *Franklin D. Roosevelt: A Rendezvous with Destiny.* Boston: Little, Brown.

Frendreis, John P., James L. Gibson, and Laura L. Vertz. 1990. "The Electoral Relevance of Local Party Organizations." *American Political Science Review* 84: 225–35.

Frendreis, John P., Alan R. Gitelson, Gregory Flemming, and Anne Layzell. 1993. "Local Political Parties and the 1992 Campaign for the State Legislature." Paper prepared for the annual meeting of the American Political Science Association, Washington, D.C., September 2–5.

Frieden, Jeff. 1988. "Sectoral Conflict and U.S. Foreign Economic Policy." *International Organization* 42: 59–90.

Gallarotti, Giutio M. 1985. "Toward a Business-Cycle Model of Tariffs." *International Organization* 39: 155–87.

Garand, James C., Kenneth Wink, and Bryan Vincent. 1993. "Changing Meanings of Electoral Marginality in U.S. House Elections, 1824–1978." *Political Research Quarterly* 46: 27–48.

Gibson, James L., Cornelius P. Cotter, John F. Bibby, and Robert J. Huckshorn. 1983. "Assessing Party Organizational Strength." *American Journal of Political Science* 27: 193–222.

———. 1985. "Whither the Local Parties? A Cross-Sectional and Longitudinal Analysis of the Strength of Party Organizations." *American Journal of Political Science* 29: 139–60.

Gibson, James L., John P. Frendreis, and Laura L. Vertz. 1989. "Party Dynamics in the 1980s: Changes in County Party Organizational Strength, 1980–1984." *American Journal of Political Science* 33: 67–90.

Gibson, James L., and Susan E. Scarrow. 1993. "State and Local Party Organizations in American Politics." In Eric M. Uslaner, ed., *American Political Parties: A Reader.* Itasca, Ill.: F. E. Peacock.

Gilmour, John B. 1990. *Reconcilable Differences? Congress, the Budget Process, and the Deficit.* Berkeley: University of California Press.

Ginsberg, Benjamin. 1976. "Elections and Public Policy." *American Political Science Review* 70: 41–49.

Ginsberg, Benjamin, and Martin Shefter. 1990. *Politics by Other Means: The Declining Importance of Elections in America.* New York: Basic Books.

Goldstein, Judith. 1986. "The Political Economy of Trade: Institutions of Protection." *American Political Science Review* 80: 161–84.

———. 1988. "Ideas, Institutions, and American Trade Policy." *International Organization* 42: 179–218.

Goldthorpe, John H. 1987. "Problems of Political Economy after the Postwar Period." In Charles S. Maier, ed., *Changing Boundaries of the Political: Essays on the Evolving Balance between the State and Society, Public and Private in Europe.* New York: Cambridge University Press.

Goodman, Saul, and Gerald H. Kramer. 1975. "Comment on Arcelus and Meltzer, The Effect of Aggregate Economic Conditions on Congressional Elections." *American Political Science Review* 69: 1255–65.

Goodwyn, Lawrence. 1978. *The Populist Moment: A Short History of the Agrarian Revolt in America.* New York: Oxford University Press.

Gordon, David M., Richard Edwards, and Michael Reich. 1982. *Segmented Work, Divided Workers: The Historical Transformation of Labor in the United States.* Cambridge: Cambridge University Press.

Gourevitch, Peter A. 1986. *Politics in Hard Times: Comparative Responses to International Economic Crises.* Ithaca: Cornell University Press.

Graham, Otis L., Jr. 1992. *Losing Time: The Industrial Policy Debate.* Cambridge: Harvard University Press.

Gramsci, Antonio. 1971. *Selections from the Prison Notebooks of Antonio Gramsci.* New York: International Publishers.

Green, John C., and James L. Guth. 1991. "Who Is Right and Who Is Left? Activist Coalitions in the Reagan Era." In Benjamin Ginsberg and Alan Stone, eds., *Do Elections Matter?* Armonk, N.Y.: M. E. Sharpe.

Gutfleish, Ron. 1986. "Roots of Trade Conflict: Technology, Market Structure, and the Politics of Industries in Competition." Paper prepared for the annual meeting of the American Political Science Association, Washington, D.C., August 28–31.

Hacker, Louis M. 1947. *The Shaping of the American Tradition.* New York: Columbia University Press.

Haggard, Stephan. 1988. "The Institutional Foundations of Hegemony: Explaining the Reciprocal Trade Agreements Act of 1934." *International Organization* 42: 91–120.

Hahn, Steven. 1983. *The Roots of Southern Populism: Yeoman Farmers and the Transformation of the Georgia Upcountry, 1850–1890.* New York: Oxford University Press.

Hall, Peter A. 1986. *Governing the Economy: The Politics of State Intervention in Britain and France.* New York: Oxford University Press.

————. 1989. "Conclusion: The Politics of Keynesian Ideas." In Peter A. Hall, ed. *The Political Power of Economic Ideas: Keynesianism across Nations.* Princeton: Princeton University Press.

Haller, H. Brandon, and Helmut Norpoth. 1994. "Let the Good Times Roll: The Economic Expectations of U.S. Voters." *American Journal of Political Science* 38: 625–50.

Hammond, Susan Webb. 1991. "Congressional Caucuses and Party Leaders in the House of Representatives." *Political Science Quarterly* 106: 277–94.

Hansen, Susan B. 1980. "Partisan Realignment and Tax Policy, 1789–1976." In Richard J. Trilling and Bruce A. Campbell, eds., *Realignment in American Politics: Toward a Theory.* Austin: University of Texas Press.

————. 1986. "The Politics of Federal Tax Policy." In James P. Pfiffner, ed., *The President and Economic Policy.* Philadelphia: Institute for the Study of Human Issues.

Hansen, Wendy L. 1990. "The International Trade Commission and the Politics of Protectionism." *American Political Science Review* 84: 21–46.

Hansen, Wendy L., and Kathy L. Powers. 1994. "Voting Behavior in the U.S. Senate on Trade Legislation." Paper prepared for the annual meeting of the American Political Science Association, New York, September 1–4.

Hardeman, D. B., and Donald C. Bacon. 1987. *Rayburn: A Biography.* Austin: Texas Monthly Press.

Hargrove, Erwin C. 1988. *Jimmy Carter as President: Leadership and the Politics of the Public Good.* Baton Rouge: Louisiana State University Press.

Hargrove, Erwin C., and Samuel A. Morley, eds. 1984. *The President and the Council of Economic Advisers: Interviews with CEA Chairmen.* Boulder, Colo.: Westview Press.

Harmel, Robert, and Kenneth Janda. 1982. *Parties and Their Environments: Limits to Reform?* New York: Longman.

Harris, Joseph P. 1964. *Congressional Control of Administration.* Washington, D.C.: Brookings Institution.

Harrison, Bennett, and Andrew Sum. 1979. "The Theory of 'Dual' or Segmented Labor Markets." *Journal of Economic Issues* 13: 687–706.

Hawley, Ellis W. 1966. *The New Deal and the Problem of Monopoly: A Study in Economic Ambivalence.* Princeton: Princeton University Press.

———. 1981. "Three Facets of Hooverian Associationalism: Lumber, Aviation, and Movies, 1921–1930." In Thomas K. McCraw, ed., *Regulation in Perspective: Historical Essays.* Boston: Harvard Business School.

Hays, Samuel P. 1981. "Politics and Society: Beyond the Political Party." In Paul Kleppner, ed., *The Evolution of American Electoral Systems.* Westport, Conn.: Greenwood Press.

Helleiner, G. K. 1977. "Transnational Enterprises and the New Political Economy of U.S. Trade Policy." *Oxford Economic Papers* 29: 102–16.

Herring, E. Pendleton. 1940. *The Politics of Democracy: American Parties in Action.* New York: Norton.

Herrnson, Paul S. 1986. "Do Parties Make a Difference? The Role of Party Organizations in Congressional Elections." *Journal of Politics* 48: 589–615.

———. 1988. *Party Campaigning in the 1980s.* Cambridge: Harvard University Press.

———. 1990. "Reemergent National Party Organizations." In L. Sandy Maisel, ed., *The Parties Respond: Changes in the American Party System.* Boulder, Colo.: Westview Press.

Hibbs, Douglas A., Jr. 1977. "Political Parties and Macroeconomic Policy." *American Political Science Review* 71: 1467–87.

———. 1987. *The American Political Economy: Macroeconomics and Electoral Politics.* Cambridge: Harvard University Press.

Hinckley, Barbara. 1990. *The Symbolic Presidency: How Presidents Portray Themselves.* New York: Routledge.

Hirschman, Albert O. 1970. *Exit, Voice, and Loyalty: Responses to Decline in Firms, Organizations, and States.* Cambridge: Harvard University Press.

Hofferbert, Richard I. 1993. "Society, Party, and Policy: Party Programs as Mechanisms of Mediation." Paper prepared for the annual meeting of the American Political Science Association, Washington, D.C., September 2–5.

Holt, James. 1975. "The New Deal and the American Anti-Statist Tradition." In

John Braeman, Robert H. Bremner, and David Brody, eds., *The New Deal: The National Level*. Columbus: Ohio State University Press.

Holt, Michael F. 1992. *Political Parties and American Political Development from the Age of Jackson to the Age of Lincoln*. Baton Rouge: Louisiana State University Press.

Horwitz, Morton J. 1977. *The Transformation of American Law, 1780–1860*. Cambridge: Harvard University Press.

Huckshorn, Robert J., James L. Gibson, Cornelius P. Cotter, and John F. Bibby. 1986. "Party Integration and Party Organizational Strength." *Journal of Politics* 48: 976–91.

Hufbauer, Gary Clyde, and Howard F. Rosen. 1986. *Trade Policy for Troubled Industries*. Washington, D.C.: Institute for International Economics.

Hughes, Kent H. 1979. *Trade, Taxes, and Transnationals: International Economic Decision Making in Congress*. New York: Praeger.

Huitt, Ralph K. 1990. *Working within the System*. Berkeley: IGS Press.

Hull, Cordell. 1934a. *International Trade and Domestic Prosperity: An Address before the National Foreign Trade Council, November 1934*. Washington, D.C.: Government Printing Office.

———. 1934b. *Report of the Delegates of the Unites States of America to the Seventh International Conference of American States*. December 3–26, 1933. Washington, D.C.: Government Printing Office.

———. 1935. *The Foreign Commercial Policy of the United States: An Address to the United States Chamber of Commerce, May 2, 1935*. Washington, D.C.: Government Printing Office.

Huntington, Samuel P. 1968. *Political Order in Changing Societies*. New Haven: Yale University Press.

———. 1973. "Congressional Responses to the Twentieth Century." In David B. Truman, ed. *The Congress and America's Future*. 2d ed. Englewood Cliffs, N.J.: Prentice-Hall.

———. 1981. *American Politics: The Promise of Disharmony*. Cambridge: Harvard University Press.

Hurley, Patricia A. 1991. "Partisan Representation, Realignment, and the Senate in the 1980s." *Journal of Politics* 53: 3–33.

Inglehart, Ronald. 1977. *The Silent Revolution: Changing Values and Political Styles among Western Publics*. Princeton: Princeton University Press.

———. 1990. *Culture Shift in Advanced Industrial Societies*. Princeton: Princeton University Press.

Ippolito, Dennis S. 1981. *Congressional Spending: A Twentieth Century Fund Report*. Ithaca: Cornell University Press.

Jackson, John E., and David C. King. 1989. "Public Goods, Private Interests, and Representation." *American Political Science Review* 83: 1143–64.

Jacobson, Gary C. 1985–1986. "Party Organization and Distribution of Campaign Resources: Republicans and Democrats in 1982." *Political Science Quarterly* 100: 603–25.

———. 1989. "Strategic Politicians and the Dynamics of U.S. House Elections, 1946–1986. "*American Political Science Review* 83: 773–93.

———. 1992. *The Politics of Congressional Elections*. 3d ed. New York: HarperCollins.

Jaenicke, Douglas W. 1986. "The Jacksonian Integration of Parties into the Constitutional System." *Political Science Quarterly* 101: 85–107.

James, Scott C. 1992. "A Party System Perspective on the Interstate Commerce Act of 1887: The Democracy, Electoral College Competition, and the Politics of Coalition Maintenance." *Studies in American Political Development* 6: 163–200.

Jeffries, John W. 1990. "The New New Deal: FDR and American Liberalism, 1937–1945." *Political Science Quarterly* 105: 397–418.

Jensen, Richard. 1981a. "The Last American Party System: Decay of Consensus, 1932–1980." In Paul Kleppner, ed., *The Evolution of American Electoral Systems*. Westport, Conn.: Greenwood Press.

———. 1981b. "Party Coalitions and the Search for Modern Values; 1820–1970." In Seymour M. Lipset, ed., *Party Coalitions in the 1980s*. San Francisco: Institute for Contemporary Studies.

Jones, Charles O. 1970. *The Minority Party in Congress*. Boston: Little, Brown.

———. 1983. "Presidential Negotiation with Congress." In Anthony King, ed., *Both Ends of the Avenue: The Presidency, the Executive Branch, and Congress*. Washington, D.C.: American Enterprise Institute.

———. 1988. *The Trusteeship Presidency: Jimmy Carter and the United States Congress*. Baton Rouge: Louisiana State University Press.

———. 1991. "Meeting Low Expectations: Strategy and Prospects of the Bush Presidency." In Colin Campbell and Bert A. Rockman, eds., *The Bush Presidency: First Appraisals*. Chatham, N.J.: Chatham House.

Kamlet, Mark S., and David Mowery. 1987. "Influences on Executive and Congressional Budgetary Priorities, 1953–1981." *American Political Science Review* 81: 155–78.

Kamlet, Mark S., David Mowery, and Tsai-Tsu Su. 1988. "Upsetting National Priorities: The Reagan Administration's Budgetary Strategy." *American Political Science Review* 82: 1293–1308.

Kane, Edward J. 1987. "External Pressure and the Operations of the Fed." In Paul E. Peretz, ed., *The Politics of American Economic Policy Making*. Armonk, N.Y.: M. E. Sharpe.

———. 1988. "Fedbashing and the Role of Monetary Arrangements in Managing Political Stress." In Thomas D. Willett, ed., *Political Business Cycles: The Political Economy of Money, Inflation, and Unemployment*. Durham, N.C.: Duke University Press.

Karl, Barry D. 1963. *Executive Reorganization and Reform in the New Deal*. Cambridge: Harvard University Press.

———. 1983. *The Uneasy State: The United States from 1915 to 1945*. Chicago: University of Chicago Press.

Katz, Richard S. 1986. "Party Government: A Rationalistic Conception." In Francis G. Castles and Rudolf Wildenmann, eds., *Visions and Realities of Party Government*. New York: Walter de Gruyter.

———. 1987. "Party Government and Its Alternatives." In Richard S. Katz, ed., *Party Governments: European and American Experiences*. New York: Walter de Gruyter.

Katznelson, Ira. 1986. "Rethinking the Silences of Social and Economic Policy." *Political Science Quarterly* 101: 307–25.

———. 1989. "'The Burdens of Urban History': Comment." *Studies in American Political Development* 3: 30–51.

Katznelson, Ira, and Bruce Pietrykowski. 1991. "Rebuilding the American State: Evidence from the 1940s." *Studies in American Political Development* 5: 301–39.

Kayden, Xandra, and Eddie Mahe Jr. 1985. *The Party Goes On: The Persistence of the Two-Party System in the United States.* New York: Basic Books.

Kazee, Thomas A., and Mary C. Thornberry. 1990. "Where's the Party? Congressional Candidate Recruitment and American Party Organizations." *Western Political Quarterly* 43: 61–80.

Keller, Robert R. 1987. "The Role of the State in the U.S. Economy during the 1920s." *Journal of Economic Issues* 21: 877–84.

Kelly, Sean Q. 1994. "Punctuated Change and the Era of Divided Government." In Lawrence C. Dodd and Calvin Jillson, eds., *New Perspectives on American Politics.* Washington, D.C.: CQ Press.

Kettl, Donald F. 1986. *Leadership at the Fed.* New Haven: Yale University Press.

Key, V. O., Jr. 1949. *Southern Politics in State and Nation.* New York: Alfred A. Knopf.

———. 1955. "A Theory of Critical Elections." *Journal of Politics* 17: 3–18.

———. 1959. "Secular Realignment and the Party System." *Journal of Politics* 21: 198–210.

———. 1964. *Politics, Parties, and Pressure Groups.* 5th ed. New York: Thomas Y. Crowell.

———. 1966. *The Responsible Electorate: Rationality in Presidential Voting, 1936–1960.* New York: Vintage.

Kiewiet, D. Roderick. 1983. *Macroeconomics and Micropolitics: The Electoral Effects of Economic Issues.* Chicago: University of Chicago Press.

Kiewiet, D. Roderick, and Mathew D. McCubbins. 1991. *The Logic of Delegation: Congressional Parties and the Appropriations Process.* Chicago: University of Chicago Press.

King, Anthony. 1969. "Political Parties in Western Democracies: Some Skeptical Reflections." *Polity* 2: 111–41.

King, Robert G., and Charles I. Plosser. 1989. "Real Business Cycles and the Test of the Adelmans." NBER Working Paper No. 3160. Cambridge: National Bureau of Economic Research.

Kingdon, John F. 1973. *Congressmen's Voting Decisions.* New York: Harper and Row.

Kirkpatrick, Jeane J. 1979. *Dismantling the Parties: Reflections on Party Reform and Party Decomposition.* Washington, D.C.: American Enterprise Institute.

Kleppner, Paul. 1981. "Critical Realignments and Electoral Systems." In Paul Kleppner, ed., *The Evolution of American Electoral Systems.* Westport, Conn.: Greenwood Press.

———. 1987. *Continuity and Change in Electoral Politics, 1893–1928.* Westport, Conn.: Greenwood Press.

Koford, Kenneth. 1989. "Dimensions in Congressional Voting." *American Political Science Review* 83: 949–65.

———. 1991. "On Dimensionalizing Roll Call Votes in the U.S. Congress." *American Political Science Review* 85: 960–75.

Kolko, Gabriel. 1963. *The Triumph of Conservatism: A Reinterpretation of American History, 1900–1916.* Chicago: Quadrangle.

Konda, Thomas M., and Lee Sigelman. 1987. "Public Evaluations of the American Parties, 1952–1984." *Journal of Politics* 49: 814–29.

Kramer, Gerald. 1971. "Short-Term Fluctuations in U.S. Voting Behavior, 1896–1964." *American Political Science Review* 65: 131–43.

Krasner, Stephen D. 1979. "The Tokyo Round: Particularistic Interests and Prospects for Stability in the Global Trading System." *International Studies Quarterly* 23: 491–531.

Kuklinski, James H., and Darrell M. West. 1981. "Economic Expectations and Voting Behavior in United States House and Senate Elections." *American Political Science Review* 75: 436–47.

Kurth, James R. 1979. "The Political Consequences of the Product Cycle: Industrial History and Political Outcomes." *International Organization* 33: 1–36.

Kuttner, Robert. 1991. *The End of Laissez-Faire: National Purpose and the Global Economy after the Cold War.* Philadelphia: University of Pennsylvania Press.

Ladd, Everett Carll, Jr. 1977. *Where Have All the Voters Gone? The Fracturing of America's Political Parties.* New York: Norton.

———. 1978. "The Shifting Party Coalitions, 1932–1976." In Seymour M. Lipset, ed., *Emerging Coalitions in American Politics.* San Francisco: Institute for Contemporary Studies.

Ladd, Everett Carll, Jr., and Charles D. Hadley. 1975. *Transformations of the American Party System: Political Coalitions from the New Deal to the 1970s.* New York: Norton.

Lake, David A. 1988a. *Power, Protection, and Free Trade: International Sources of U.S. Commercial Strategy, 1887–1939.* Ithaca, N.Y.: Cornell University Press.

———. 1988b. "The State and American Trade Strategy in the Pre-hegemonic Era." *International Organization* 42: 33–58.

Lavergne, Real P. 1983. *The Political Economy of U.S. Tariffs.* Toronto: Academic Press.

Lawrence, David G., and Richard Fleisher. 1987. "Puzzles and Confusions: Political Realignment in the 1980s." *Political Science Quarterly* 102: 79–92.

Layman, Geoffrey, and Edward G. Carmines. 1992. "Value Change and Partisan Realignment in the United States." Paper prepared for the annual meeting of the Midwest Political Science Association, Chicago, April 9–11.

Lee, Bradford A. 1989. "The Miscarriage of Necessity and Invention: Proto-Keynesianism and Democratic States in the 1930s." In Peter A. Hall, ed. *The Political Power of Economic Ideas: Keynesianism across Nations.* Princeton: Princeton University Press.

LeLoup, Lance T. 1982. "After the Blitz: Reagan and the U.S. Congressional Budget Process." *Legislative Studies Quarterly* 7: 321–39.

———. 1983. "Congress and the Dilemma of Economic Policy." In Allen Schick, ed., *Making Economic Policy in Congress.* Washington, D.C.: American Enterprise Institute.

———. 1988. "From Microbudgeting to Macrobudgeting: Evolution in Theory and Practice." In Irene Rubin, ed., *New Directions in Budget Theory.* Albany: State University of New York Press.

Lenway, Stephanie. 1982. "The Politics of Protection, Expansion, and Escape: International Collaboration and Business Power in U.S. Trade Policy." Ph.D. diss., University of California, Berkeley.

Leuchtenburg, William E. 1963. *Franklin D. Roosevelt and the New Deal, 1932–1940.* New York: Harper and Row.

Lewis, Justin, and Michael Morgan. 1992. "Images/Issues/Impact: The Media and Campaign '92 (survey)." Center for the Study of Communication, University of Massachusetts, Amherst. Manuscript.

Lewis-Beck, Michael S. 1988. *Economics and Elections: The Major Western Democracies.* Ann Arbor: University of Michigan Press.

Lewis-Beck, Michael S., and Tim W. Rice. 1992. *Forecasting Elections.* Washington, D.C.: CQ Press.

Lewis-Beck, Michael S., and Peverill Squire. 1991. "The Transformation of the American State: The New Era–New Deal Test." *Journal of Politics* 53: 106–21.

Lipset, Seymour Martin. 1968. *Revolution and Counterrevolution: Change and Persistence in Social Structures.* New York: Basic Books.

Lipset, Seymour Martin, and Stein Rokkan. 1967. "Cleavage Structures, Party Systems, and Voter Alignments: An Introduction." In Seymour Martin Lipset and Stein Rokkan, eds., *Party Systems and Voter Alignments: Cross-National Perspectives.* New York: Free Press.

Lipset, Seymour Martin, and William Schneider. 1983. "The Decline of Confidence in American Institutions." *Political Science Quarterly* 98: 379–402.

———. 1987. "The Confidence Gap during the Reagan Years, 1981–1987." *Political Science Quarterly* 102: 1–23.

Lohmann, Susanne, and Sharyn O'Halloran. 1991. "Delegation Mechanisms in International Trade: Congress, the President, and U.S. Protectionism." Paper prepared for the annual meeting of the American Political Science Association, Washington, D.C., August 29–September 1.

Longley, Lawrence D. 1992. "The Institutionalization of the National Democratic Party: A Process Stymied, Then Revitalized." *Wisconsin Political Scientist* 7: 9–15.

Loomis, Burdett. 1988. *The New American Politician: Ambition, Entrepreneurship, and the Changing Face of Political Life.* New York: Basic Books.

Lowery, David, Samuel Bookheimer, and James Malachowski. 1985. "Partisanship in the Appropriations Process: Fenno Revisited." *American Politics Quarterly* 13: 188–99.

Lowi, Theodore J. 1975. "Party, Policy, and Constitution in America." In William N. Chambers and Walter Dean Burnham, eds., *The American Party Systems: Stages of Political Development.* 2d ed. New York: Oxford University Press.

———. 1979. *The End of Liberalism: The Second Republic of the United States* 2d ed. New York: Norton.

Macdonald, Stuart Elaine, and George Rabinowitz. 1987. "The Dynamics of Structural Realignment." *American Political Science Review* 81: 775–96.

MacKuen, Michael B., Robert S. Erikson, and James A. Stimson. 1989. "Macropartisanship." *American Political Science Review* 83: 1125–42.

MacNeil, Neil. 1982. *Dirksen: Portrait of a Public Man.* New York: World Publishing.

MacRae, Duncan, Jr. 1970. *Issues and Parties in Legislative Voting: Methods of Statistical Analysis*. New York: Harper and Row.

Maggiotto, Michael A., and Gary D. Wekkin. 1993. "'His to Lose': The Failure of George Herbert Walker Bush, 1992." *American Review of Politics* 14: 163–82.

Mahler, Vincent, and Claudio J. Katz. 1984. "The Impact of Government Expenditures on Growth and Distribution in Developed Market Economy Countries: A Cross-National Study." Paper prepared for the annual meeting of the American Political Science Association, Washington, D.C., August 30–September 2.

Mair, Peter, ed. 1990. *The West European Party System*. New York: Oxford University Press.

Malbin, Michael J. 1993. "Political Parties across the Separation of Powers." In Peter W. Schramm and Bradford P. Wilson, eds., *American Political Parties and Constitutional Politics*. Lanham, Md.: Rowman and Littlefield.

Martin, Andrew. 1973. "The Politics of Economic Policy in the United States: A Tentative View from a Comparative Perspective." Sage Professional Paper in Comparative Politics, series 01–040. Beverly Hills, Calif.: Sage Publications.

Martin, Elizabeth M. 1994. "Congressional Delegation: Lessons from Fast Track." Paper prepared for the annual meeting of the American Political Science Association, New York, September 1–4.

Mayhew, David R. 1974. *Congress: The Electoral Connection*. New Haven: Yale University Press.

McAdams, John C., and John R. Johannes. 1988. "Congressmen, Perquisites, and Elections." *Journal of Politics* 50: 412–39.

McCleskey, Clifton, and Pierce McCleskey. 1984. "Jimmy Carter and the Democratic Party." In M. Glenn Abernathy, Dilys M. Hill, and Phil Williams, eds., *The Carter Years: The President and Policy Making*. New York: St. Martin's Press.

McCormick, Richard L. 1986. *The Party Period and Public Policy: American Politics from the Age of Jackson to the Progressive Era*. New York: Oxford University Press.

McDonald, Forrest. 1965. *The Formation of the American Republic, 1776–1790*. Baltimore: Penguin Books.

McKeown, Timothy. 1984. "Firms and Tariff Regime Change: Explaining the Demand for Protection." *World Politics* 36: 215–33.

Meier, Kenneth J., and Kenneth W. Kramer. 1980. "The Impact of Realigning Elections on Public Bureaucracies." In Richard J. Trilling and Bruce A. Campbell, eds., *Realignment in American Politics: Toward a Theory*. Austin: University of Texas Press.

Milkis, Sidney M. 1981. "The New Deal, The Decline of Parties, and the Administrative State." PhD. diss., University of Pennsylvania.

———. 1984. "Party Leadership, Policy Reform, and the Development of the Modern Presidency: The Impact of the Roosevelt and Johnson Presidencies on the American Party System." Paper prepared for the annual meeting of the American Political Science Association, Washington, D.C., August 30–September 2.

——. 1993. *The President and the Parties: The Transformation of the American Party System since the New Deal*. New York: Oxford University Press.

Milner, Helen V. 1988. *Resisting Protectionism: Global Industries and the Politics of International Trade*. Princeton: Princeton University Press.

Milner, Helen, and David B. Yoffie. 1989. "Between Free Trade and Protectionism: Strategic Trade Policy and a Theory of Corporate Trade Demands." *International Organization* 43: 239–72.

Moe, Terry M. 1989. "The Politics of Bureaucratic Structure." In John E. Chubb and Paul E. Peterson, eds., *Can the Government Govern?* Washington, D.C.: Brookings Institution.

Mollenkopf, John, James O'Connor, and Alan Wolfe. 1976. "The Crisis of Party Politics: Towards a Historical Materialist Theory of Political Parties and the Capitalist State." Paper prepared for the annual meeting of the American Political Science Association, Chicago, September 1–5.

Morgan, Iwan W. 1990. *Eisenhower versus "The Spenders": The Eisenhower Administration, The Democrats, and the Budget, 1953–60*. New York: St. Martin's Press.

Morone, James A. 1990. *The Democratic Wish: Popular Participation and the Limits of American Government*. New York: Basic Books.

Morris, Richard B. 1946. *Government and Labor in Early America*. New York: Columbia University Press.

Mutz, Diana C. 1994. "Contextualizing Personal Experience: The Role of Mass Media." *Journal of Politics* 56: 689–714.

Nash, Gerald D. 1981. "The Managerial State: Government and Business since 1940." In Robert Weible, Oliver Ford, and Paul Marion, eds., *Essays from the Lowell Conference on Industrial History, 1980 and 1981*. Lowell, Mass.: Lowell Conference on Industrial History.

Nau, Henry B. 1992. *The Myth of America's Decline: Leading the World Economy into the 1990s*. New York: Oxford University Press.

Nelson, Douglas. 1988. "Endogenous Tariff Theory: A Critical Survey." *American Journal of Political Science* 32: 796–837.

Nexon, David H. 1980. "Methodological Issues in the Study of Realignment." In Richard J. Trilling and Bruce A. Campbell, eds., *Realignment in American Politics: Toward a Theory*. Austin: University of Texas Press.

Nie, Norman H., Sidney Verba, and John R. Petrocik. 1979. *The Changing American Voter*. 2d ed. Cambridge: Harvard University Press.

Nivola, Pietro S. 1993. *Regulating Unfair Trade*. Washington, D.C.: Brookings Institution.

Nordhaus, William D. 1989. "Alternative Approaches to the Political Business Cycle." In William C. Brainard and George L. Perry, eds., *Brookings Papers on Economic Activity*. Vol. 2. Washington, D.C.: Brookings Institution.

Norton, Hugh S. 1977. *The Employment Act and the Council of Economic Advisers, 1946–1976*. Columbia: University of South Carolina Press.

Noyelle, Thierry J. 1982. "Rethinking Public Policy for the Service Economy with a Special Focus on People and Places." Paper presented to the Committee on New Realities, National Planning Association.

——. 1983. "The Implications of Industry Restructuring for Spatial Organization in the United States." In Frank Moulaert and Patricia Salinas, eds., *Regional Analysis and the New International Division of Labor.* Boston: Kluwer-Nijoff.

Oestreicher, Richard. 1988. "Urban Working-Class Political Behavior and Theories of American Electoral Politics." *Journal of American History* 74: 1257–86.

Offe, Claus. 1983. "Competitive Party Democracy and the Keynesian Welfare State: Factors of Stability and Disorganization." *Policy Sciences* 15: 225–46.

———. 1984. *Contradictions of the Welfare State,* ed. and trans. by John Keane. Cambridge: MIT Press.

———. 1987. "Challenging the Boundaries of Institutional Politics: Social Movements since the 1960s." In Charles S. Maier, ed., *Changing Boundaries of the Political: Essays on the Evolving Balance between the State and Society, Public and Private in Europe.* New York: Cambridge University Press.

O'Halloran, Sharyn. 1991. "Congress, Parties, and the Tariff, 1878–1934." Paper prepared for the annual meeting of the American Political Science Association, Washington, D.C., August 29–September 1.

———. 1994. *Politics, Process, and American Trade Policy.* Ann Arbor: University of Michigan Press.

Okun, Arthur M. 1970. *The Political Economy of Prosperity.* Washington, D.C.: Brookings Institution.

O'Neill, Thomas P. Jr. 1987. *Man of the House: The Life and Political Memoirs of Speaker Tip O'Neill.* New York: Random House.

Ornstein, Norman J., and David W. Rohde. 1978. "Political Parties and Congressional Reform." In Jeff Fishel, ed., *Parties and Elections in an Anti-Party Age: American Politics and the Crisis of Confidence.* Bloomington: Indiana University Press.

Orren, Gary R. 1982. "The Changing Styles of American Party Politics." In Joel Fleischman, ed., *The Future of American Political Parties: The Challenge of Governance.* Englewood Cliffs, N.J.: Prentice-Hall.

Orren, Karen, and Stephen Skowronek. 1994. "Beyond the Iconography of Order: Notes for a 'New Institutionalism.'" In Lawrence C. Dodd and Calvin Jillson, eds., *The Dynamics of American Politics: Approaches and Interpretations.* Boulder, Colo.: Westview Press.

Ostrom, Charles W., Jr. 1990. *Time Series Analysis: Regression Techniques.* 2d ed. Newbury Park, Calif.: Sage Publications.

Pach, Chester J., Jr., and Elmo Richardson. 1991. *The Presidency of Dwight D. Eisenhower.* Rev. ed. Lawrence: University Press of Kansas.

Palazzolo, Daniel J. 1992. *The Speaker and the Budget: Leadership in the Post-Reform House of Representatives.* Pittsburgh: University of Pittsburgh Press.

Panebianco, Angelo. 1989. *Political Parties: Organization and Power.* New York: Cambridge University Press.

Parker, Glenn R. 1986. "Economic Partisan Advantages in Congressional Contests, 1938–1978." *Public Opinion Quarterly* 50: 387–401.

———. 1989. "Members of Congress and Their Constituents: The Home-Style Connection." In Lawrence C. Dodd and Bruce I. Oppenheimer, eds., *Congress Reconsidered.* 4th ed. Washington, D.C.: CQ Press.

Pasquino, Gianfranco. 1986. "The Impact of Institutions on Party Government:

Tentative Hypotheses." In Francis G. Castles and Rudolf Wildenmann, eds., *Visions and Realities of Party Government*. New York: Walter de Gruyter.

Pastor, Robert. 1980. *Congress and the Politics of U.S. Foreign Economic Policy.* Berkeley: University of California Press.

Patterson, James T. 1967. *Congressional Conservatism and the New Deal: The Growth of the Conservative Coalition in Congress, 1933–1939.* Lexington: University of Kentucky Press.

Patterson, Samuel C. 1989. "The Persistence of State Parties." In Carl E. Van Horn, ed., *The State of the States*. Washington, D.C.: CQ Press.

Patterson, Samuel C., and Gregory A. Caldeira. 1988. "Party Voting in the United States Congress." *British Journal of Political Science* 17: 111–31.

Penner, Rudolph G. 1990. Statement before the Committee on Rules, Subcommittee on the Legislative Process, United States Congress, House of Representatives, March 21. Manuscript.

Peterson, Mark A. 1990. *Legislating Together: The White House and Capitol Hill from Eisenhower to Reagan.* Cambridge: Harvard University Press.

Peterson, Paul E. 1985. "The New Politics of Deficits." In John E. Chubb and Paul E. Peterson, eds., *The New Direction in American Politics*. Washington, D.C.: Brookings Institution.

Peterson, Paul E., and Mark Rom. 1989. "Macroeconomic Policymaking: Who Is in Control?" In John E. Chubb and Paul E. Peterson, eds., *Can the Government Govern?* Washington, D.C.: Brookings Institution.

Petrocik, John R. 1981. *Party Coalitions: Realignments and the Decline of the New Deal Party System.* Chicago: University of Chicago Press.

———. 1987. "Realignment: New Party Coalitions and the Nationalization of the South." *Journal of Politics* 49: 347–75.

Phillips, Kevin P. 1969. *The Emerging Republican Majority.* New Rochelle, N.Y.: Arlington House.

———. 1975. *Mediacracy: American Parties and Politics in the Communications Age.* Garden City, N.Y.: Doubleday.

———. 1990. *The Politics of Rich and Poor: Wealth and the American Electorate in the Reagan Aftermath.* New York: HarperPerennial.

Pincus, J. J. 1977. *Pressure Groups and Politics in Antebellum Tariffs.* New York: Columbia University Press.

Piore, Michael J., and Charles F. Sabel. 1984. *The Second Industrial Divide: Possibilities for Prosperity.* New York: Basic Books.

Piven, Frances Fox. 1992. "Structural Constraints and Political Development: The Case of the American Democratic Party." In Frances Fox Piven, ed., *Labor Parties in Postindustrial Societies*. New York: Oxford University Press.

Piven, Frances Fox, and Richard A. Cloward. 1977. *Poor People's Movements: Why They Succeed, How They Fail.* New York: Pantheon.

———. 1988. *Why Americans Don't Vote.* New York: Pantheon Books.

Pizzorno, Alessandro. 1981. "Interests and Parties in Pluralism." In Suzanne Berger, ed., *Organizing Interests in Western Europe: Pluralism, Corporatism, and the Transformation of Politics*. New York: Cambridge University Press.

Poggi, Gianfranco. 1978. *The Development of the Modern State: A Sociological Introduction.* Stanford: Stanford University Press.

Poguntke, Thomas. 1993. "Explorations into a Minefield: Anti-Party Sentiment." Paper prepared for the annual meeting of the American Political Science Association, Washington, D.C., September 2–5.

Polenberg, Richard. 1966. *Reorganizing Roosevelt's Government.* Cambridge: Harvard University Press.

———. 1975. "The Decline of the New Deal, 1937–1940." In John Braeman, Robert H. Bremner, and David Brody, eds., *The New Deal: The National Level.* Columbus: Ohio State University Press.

Polsby, Nelson W. 1968. "The Institutionalization of the U.S. House of Representatives." *American Political Science Review* 62: 144–68.

———. 1983. *Consequences of Party Reform.* New York: Oxford University Press.

Pomper, Gerald M. 1992. *Passions and Interests: Political Party Concepts of American Democracy.* Lawrence: University Press of Kansas.

Poole, Keith T., and R. Steven Daniels. 1985. "Ideology, Party, and Voting in the U.S. Congress, 1959–1980." *American Political Science Review* 79: 373–99.

Poole, Keith T., and Howard Rosenthal. 1991. "On Dimensionalizing Roll Call Votes in the U.S. Congress." *American Political Science Review* 85: 955–60.

Porter, Roger B. 1980. *Presidential Decision-Making: The Economic Policy Board.* New York: Cambridge University Press.

Poulshock, S. Walter. 1965. *The Two Parties and the Tariff in the 1880s.* Syracuse, N.Y.: Syracuse University Press.

Rabinowitz, George, Stuart Elaine Macdonald, and Ola Listhaug. 1993. "Competing Theories of Issue Voting: Is Discounting the Explanation?" Paper prepared for the annual meeting of the American Political Science Association, Washington, D.C., September 2–5.

Radcliff, Benjamin. 1988. "Solving a Puzzle: Aggregate Analysis and Economic Voting Revisited." *Journal of Politics* 50: 440–55.

Rae, Nicol C. 1989. *The Decline and Fall of the Liberal Republicans from 1952 to the Present.* New York: Oxford University Press.

Ranney, Austin. 1975. *Curing the Mischief of Faction.* Berkeley: University of California Press.

———. 1983. "The President and His Party." In Anthony King, ed., *Both Ends of the Avenue: The Presidency, the Executive Branch, and Congress.* Washington, D.C.: American Enterprise Institute.

Ratner, Sidney. 1972. *The Tariff in American History.* New York: Van Nostrand.

Ray, Edward John. 1981. "Determinants of Tariff and Nontariff Trade Restrictions in the United States." *Journal of Political Economy* 81: 105–21.

Reich, Robert B. 1992. *The Work of Nations: Preparing Ourselves for 21st-Century Capitalism.* New York: Vintage.

Reichard, Gary W. 1975. *The Reaffirmation of Republicanism: Eisenhower and the Eighty-Third Congress.* Knoxville: University of Tennessee Press.

Reichley, A. James. 1981. *Conservatives in an Age of Change: The Nixon and Ford Administrations.* Washington, D.C.: Brookings Institution.

———. 1985. "The Rise of National Parties." In John E. Chubb and Paul E. Peterson, eds., *The New Direction in American Politics.* Washington, D.C.: Brookings Institution.

Reiter, Howard L. 1991. "The Rise of the New Agenda and the Decline of Partisanship." Paper prepared for the annual meeting of the American Political Science Association, Washington, D.C., August 29–September 1.

Reynolds, John F. 1988. *Testing Democracy: Electoral Behavior and Progressive Reform in New Jersey, 1880–1920.* Chapel Hill: University of North Carolina Press.

Richardson, Bradley M. 1991. "European Party Loyalties Revisited." *American Political Science Review* 85: 751–76.

Rieder, Jonathan. 1989. "The Rise of the 'Silent' Majority." In Steve Fraser and Gary Gerstle, eds., *The Rise and Fall of the New Deal Order, 1930–1980.* Princeton: Princeton University Press.

Rohde, David W. 1991. *Parties and Leaders in the Postreform House.* Chicago: University of Chicago Press.

———. 1992. "Electoral Forces, Political Agendas, and Partisanship in the House and Senate." In Roger H. Davidson, ed., *The Postreform Congress.* New York: St. Martin's Press.

Rose, Richard. 1980. *Do Parties Make a Difference?* Chatham, N.J.: Chatham House.

Rubin, Irene. 1988. "Reauthorizations: Implications for Budget Theory." In Irene Rubin, ed., *New Directions in Budget Theory.* Albany: State University of New York Press.

Sabato, Larry J. 1981. *The Rise of Political Consultants: New Ways of Winning Elections.* New York: Basic Books.

———. 1988. *The Party's Just Begun: Shaping Political Parties for America's Future.* Glenview, Ill.: Scott, Foresman.

Salant, Walter S. 1989. "The Spread of Keynesian Doctrines and Practices in the United States." In Peter A. Hall, ed., *The Political Power of Economic Ideas: Keynesianism across Nations.* Princeton: Princeton University Press.

Sartori, Giovanni. 1990. "The Sociology of Parties: A Critical Review." In Peter Mair, ed., *The West European Party System.* New York: Oxford University Press.

Savage, James D. 1988. *Balanced Budgets and American Politics.* Ithaca, N.Y.: Cornell University Press.

Schattschneider, E. E. 1935. *Politics, Pressures, and the Tariff.* New York: Prentice-Hall.

———. 1942. *Party Government.* New York: Rinehart.

———. 1960. *The Semi-Sovereign People: A Realist's View of Democracy in America.* New York: Holt, Rinehart, and Winston.

Scheiber, Harry N. 1981. "Government and the American Economy: Three Stages of Historical Change, 1790–1941." In Robert Weible, Oliver Ford, and Paul Marion, eds., *Essays from the Lowell Conference on Industrial History, 1980 and 1981.* Lowell, Mass.: Lowell Conference on Industrial History.

Schick, Allen. 1980. *Congress and Money: Budgeting, Spending and Taxing.* Washington, D.C.: Urban Institute.

———. 1983. "The Distributive Congress." In Allen Schick, ed., *Making Economic Policy in Congress.* Washington, D.C.: American Enterprise Institute.

———. 1990. *The Capacity to Budget.* Washington, D.C.: Urban Institute.

Schlesinger, Arthur M., Jr. 1984. "The Crisis of the American Party System." In Richard L. McCormick, ed., *Political Parties and the Modern American State.* New Brunswick, N.J.: Rutgers University Press.

Schlesinger, Joseph A. 1991. *Political Parties and the Winning of Office.* Ann Arbor: University of Michigan Press.

Schmidt, Manfred G. 1982. "The Role of Parties in Shaping Macroeconomic Policy." In Francis G. Castles, ed., *The Impact of Parties: Politics and Policies in Democratic Capitalist States.* Beverly Hills, Calif.: Sage Publications.

Schneider, William. 1984. "Antipartisanship in America." In Vernon Bogdanor, ed., *Parties and Democracy in Britain and America.* New York: Praeger.

Schonfeld, William R. 1983. "Political Parties: The Functional Approach and the Structural Alternative." *Comparative Politics* 15: 477–99.

Segal, David R. 1968. "Partisan Realignment in the United States: The Lesson of the 1964 Election." *Public Opinion Quarterly* 33: 441–44.

Seligman, Lester G., and Michael R. King. 1980. "Political Realignment and Recruitment to the U.S. Congress, 1870–1970." In Richard J. Trilling and Bruce A. Campbell, eds., *Realignment in American Politics: Toward a Theory.* Austin: University of Texas Press.

Shafer, Byron E., ed. 1991a. *The End of Realignment? Interpreting American Electoral Eras.* Madison: University of Wisconsin Press.

——. 1991b. "The Notion of an Electoral Order: The Structure of Electoral Politics at the Accession of George Bush." In Byron E. Shafer, ed., *The End of Realignment? Interpreting American Electoral Eras.* Madison: University of Wisconsin Press.

Shafer, Byron E., and William J. M. Claggett. 1994. "The Split Two-Party System: Partisans, Independents, and Policy Preferences." Paper prepared for the annual meeting of the American Political Science Association, New York, September 1–4.

Shaffer, William R. 1980. *Party and Ideology in the United States Congress.* Lanham, Md.: University Press of America.

Shea, Daniel M., and John C. Green, eds. 1994. *The State of the Parties: The Changing Role of Contemporary American Parties.* Lanham, Md.: Rowman and Littlefield.

Shefter, Martin. 1984. "Political Parties, Political Mobilization, and Political Demobilization." In Thomas Ferguson and Joel Rogers, eds., *The Political Economy: Readings in the Politics and Economics of American Public Policy.* Armonk, N.Y.: M. E. Sharpe.

——. 1994. *Political Parties and the State: The American Historical Experience.* Princeton: Princeton University Press.

Shepsle, Kenneth A. 1989. "The Changing Textbook Congress." In John E. Chubb and Paul E. Peterson, eds., *Can the Government Govern?* Washington, D.C.: Brookings Institution.

Shonfield, Andrew. 1965. *Modern Capitalism: The Changing Balance of Public and Private Power.* New York: Oxford University Press.

Shuman, Howard E. 1988. *Politics and the Budget: The Struggle between the President and the Congress.* 2d ed. Englewood Cliffs, N.J.: Prentice-Hall.

Silbey, Joel H. 1984. "'The Salt of the Nation' : Political Parties in Ante-bellum

America." In Richard L. McCormick, ed., *Political Parties and the Modern State.* New Brunswick, N.J.: Rutgers University Press.

———. 1990. "The Rise and Fall of American Political Parties, 1790–1990." In L. Sandy Maisel, ed., *The Parties Respond: Changes in the American Party System.* Boulder, Colo.: Westview Press.

———. 1991. *The American Political Nation, 1838–1893.* Stanford, Calif.: Stanford University Press.

Sinclair, Barbara. 1977. "Determinants of Aggregate Party Cohesion in the U.S. House of Representatives, 1901–1956." *Legislative Studies Quarterly* 2: 155–75.

———. 1978. "From Party Voting to Regional Fragmentation: The House of Representatives, 1933–1956." *American Politics Quarterly* 6: 125–46.

———. 1981. "Agenda and Alignment Change: The House of Representatives, 1925–1978." In Lawrence C. Dodd and Bruce Oppenheimer, eds., *Congress Reconsidered.* 2d ed. Washington, D.C.: CQ Press.

———. 1983. *Majority Leadership in the U.S. House.* Baltimore: Johns Hopkins University Press.

———. 1989. *The Transformation of the U.S. Senate.* Baltimore: Johns Hopkins University Press.

Skidelsky, Robert. 1979. "The Decline of Keynesian Politics." In Colin Crouch, ed., *State and Economy in Contemporary Capitalism.* London: Croon Helm.

Skocpol, Theda. 1980. "Political Responses to the New Deal: Neo-Marxist Theories of the State and the Case of the New Deal." *Politics and Society* 10: 155–201.

———. 1985. "Bringing the State Back In: Strategies of Analysis in Current Research." In Peter B. Evans, Dietrich Rueschemeyer, and Theda Skocpol, eds., *Bringing the State Back In.* New York: Cambridge University Press.

Skocpol, Theda, and Kenneth Finegold. 1982. "State Capacity and Economic Intervention in the Early New Deal." *Political Science Quarterly* 97: 255–78.

Skocpol, Theda, and John Ikenberry. 1983. "The Political Formation of the American Welfare State in Historical and Comparative Perspective." *Comparative Social Research* 6: 87–148.

Skowronek, Stephen. 1982. *Building a New American State: The Expansion of National Administrative Capacities.* New York: Cambridge University Press.

———. 1993. *The Politics Presidents Make: Leadership from John Adams to George Bush.* Cambridge: Harvard University Press.

Sloan, John W. 1991. *Eisenhower and the Management of Prosperity.* Lawrence: University Press of Kansas.

Smith, Gordon. 1986. "The Futures of Party Government: A Framework for Analysis." In Francis G. Castles and Rudolf Wildenmann, eds., *Visions and Realities of Party Government.* New York: Walter de Gruyter.

Sorauf, Frank J. 1975. "Political Parties and Political Analysis." In William N. Chambers and Walter Dean Burnham, eds., *The American Party Systems: Stages of Political Development.* 2d ed. New York: Oxford University Press.

Sorauf, Frank J., and Scott A. Wilson. 1990. "Campaigns and Money: A Changing Role for the Political Parties?" In L. Sandy Maisel, ed., *The Parties Respond: Changes in the American Party System.* Boulder, Colo.: Westview Press.

Spiliotes, Constantine J. 1993. "Presidential Choice in Macroeconomic Policy-making." Paper prepared for the annual meeting of the American Political Science Association, Washington, D.C., September 2–5.

Springer, William M. 1892. *Tariff Reform, the Paramount Issue: Speeches and Writings on the Questions Involved in the Presidential Contest of 1892*. New York: Charles L. Webster and Company.

Stanback, Thomas M., Jr., and Thierry J. Noyelle. 1982. *Cities in Transition*. Totowa, N.J.: Allanheld, Osmun.

Stanga, John E., and James F. Sheffield. 1987. "The Myth of Zero Partisanship: Attitudes toward American Political Parties, 1964–84." *American Journal of Political Science* 31: 829–55.

Stanley, Harold W., and Richard G. Niemi. 1990. *Vital Statistics on American Politics*. 2d ed. Washington, D.C.: CQ Press.

Starr, Martin K., ed. 1988. *Global Competitiveness: Getting the U.S. Back on Track*. New York: Norton.

Steel, Brent, and Taketsugu Tsurutani. 1986. "From Consensus to Dissensus: A Note on Postindustrial Political Parties." *Comparative Politics* 18: 235–48.

Stein, Herbert. 1969. *The Fiscal Revolution in America*. Chicago: University of Chicago Press.

Stewart, Charles H., III. 1989. *Budget Reform Politics: The Design of the Appropriations Process in the House of Representatives, 1865–1921*. New York: Cambridge University Press.

Stewart, Charles, III, and Barry R. Weingast. 1992. "Stacking the Senate, Changing the Nation: Republican Rotten Boroughs, Statehood Politics, and American Political Development." *Studies in American Political Development* 6: 223–71.

Stock, James H., and Mark W. Watson. 1989. "New Indexes of Coincident and Leading Economic Indicators." In Oliver Jean Blanchard and Stanley Fischer, eds., *NBER Macroeconomics Annual 1989*. Cambridge: MIT Press.

Stockman, David A. 1986. *The Triumph of Politics: How the Reagan Revolution Failed*. New York: Harper and Row.

Stone, Alan. 1984. "Capitalism, Case Studies, and Public Policy: Trade Expansion Legislation Re-examined." In Thomas Ferguson and Joel Rogers, eds., *The Political Economy: Readings in the Politics and Economics of American Public Policy*. Armonk, N.Y.: M. E. Sharpe.

Summers, Lawrence H. 1990. *Understanding Unemployment*. Cambridge: MIT Press.

Sundquist, James L. 1968. *Politics and Policy: The Eisenhower, Kennedy, and Johnson Years*. Washington, D.C.: Brookings Institution.

———. 1973. *Dynamics of the Party System: Alignment and Realignment of Political Parties in the United States*. Washington, D.C.: Brookings Institution.

———. 1981. *The Decline and Resurgence of Congress*. Washington, D.C.: Brookings Institution.

———. 1983. *Dynamics of the Party System: Alignment and Realignment of Political Parties in the United States*. 2d ed. Washington, D.C.: Brookings Institution.

———. 1983–1984. "Whither the American Party System?—Revisited." *Political Science Quarterly* 98: 573–93.

Terrill, Tom E. 1973. *The Tariff, Politics, and American Foreign Policy, 1874–1901*. Westport, Conn.: Greenwood Press.

Thompson, Robert J. 1991. "Contrasting Models of White House Staff Organization: The Eisenhower, Ford, and Carter Experiences." Paper prepared for the annual meeting of the American Political Science Association, Washington, D.C., August 29–September 1.

Thurow, Lester C. 1983. *Dangerous Currents: The State of Economics*. New York: Random House.

Trilling, Richard J., and Bruce A. Campbell. 1980. "Toward a Theory of Realignment: An Introduction." In Richard J. Trilling and Bruce A. Campbell, eds., *Realignment in American Politics: Toward a Theory*. Austin: University of Texas Press.

Tufte, Edward R. 1975. "Determinants of the Outcomes of Midterm Congressional Elections." *American Political Science Review* 69: 812–26.

Tyson, Laura D Andrea. 1993. *Who's Bashing Whom? Trade Conflict in High-Technology Industries*. Washington, D.C.: Institute for International Economics.

Unekis, Joseph K., and James L. Franke. 1994. "Universalism and the Parties in the Committees of the Post-Reform U.S. House of Representatives: 1971–1992." Paper prepared for the annual meeting of the American Political Science Association, New York, September 1–4.

United States. Congress. Joint Economic Committee. 1963. *The Federal Budget as an Economic Document*. Washington, D.C.: Government Printing Office.

———. 1969. *The Federal Budget, Inflation, and Full Employment*. Washington, D.C.: Government Printing Office.

———. 1980. *Hearings before the Joint Economic Committee on the Economic Report of the President: February 1–5*. Washington, D.C.: Government Printing Office.

United States. Office of Management and Budget. 1994. *Budget of the United States Government*. Washington, D.C.: Government Printing Office.

Verdier, Daniel. 1992. "The Politics of Trade Preference Formation: The Case of the United States from the Civil War to the New Deal." Paper prepared for the annual meeting of the American Political Science Association, Chicago, September 3–6.

———. 1994. *Democracy and International Trade: Britain, France, and the United States, 1860–1990*. Princeton: Princeton University Press.

Wallis, John Joseph. 1987. "Laws, Legislatures, and Relief: Some Determinants of Institutional Change in the New Deal." University of Maryland, Department of Economics. Manuscript.

Ware, Alan. 1985. *The Breakdown of Democratic Party Organization, 1940–1980*. New York: Oxford University Press.

———. 1988. *Citizens, Parties, and the State: A Reappraisal*. Princeton: Princeton University Press.

Waterman, Richard W., Bruce I. Oppenheimer, and James A. Stimson. 1991. "Sequence and Equilibrium in Congressional Elections: An Integrated Approach." *Journal of Politics* 53: 372–93.

Wattenberg, Martin P. 1990. *The Decline of American Political Parties, 1952–1988*. Cambridge: Harvard University Press.

Way, Christopher. 1994. "Central Banks, Partisan Politics, and Macroeconomic Performance." Paper prepared for the annual meeting of the American Political Science Association, New York, September 1–4.

Weatherford, M. Stephen. 1988. "Political Business Cycles and the Process of Economic Policymaking." *American Politics Quarterly* 16: 99–136.

Weaver, R. Kent. 1988. *Automatic Government: The Politics of Indexation.* Washington, D.C.: Brookings Institution.

Weir, Maragret. 1989. "Ideas and Politics: The Acceptance of Keynesianism in Britain and the United States." In Peter A. Hall, ed. *The Political Power of Economic Ideas: Keynesianism across Nations.* Princeton: Princeton University Press.

Weir, Margaret, Ann Shola Orloff, and Theda Skocpol, eds. 1988. *The Politics of Social Policy in the United States.* Princeton: Princeton University Press.

Weir, Margaret, and Theda Skocpol. 1985. "State Structures and the Possibilities for Keynesian Responses to the Great Depression in Sweden, Britain, and the United States." In Peter B. Evans, Dietrich Rueschemeyer, and Theda Skocpol, eds., *Bringing the State Back In.* New York: Cambridge University Press.

Weisberg, Herbert F. 1978. "Evaluating Theories of Congressional Roll-Call Voting." *American Journal of Political Science* 22: 554–77.

Weissberg, Robert. 1991. "The Democratic Party and the Conflict over Racial Policy." In Benjamin Ginsberg and Alan Stone, eds., *Do Elections Matter?* 2d ed. Armonk, N.Y.: M. E. Sharpe.

White, Joseph, and Aaron Wildavsky. 1989. *The Deficit and the Public Interest: The Search for Responsible Budgeting in the 1980s.* Berkeley: University of California Press.

Wilcox, Clyde. 1989. "Share the Wealth: Contributions by Congressional Incumbents to the Campaigns of Other Candidates." *American Politics Quarterly* 17: 386–408.

Wildenmann, Rudolf. 1986. "The Problematic of Party Government." In Francis G. Castles and Rudolf Wildenmann, eds., *Visions and Realities of Party Government.* New York: Walter de Gruyter.

Williams, John T. 1990. "The Political Manipulation of Macroeconomic Policy." *American Political Science Review* 84: 767–95.

Williams, Philip. 1984. "Review Article: Party Realignment in the United States and Britain." *British Journal of Political Science* 15: 97–115.

Wilson, Frank L. 1979. "The Revitalization of French Parties." *Comparative Political Studies* 12: 82–103.

Winch, Donald. 1989. "Keynes, Keynesianism, and State Intervention." In Peter A. Hall, ed. *The Political Power of Economic Ideas: Keynesianism across Nations.* Princeton: Princeton University Press.

Witte, John F. 1985. *The Politics and Development of the Federal Income Tax.* Madison: University of Wisconsin Press.

————. 1986. "The President versus Congress on Tax Policy." In James P. Pfiffner, ed., *The President and Economic Policy.* Philadelphia: Institute for the Study of Human Issues.

Wolfe, Alan. 1977. *The Limits of Legitimacy: Political Contradictions of Late Capitalism.* New York: Free Press.

Wolman, Paul. 1992. *Most Favored Nation: The Republican Revisionists and U.S. Tariff Policy, 1897–1912*. Chapel Hill: University of North Carolina Press.

Woolcock, Stephen. 1984. "The Economic Policies of the Carter Administration." In M. Glenn Abernathy, Dilys M. Hill, and Phil Williams, eds., *The Carter Years: The President and Policy Making*. New York: St. Martin's Press.

Woolley, John T. 1988. "Partisan Manipulation of the Economy: Another Look at Monetary Policy with Moving Regression." *Journal of Politics* 50: 335–60.

———. 1993. "The Study of the Politics of Monetary Policy: A Critical Review of Our Achievements." Paper prepared for the annual meeting of the Midwest Political Science Association, Chicago, April 15–17.

Wright, Gerald C. 1994. "The Meaning of 'Party' in Congressional Roll Call Voting." Paper prepared for the annual meeting of the Midwest Political Science Association, Chicago, April 14–16.

Yans-McLaughlin, Virginia. 1977. *Family and Community: Italian Immigrants in Buffalo, 1880–1930*. Ithaca: Cornell University Press.

Yarbrough, Tinsley E. 1984. "Carter and the Congress." In M. Glenn Abernathy, Dilys M. Hill, and Phil Williams, eds., *The Carter Years: The President and Policy Making*. New York: St. Martin's Press.

Yoffie, David B. 1989. "American Trade Policy: An Obsolete Bargain?" In John E. Chubb and Paul E. Peterson, eds., *Can the Government Govern?* Washington, D.C.: Brookings Institution.

Index

About the Author

JOHN J. COLEMAN is Assistant Professor of Political Science at the University of Wisconsin-Madison.